OLD GOLD
GLORY

WOLVES LEAGUE CHAMPIONS 1953-54

A

britesp t
PUBLICATION

Dedicated to
Robbie and Hannah

OLD GOLD GLORY

by Steve Gordos
A Britespot Publication

First Published in Great Britain by
Britespot Publishing Solutions Limited
Chester Road, Cradley Heath, West Midlands B64 6AB

ISBN 1 904103 27 8

Cover design and layout
© Britespot Publishing Solutions Limited

Printed and bound in the UK by Cromwell Press Limited

Steve Gordos Acknowledgments:
This book would not have been possible without the help of many people – primarily, the former players who so willingly provided
their memories and to whose talents this book is hopefully a fitting tribute: Peter Broadbent, Norman Deeley, Ron Flowers, Bill
Shorthouse, Nigel Sims, Bill Slater, Eddie Stuart, Roy Swinbourne, Dennis Wilshaw and Bert Williams.

Thanks also to: Tony Brown of SoccerData, for the 1953-4 season's results and attendances. Peter Creed, honorary secretary of
the Wolves Former Players' Association, for his advice, assistance and proof reading. Harry Donkersley, long-time – and suffering –
Huddersfield Town fan for his recollections. Lindsay Gordos, for additional proof reading. John Hendley of Wolves for use of
his programme collection. Graham Hughes, Wolves' club historian. Tony Matthews, for research on the match reports.
Christine Povey, for use of pictures collected by her late father, Jack Howley. John Sambrooks, for his considerable help in
assembling the many photographs.

From Britespot Publishing: Roger Marshall, Paul Burns, Darren Cartwright, Chris Sweet, Chris Russell, Chris Ivens and Linda Perkins

Photos © Graham Hughes, Christine Povey, Eddie Stuart and Bert Williams

Sources:
*Arsenal, A Complete Record, Fred Ollier. Aston Villa, A Complete Record 1874-1988, David Goodyear and Tony Matthews.
Billy Wright, A Hero For All Seasons, The Official Biography, Norman Giller. Blackpool, A Complete Record, Roy Calley.
Bolton Wanderers FC, The Official History 1877-2002, Simon Marland. The Breedon Book of Football Managers, Dennis Turner and Alex White.
Clown Prince of Soccer, Len Shackleton, His Autobiography, edited by David R Jack. The Definitive Cardiff City FC, Richard Shepherd.
England, The Complete Post-War Record, Mike Payne. England, The Football Facts, Nick Gibbs.
The Essential History of Middlesbrough, Richard Jones. The Football League 1888-1988, The Official Illustrated History, by Bryon Butler.
Football League Players Records 1946-92, editor Barry J Hugman. The Football Managers, Tony Pawson.
For Wolves And England, Ron Flowers. The History of Sunderland AFC, revised and updated by Bob Graham.
It's All In The Game, Johnny Haynes. League Football, The Official Centenary History of the Football League, Simon Inglis.
Manchester City, A Complete Record, Ray Goble and Andrew Ward. Manchester United, A Complete Record 1878-1992, Ian Morrison and Alan Sury.
Newcastle United, A Complete Record 1882-1990, Paul Joannou, Bill Swann, Steve Corke. One Hundred Caps And All That, Billy Wright.
Proud Preston, Preston North End's One Hundred Seasons of Football League History, Ian Rigby, Mike Payne.
The Sunday Chronicle Football Annual 1953-4. Soccer In The Fifties, Geoffrey Green. Spurs, A Complete Record, Bob Goodwin.
West Bromwich Albion by Peter Morris. West Bromwich Albion The First Hundred Years, G A Willmore.*

CONTENTS

SIR JACK HAYWARD OBE

I write this as we at Molineux prepare for our first season in the FA Premiership. Obviously, the present and the future of the club are what concern us but I, and all at Molineux, am only too aware of our great heritage. That is why it is so fitting that our return to the top flight should coincide with the fiftieth anniversary of Wolves becoming champions of England for the first time.

When I began going to Molineux as a young boy, Wolves were hardly the most talked about club in the land but I was fortunate enough to see them rise to greatness. Under Major Buckley and then Ted Vizard we came so very close to winning the First Division championship. It was left to the team managed by Stan Cullis and captained by my great pal Billy Wright to put Wolves finally at the top of the tree in 1953-4.

Many Wolves fans will share my memories of Billy's team. The marvellous Bert Williams was in goal, we had the best pair of wingers in the land in Johnny Hancocks and Jimmy Mullen, fine inside forwards in Peter Broadbent and Dennis Wilshaw, a wonderful centre-forward in Roy Swinbourne, half-back strength through the three Bills, Wright, Shorthouse and Slater, as well as young Ron Flowers, and stalwart full-backs in Jack Short, Roy Pritchard and Eddie Stuart.

In this book, older fans, like me, can relive the memories of our triumph as we pipped our good friends from West Bromwich for the title, while young fans can learn about the men who set the football world talking in the Fabulous Fifties.

While Billy, Jack, Roy, Johnny and Jimmy are sadly no longer with us, the majority of that wonderful 1953-4 team are alive and well and are active members of the Wolverhampton Wanderers Former Players' Association under the honorary secretaryship of Peter Creed. We were happy to have so many of those great players at the Millennium Stadium in Cardiff on May 26, 2003, to see us win the First Division play-off final. I gather the old players have willingly contributed their recollections to this book which will be a lasting tribute to what they achieved.

I hope we have paid due honour at Molineux to Stan Cullis and Billy Wright by naming two of our stands after them and by the erection of two superb statues. This book will be a further salute to them and their colleagues.

As I said at the start, the present and future are what matter most now at Molineux but we will always find time to salute the past and those men who first helped Wolves rule English football.

Sir Jack
President and Chairman of Wolverhampton Wanderers FC, August 2003

INTRODUCTION

Before telling the story of how Wolverhampton Wanderers became champions of England for the first time it might help to explain a few things about English football in 1953 as Stan Cullis's side began their quest for that elusive First Division title.

There was no European competition at either club or national level in those days, no Premiership, no League Cup, no play-offs, no automatic entry into the League for the top non-League club in the country. There were still people around who remembered the founding of the Football League, for it had come about just 65 years earlier. Of the 12 clubs who pioneered a championship that would be copied throughout the world, six remained in the top flight. As well as Wolves, there were Aston Villa, whose William McGregor had been the founding father of League, West Bromwich Albion and the Lancashire trio of Bolton, Burnley and Preston.

Extra clubs in 1892 had brought about the setting-up of a First Division and Second Division In 1920 came the Third Division Southern section and in 1921 a Third Division Northern section. That's the way it had stayed. Only two teams were relegated from the top two divisions each season while only the champions of the two Third Division sections were promoted to the Second.

The bottom Third Division sides did not automatically drop out, either. Each season the bottom two of each section had to stand at the League AGM for re-election and they usually got it despite non-League clubs being able to seek election, too. In 1953 Accrington (45 votes) and Workington (36) retained their places in the Northern section, though Wigan Athletic obtained a respectable 17 votes. Shrewsbury (46) and Walsall (41) stayed in the Southern section with hopefuls Peterborough United (6), Bath City (2), Yeovil Town (2) and Hereford United (1) disappointed.

Wolves were the only side in the First Division in 1953-4 who had won both a Third Division title and that of the Second Division. So a unique treble beckoned. There were other differences in the League set-up compared with today. Only two points were awarded for a win and goal average separated teams level on points. That was arrived at by dividing the number of goals scored by those conceded. So a club who scored 80 goals and let in 40 would have a goal average of 2.0.

On the field, it was also a very different game. Players could freely pass back to their goalkeeper, the tackle from behind was still a feature and shoulder charging goalkeepers was quite in order. However, there were signs of growing concern for that very British aspect of soccer as evidenced by the 1953-4 edition of the Sunday Chronicle Football Annual, forerunner of the News of the World Annual, which is happily still going strong today and is a pocket-sized fount of football knowledge. In that 1953-4 edition, respected soccer write Ivan Sharpe, for many years a regular contributor to the Wolves match-day programme, called for something to be done to reduce the number of collisions between goalkeepers and other players.

He lists the considerable number of keepers who suffered broken bones in 1952-3 as well as pointing out that Blackpool's Allan Brown had broken his leg when he clashed with the the goalkeeper in scoring a winning FA Cup goal against Arsenal. As a result, he missed the memorable 'Matthews Final' at Wembley. Most serious of all, Sheffield Wednesday scoring sensation Derek Dooley had broken his leg when he collided with the Preston keeper and, after gangrene set in, had to have the leg amputated.

Sharpe did not advocate that charging of the keeper should be outlawed but that it should not be allowed in the goal area. Wrote Sharpe: "This offers a compromise to the many foreign countries which prohibit all charges on the goalkeepers."

One shudders to think what Sharpe would make of today's regulations regarding keepers as he went on to write; "It is absurd that, abroad, a goalkeeper can collect the ball and dance his way to the penalty (18 yards) line without interference of any kind. Attackers turn on their heel and walk away – a silly situation. This is wrapping the goalkeeper in cotton wool. It is giving him the freedom of the (extensive) penalty area . . . too much protection. There is nothing skilful in such play, nothing attractive to the the spectator. And it has the further disadvantage of reducing goalscoring."

At the Football League's annual meeting in 1953 Sunderland chairman Bill Ditchburn proposed that teams in the FA Cup final should each receive no fewer than 20,000 tickets. He attacked the allocation of 43,000 tickets to amateur organisations and also criticised the FA for not looking to the future and building a national stadium of their own. Such a ground should have a capacity of 250,000, said Ditchburn. He was, of course, talking in the days when the majority of football fans stood at grounds. The Sunderland man had few supporters for his views at the meeting. His resolution failed.

Sunderland did have the backing of Newcastle in a proposal to have the bonus paid to players whose clubs reached the FA Cup semi-final raised from £15 to £20 and that for the final from £20 to £25. That, too was thrown out, so it's not surprising the League was also resisting the latest players' bid to increase the maximum weekly wage of £14! The most recent claim had been referred to the Ministry of Labour and League president Arthur Drewry commented: "It would appear that we are to be continually exposed to these irresponsible claims so long as any particular one is refused." Different days indeed!

The Sunday Chronicle Annual also notes that five-figure transfer fees had become so numerous that there was not enough space to list them all. The record fee was still the £34,000 Sheffield Wednesday had paid to Notts County for Jackie Sewell in 1951. The book still included in its 'Transfer Trail' section the £14,000 fee Wolves received from Arsenal for Bryn Jones in 1938, which was a record at the time.

Sunderland were the big spenders in 1953, having splashed out in June £27,000 for Arsenal centre-half Ray Daniel and £26,000 for Burnley winger Billy Elliott. It was a far cry from the eight-figure transfers of 2003, though the League did have its share of non-English players – the difference was that most of the 'imports' came from Scotland, Wales or Ireland.

Such then was the football scene in England fifty years ago as Wolves embarked upon what was to be the most famous season in their history.

CHAPTER ONE

PERCHANCE TO DREAM

Some years stand out more than others. Such a year was 1953 and not just because it saw the coronation of HRH Queen Elizabeth II and the conquest of Mount Everest by a British-led expedition.

It also saw sporting dreams come true. Stanley Matthews, that doyen among wingers, finally collected an FA Cup winner's medal, at the age of 38, as Blackpool came from 3-1 down to win an epic final 4-3 against Bolton at Wembley. Shropshire-born jockey Sir Gordon Richards at last rode a Derby winner – Pinza – and England's cricketers recaptured the Ashes after 19 long years. So it was a time for sportsmen to dare to dream – and Wolves had dared to dream of one day being Football League champions. They had been runners-up under the managership of Major Frank Buckley and captaincy of Stan Cullis in the final two seasons before World War II. When league football resumed in 1946-7, Wolves went close again and needed a win from their final game of the season to become champions. To add drama to the occasion Cullis announced he was retiring but his men were beaten 2-1 by Liverpool, who eventually took the title when Stoke failed to win their final match.

After Cullis had taken over the managerial reins from Ted Vizard, the FA Cup had come to Molineux for a third time – in 1949 – and talk was of that elusive league crown at last coming to Wolverhampton the following season. It nearly did too, as the men in old gold and black went closest yet, finishing second to Portsmouth on goal average.

Then came a couple of indifferent seasons as Wolves had no say in the title races which saw first Tottenham and then Manchester United top the table. Things looked more promising in 1952-3 and Cullis's team led the table early in the season but it was the ageing Arsenal side, captained by Joe Mercer, who finished top of the pile, with Wolves third.

So 1953-4 arrived with Wolves definitely among the fancied sides along with their arch rivals a few miles down the road in West Bromwich. Cullis had not made any major signings during the close season though young Irish goalkeeper Noel Dwyer joined the club in August after five days of a month's trial.

The Wolves team who would start the campaign were packed with experience. Three of them, goalkeeper Bert Williams, right-winger Johnny Hancocks and left-winger Jimmy Mullen had played League football before the War. The average age of the side who played in the opening game was over 28, with four of them aged 30 or more. The arrival of 20-year-old Peter Broadbent in preference to 22-year-old Ron Stockin in the fourth game of the season would lower the average age only slightly. Towards the end of the season the emergence of 19-year-old Ron Flowers and 22-year-old Eddie Stuart would lower it a bit more. Manager Cullis, who always looked older than his years, was still only 36.

Six of the squad, Williams, Mullen, Hancocks, Roy Pritchard, Billy Wright and Bill Shorthouse, had appeared in the 1949 Cup Final. Six players, Williams, Pritchard, Wright, Ray Chatham, Hancocks and Mullen had made League appearances in each of the previous seven seasons, while Shorthouse had been a first team regular for the past six. As well as experience there was a high pedigree among the playing staff. Williams, Wright, Hancocks and Mullen were already full internationals. Six of them would be full internationals by the time the 1950s ended – Flowers, Bill Slater, Broadbent, Dennis Wilshaw, Norman Deeley and Eddie Clamp. Another interesting aspect of the team was the preponderance of Englishmen in the squad. Only exceptions were Scottish-born Bill Baxter and South African Stuart.

Dover-born Broadbent was the only Southerner among the players mainly responsible for winning the title. Three of them were from Shropshire (Hancocks, Wright and Pritchard), three from Yorkshire (Jack Short, Roy Swinbourne and Flowers, three from Staffordshire (Williams, Wilshaw and Bill Shorthouse), there was one Lancastrian (Slater), a Geordie (Mullen) and Stuart from Johannesburg.

It was an unusual start to the new season – games were played in midweek. The previous season the FA had moved the Cup Final to the last day of the season and, as it was televised live, several clubs with league fixtures the same day, found their attendances affected. As there was a similar arrangement for the 1954 final, the Football League agreed matches arranged for the last Saturday of the season could be brought forward to the week before the scheduled kick-off.

Wolves therefore started their title quest at Burnley on Wednesday, August 19 – not that there was much interest nationally in the winter game. All focus was on the Oval cricket ground where Middlesex aces Bill Edrich and Denis Compton saw England home in the fifth and final Test of the season to grab back the Ashes at last from the Aussies. The previous four Tests had ended in draws. The defining moment in the series had featured two cricketers who were also pretty useful footballers. On the final day of the second Test, at Lord's, England were staring defeat in the face when they slumped to 12-3 and then 73-4. Then Willie Watson, the Sunderland wing-half who had also played for his country at football, and Trevor Bailey a member of the Walthamstow Avenue side who won the FA Amateur Cup at Wembley in 1952, came together in a fifth-wicket stand of 163 to frustrate the Aussies. It was an act of defiance which has gone down in cricket folklore.

It was a case of LBW up at Turf Moor – Lively Burnley Won! Wolves fielded the forward line who had played in the final 13 games of the previous season and they got off to a dream start. Roy Swinbourne scored after one minute 50 seconds – the season's first goal anywhere in the country. It was a false omen. A match played in driving rain for much of the time, saw Wolves miss chances and pay the price. Les Shannon and Bill Holden scored in the space of two minutes around the hour mark and 20-year-old winger Brian Pilkington and Shannon completed a 4-1 win.

On the same evening Albion beat champions Arsenal 2-0 at The Hawthorns thanks to two goals from Wolverhampton-born Johnny Nicholls, to give early notice that they would be in contention for honours. Newly-promoted Huddersfield began with a 2-1 win at Preston while the biggest goal spree of the night was at The Valley where Charlton beat Sunderland 5-3. Centre-forward Eddie Firmani scoring twice. South African-born Firmani, just 20 years old, would two years later move to Italian giants Sampdoria and earn caps for Italy, through his parentage.

12

Three days later, Saturday, August 22, Albion were held 1-1 at home by the previous season's beaten FA Cup finalists Bolton. On the same day an unchanged Wolves side, with Nigel Sims continuing to deputise in goal for the injured Bert Williams, won 4-0 against Manchester City at Maine Road. Dennis Wilshaw and Bill Slater were on target in the first half while Roy Swinbourne scored two in the second when Wilshaw and Billy Wright also had the ball in the net only to be denied by off-side flags. There was also a confident appeal for a penalty when home full-back Ken Branagan appeared to punch the ball off the line.

City included a couple of the game's best known post-War names – Don Revie and Ivor Broadis. Revie, later to manage Leeds during their glory years, and England during their not-so-glorious years, was operating at right-half. He would later in the season switch to inside left and the following season create a lot of interest by playing as a deep-lying centre-forward in what became known as 'The Revie Plan'. Born in Poplar, Broadis was only 23 when Carlisle made him player-manager in 1946. He was able to create a little bit of football history by later transferring himself to Sunderland for £19,000 in 1949. City had then signed him for a club record £25,000 but in October 1953, he moved to Newcastle and would face Wolves at Molineux later in the season

While Wolves were beating City, Liverpool, who had won their opening game 3-1 at home to Portsmouth, shared eight goals with Manchester United at Anfield, Louis Bimpson hitting all four home goals. The Scouse fans could hardly have dreamed that this would be a season of struggle, ending in relegation. The previous season's Second Division champions Sheffield United opened their campaign with a win – 4-3 over Portsmouth at Fratton Park.

There was one more trip before Wolves could make their Molineux bow for the new season. This time it was to the North East and a packed Roker Park, the home fans hoping to see if their costly line-up could at last make an impact. In the close season they had signed goalkeeper Jimmy Cowan from Morton, centre-half Ray Daniel from Arsenal and winger Billy Elliott from Burnley, internationals all. The fans must have been pretty well convinced that the good times were about to roll when Tommy Wright, the mercurial Len Shackleton and Welsh centre-forward Trevor Ford put the Wearsiders three goals up. However, Wolves were not done and when Dennis Wilshaw was tripped as he glided his way through the home defence, Johnny Hancocks fired home the penalty. Then Wilshaw scored after Roy Swinbourne had headed down a Billy Wright lob.

Shackleton had one of his better games that night, He was one of the most talented inside forwards of his era. He had amazing control, loved to do tricks with the ball and was, in many ways, the Joe Cole of his day. However, Shackleton never went out of his way to please the game's authorities. His autobiography, Clown Prince of Soccer (Kaye), published in 1955, included a one-page chapter headed 'The average director's knowledge of football'. At Shackleton's instruction, the page was left blank.

Over at Old Trafford, Albion played their first away game of the season and were 3-1 winners over Manchester United. However, newly-promoted Huddersfield, whose six-man defence had played in every league game during the previous season, maintained their unbeaten start to the campaign with a 2-0 home win over Cardiff while Preston followed up a 4-0 away win at Middlesbrough with a 6-0 home win over Sheffield Wednesday, Jimmy Baxter scoring three times This is how the top of the table looked after just three games:

	P	W	D	L	F	A	Pt
Huddersfield	3	2	1	0	4	1	5
Albion	3	2	1	0	6	2	5
Preston	3	2	0	1	11	2	4

Huddersfield led because they had a goal average of 4.0 compared with Albion's 3.0.

For the opening Molineux outing of the season, against Cardiff, on Saturday, August 29, manager Stan Cullis decided to make a change to his forward line for the first time in 17 games. Ron Stockin, who had missed a couple of good chances in the first half at Sunderland made way for Peter Broadbent in a match played in drizzle after early morning rain. That forward line of Hancocks, Broadbent, Swinbourne, Wilshaw and Mullen would play in 29 games in 1953-4.

The Welshmen had a shock in store for the home side when centre-forward Wilf Grant picked up a clearance from goalkeeper Ron Howells to give them a 13th-minute lead. That shook Wolves into life and three goals in the space of five minutes, starting after 34, put Wolves in control. Dennis Wilshaw, Jimmy Mullen and Johnny Hancocks (penalty) were the scorers and only the brilliance of Howells prevented a rout. Wolves might have paid for a series of near things when Cardiff twice went close to goals late in the game. The home fans did not know it but their side were about to put together the long unbeaten run which would form the backbone of their title quest.

Huddersfield were enjoying their stay at the top of the table and beat Portsmouth 5-1 at Leeds Road, where centre-forward Jimmy Glazzard struck three times. Albion kept up the pressure with that man Nicholls twice on target in a 2-0 win at Preston. Arsenal suffered their third defeat in four games when they went down 2-1 away to Villa.

Cullis gave his winning line-up a vote of confidence for the return fixture with Sunderland at Molineux two days later. Again there was a shock in store for the home side as visiting centre-forward Tommy Wright, deputising for the injured Ford, scored after just 90 seconds. That did not put off Wolves who proceeded to bombard the visiting goal with Jimmy Mullen having a point-blank shot saved by Cowan, sending a running header just wide and seeing a centre hit the upright. Others went close too before, after 35 minutes Daniel and Cowan failed to cope with a Broadbent pass and the persistent Dennis Wilshaw took advantage to equalise.

The pattern continued in the second half but the goals that gave Wolves a 3-1 win arrived in the space of a couple of minutes. Mullen, in scintillating form, drove the ball home on 68 minutes after Cowan had pushed it out then Roy Swinbourne scored from a Broadbent pass. So ended August, and, two days into September, Albion went top for the first time when their Wednesday night home clash with Manchester United brought a 2-0 win thanks to goals from Ronnie Allen and Ken Hodgkisson, the latter making a rare appearance for the club who would

14

later sell him to Walsall where he became a stalwart servant. Albion's elevation owed itself to Huddersfield losing for the first time in the campaign – 2-1 at Cardiff.

There was also a Thursday match that week and Tottenham's win at Charlton saw them go second in the table. The only goal of the game came from a young amateur, Vic Groves, who would a few years later make his name with Leyton Orient before becoming a big money buy for Spurs' arch rivals Arsenal. This was how the of the table looked on September 3:

	P	W	D	L	F	A	Pt
Albion	5	4	1	0	10	2	9
Tottenham	5	4	0	1	10	4	8
Huddersfield	5	3	1	1	10	4	7

Then came one of the high spots of Wolves' season, the visit to Highbury where they had not won for twenty years. There had hardly been a better chance to beat the Gunners on their own patch, however. Champions the previous season, Tom Whittaker's team had made a dreadful start this time with three defeats and two draws in five games to lie rock bottom in the table.

They were also without their inspirational skipper Joe Mercer, for whom Welshman Dave Bowen deputised. So it was no real surprise that Wolves did at last triumph at Highbury though it was something of a surprise that their win, on September 5, was by only 3-2. It was climaxed with that footballing rarity – a Johnny Hancocks header and a flying one at that. The little winger nodded in Jimmy Mullen's cross with just two minutes left.

15

Twice Arsenal had quickly answered Wolves goals. Peter Broadbent struck his first of the season, on 22 minutes, only for Don Roper to level three minutes later and Dennis Wilshaw's 32nd-minute header was cancelled out by Cliff Holton. Yet Wolves ought to have won comfortably but Wilshaw, Broadbent, Mullen (twice) and Hancocks all missed chances before Hancocks's final flourish. The match saw the return to first team action of Bert Williams and the goalkeeper showed he was still a potential England man.

Williams recalls: "I'd had a bad start to the season. I think it was the time I'd got a shoulder injury and for a time I even thought I might not play again. I was in agony."

Arsenal's start would get worse before it got better as a week after the Wolves reverse they went to Sunderland and were hammered 7-1, Trevor Ford scoring three. Manager Whittaker's reaction was to sign veteran former England centre-forward Tommy Lawton from Brentford. It was an unexpected return to top flight action for the man many rated England's best ever No 9.

To complete a Black Country double over North London, Albion beat Tottenham 3-0 at The Hawthorns, helped by an Alf Ramsey own goal. That put Albion three points clear at the top as Blackpool had become the latest side to beat Huddersfield to put themselves second on eight points, the same total as Burnley and Wolves. Preston again demonstrated their goal potential with a 5-1 win at Anfield, where England winger Tom Finney was on target twice.

The week beginning, Monday September 7, saw all 22 clubs in midweek action with Albion unexpectedly held 2-2 at home by Newcastle on the Wednesday, two days after Wolves had beaten Liverpool 2-1 at Molineux in a match of incident featuring a finish even more dramatic than that at Highbury and a display of high courage from full-back Jack Short.

He sustained a torn thigh muscle after 23 minutes, switched to outside right and had to persuade manager Stan Cullis to let him return to the action after failing to start the second half. The Yorkshireman got his way and operated as nuisance value at centre-forward. The injury also highlighted the versatility of others, particularly Dennis Wilshaw who moved to right-half, with Bill Slater switching to left-half, Billy Wright moving to right-back and Roy Swinbourne to inside-right.

The reshuffle probably had much to do with Wolves making hard work of beating a Liverpool side who had won only one of their previous six league games. Swinbourne opened the scoring right on half-time but the Anfield men silenced the home fans when, three minutes from time, Brian Jackson ran on to a long pass from centre-forward Louis Bimpson and fired the ball past Williams. Within 30 seconds, it was Wolves fans who were in full voice as Short managed to prod the ball towards goal after a poor clearance header. Swinbourne and Broadbent both rushed in for the kill, Broadbent applying the finishing touch after brushing his team-mate to one side.

16

Short paid the price for his gallantry and when Portsmouth visited Molineux on Saturday, September 12, it was Len Gibbons who lined up at right-back. There was another enforced change – Bill Slater was on duty for England in the amateur international against Ireland. In those days England still played amateur internationals and they were ranked of major importance by the FA. So if your country called – you had to answer. There was no suggestion of postponing games because clubs had players on international duty. So while Wolves and Pompey staged a seven-goal thriller, Slater was in Coleraine at left-half in an England side beaten 2-1 by the Irish.

Norman Deeley, on leave from the army, came in for his first game of the season, as Slater's deputy as, for a third game running, Wolves won with a late goal. Roy Swinbourne was the scorer to give his side a 4-3 victory after they had led 2-0 and 3-1, thanks to a Dennis Wilshaw treble. His first two goals had come within three minutes of the start but Johnny Gordon had quickly reduced the deficit. When Wilshaw made it 3-1, Portsmouth's answer was a goal from Peter Harris just before the break and another from Gordon three minutes into the second half.

Wolves were not at their best despite young Deeley giving Johnny Hancocks fine service on the right wing. Chances came and went in the second half and the defence looked vulnerable at times. However, Swinbourne had the last word and so Pompey had lost 4-3 for the third time in eight games. For good measure, their next game brought a 4-4 home draw with Blackpool. While Wolves were struggling to get the better of Portsmouth, Albion were back to their best, beating Burnley 4-1 at Turf Moor. That setback for the Lancashire side saw them lose their second spot in the table to Wolves. Biggest win of the day was at The Valley where Charlton beat Middlesbrough 8-1, Eddie Firmani grabbing a hat-trick. The top of the table:

	P	W	D	L	F	A	Pt
Albion	8	6	2	0	19	5	14
Wolves	8	6	0	2	22	15	12
Huddersfield	8	4	2	2	15	9	10
Bolton	7	4	2	1	13	9	10
Burnley	8	5	0	3	19	15	10
Tottenham	8	5	0	3	14	12	10

Both Wolves and Albion were away from home the following Wednesday, September 16, and while Wolves ought to have won at Liverpool, only to be held 1-1, Albion were in sparkling form at St James' Park against Newcastle. Leading 3-0 at the break, the Baggies conceded three second-half goals but it mattered little as they collected another four themselves to run out 7-3 winners. Johnny Nicholls scored three that night.

Dennis Wilshaw took his scoring spree to nine goals in nine games when he gave Wolves a 40th-minute lead over Liverpool. He beat a couple of opponents before clipping the ball past goalkeeper Russell Crossley. With Slater back from amateur international duty, Norman Deeley kept his place at right half, with Slater on the left and Billy Wright in the unfamiliar role of right-back. The new-look formation did well and in the 20 minutes after half-time ought to have added to their lead. They did not and paid the price 21 minutes from time when inside left Bill Jones prodded the ball home through a sea of legs after a Brian Jackson centre had been headed back across goal by young left-winger Alan A'Court.

The evening before, champions Arsenal at last won a match. They chose an ideal place to do it – at Stamford Bridge, beating London rivals Chelsea 2-0 in front of a crowd of more than 60,000, former Walsall inside-forward Doug Lishman scoring the goals.

Wolves were held again, on Saturday, September 19. They drew 0-0 at Blackpool having again had to make changes in defence. Once again the England amateur side had first call on Slater – he played left-half in the side beaten 4-0 at Crystal Palace by the touring South Africans – and so Ray Chatham and Bill Baxter were given their first outings of the season at right-half and left-half respectively with Wright continuing at right back.

Before a crowd of 35,074, at Bloomfield Road, the Seasiders must have been optimistic of success fielding a forward line of five current or future internationals – Matthew, Taylor, Mortensen, Mudie, Perry – yet Wolves held them, Bill Shorthouse keeping a tight rein on Stanley Mortensen, who was on top form at the time, having hit 11 goals in his previous eight games. Wolves were handicapped by an injury to Wilshaw just before half-time, a thigh strain causing him to operate at centre-forward in the second half. There was plenty of entertainment but goals would not come.

There may have been some disappointment as Wolves slipped to third place following Huddersfield's 6-3 win at Sheffield United, where Jimmy Glazzard hit three goals, yet they still made up some ground on Albion. Charlton became the first side to beat them this season when they won by the odd goal in five at The Hawthorns.

Four days after the Blackpool draw came the first representative game of the season when the Football League took on the Irish League at Windsor Park, Belfast, and ran out 5-0 winners thanks to goals from Bolton pair Nat Lofthouse (three) and Harold Hassall (two). Billy Wright was at right-half in the following side: Merrick (Birmingham); Green (Birmingham), Eckersley (Blackburn); Wright, Johnston (Blackpool), Dickinson (Portsmouth), Finney (Preston), Quixall (Sheffield Wednesday), Lofthouse, Hassall, Robb (Tottenham).

Wright was back in his familiar club position the following Saturday – September 26 – when Wolves did what they had been threatening to do for some time – hit a load of goals, Chelsea were on the receiving end, losing 8-1 to register the heaviest league defeat in their history. Johnny Hancocks had a field day, scoring three times, starting with a third-minute penalty. He hit a second on the half hour and the other four forwards were on target in the second half, Roy Swinbourne twice and Peter Broadbent, Dennis Wilshaw and Jimmy Mullen collecting one each. With the score 6-0, Roy Bentley pulled one back via a rebound from a penalty saved by Bert Williams, but it had been a harrowing day for a Chelsea defence who had future West Ham and England manager Ron Greenwood at centre-half.

An added sidelight to the match was the presence on the field of three England skippers, Billy Wright, of course, was England's leader, while Bill Slater captained England amateurs, a role previously fulfilled by Chelsea's Derek Saunders. It was only the sixth time in the club's history that all five forwards had scored in a League match.

The goal spree was still not enough to edge Huddersfield out of second place. They won 3-2 at home to Middlesbrough thanks to goals from the prolific Jimmy Glazzard, while Albion were 3-2 winners at Sheffield Wednesday with wingers Frank Griffin and George Lee on target along with the inevitable Johnny Nicholls. Charlton also went on another goal spree at The Valley, Stuart Leary scoring four times as Liverpool were beaten 6-0, a defeat that put the Merseysiders bottom but one in the table.

18

CHAPTER TWO
SOME LIGHT RELIEF

Centre-forward Jimmy Glazzard was at it again on the first Saturday in October, with a hat-trick as Huddersfield beat Villa 4-0 at Leeds Road, while Albion were beating Middlesbrough 2-1 at The Hawthorns. On the same day, Wolves grabbed a useful point when they shared six goals with Sheffield United at Bramall Lane.

Before that game, however, had come a notable event in Wolves history when they played the first floodlit game at Molineux. The South African touring side were the visitors and Wolves' own Springbok, Eddie Stuart, was given the honour of captaining the side against his fellow countrymen. Stuart was celebrating his return to health after a mystery illness had brought him close to death during the previous season. Regular centre-half Bill Shorthouse agreed to step down so that Stuart could have his moment.

"It was a great honour," recalls Stuart, "to be captain of Wolves in the very first floodlit game. Some might have said it was the obvious thing to do with me be being a South African and the game being against South Africa but the club didn't have to do it. It was a tremendous gesture and so good of Bill Shorthouse to agree to step down. It's something I'll never forget."

The game on Wednesday, September 30, saw Wolves, wearing special luminous gold shirts, triumph 3-1. The tourists never managed to curb the wing magic of Johnny Hancocks and Jimmy Mullen. Wolves might well have scored more goals than those that came from Mullen (32 minutes), Peter Broadbent (34), with a narrow-angle cross shot, and Roy Swinbourne (86) who turned in a Hancocks centre. Brian Gibson had replied for South Africa soon after half-time.

19

"It was a very colourful occasion," adds Stuart, "us in our fluorescent shirts, South Africa in their famous green shirts and the novelty of the floodlights."

There was much praise for the Molineux lights, the club having taken their time to find the best system before installing them. South African FA president Fred Fell rated the system one of the best he had seen. South African skipper Ross Dow said the lighting was first class while his opposite number, Billy Wright, rated them the best under which he had played in England. Teams that night:

Wolves: Williams; Short, Pritchard; Slater, Stuart, Wright; Hancocks, Broadbent, Swinbourne, Stockin, Mullen.
South Africa: Rudham; Machanik, Jacobson; Dow, Naish, Jacques; Claasens, Warren, Salton, Gibson, Le Roux.

Referee: F Read (Willenhall).

Shorthouse returned to the side for the trip to Bramall Lane, as did Dennis Wilshaw, but Wolves had once again to rely upon a late goal to gain something from the match. Johnny Hancocks had scored after 10 minutes but goals from Irish winger Alf Ringstead and Arthur Bottom, later to help York on their FA Cup giant-killing run of 1955, put the Blades ahead, only for Wilshaw to make it 2-2 on the half-hour.

Jimmy Hagan, a masterly inside forward who had won many war-time caps for England but only one official one, was in top form and his promptings kept Wolves on their toes. Ringstead struck again three minutes into the second half only for Swinbourne to equalise with four minutes to go. Top of the table:

	P	W	D	L	F	A	Pt
Albion	12	9	2	1	33	14	20
Huddersfield	12	8	2	2	28	13	18
Wolves	12	7	3	2	34	20	17

Here, one again has to emphasise how different were times in the 1950s when country took precedent over club and there was never a suggestion that international calls could mean the postponement of a league match. So when Dennis Wilshaw's fine early form brought its deserved reward in the shape of place in the England team to face Wales at Ninian Park Cardiff, on Saturday, October 10, along with Billy Wright and Jimmy Mullen, there was no suggestion of calling off Wolves' match that same day at Newcastle.

It was a case of 'Get on with it' so Wolves drafted in Ron Stockin and Les Smith to form a left-wing partnership while teenager Ron Flowers played his first game of the season as Wright's deputy. A side captained by the redoubtable Bill Shorthouse had Bert Williams, as much as anyone, to thank for their 2-1 win – the club's first at St James' Park for 30 years. The goalkeeper was in top form even though he was beaten by Tommy Mulgrew on seven minutes. That was Mulgrew's first goal for the Geordies in what proved to be his last first-team appearance for them.

Once more, late goals brought Wolves success. Smith cut inside to go down the middle of the field and then fire the equaliser with a right-foot shot on 81 minutes and, two minutes from time, Roy Swinbourne turned in a cunning Johnny Hancocks free kick. The winger looked as though he would lob the ball into the penalty area but instead fired it low to take the home defence by surprise as Swinbourne nipped in to turn the ball past Ronnie Simpson. Though the reserves rose to the occasion, full-back Roy Pritchard was the real hero. He got a nasty kick early in the match but carried on to play a key part in the win. He paid the price, though and could hardly walk afterwards.

The win was enough to take Wolves back to second place as the top-of-the-table showdown at The Hawthorns saw Albion beat Huddersfield 4-0, helped by three goals from Ronnie Allen. Liverpool found a a rare goal touch at Anfield, before slipping back into relegation mode, as they beat Villa 6-1, helped by two goals from Wolves' 1949 Cup Final hero Sammy Smyth and an own goal from Danny Blanchflower.

While all this was going on, Dennis Wilshaw was marking his international debut with two goals in England's 4-1 win in Cardiff. The other two came from Nat Lofthouse but the England side got little praise afterwards as three of their goals came while Welsh full-back Alf Sherwood was off the field injured. Wilshaw had been called into the side on the Thursday before the match when Bolton's Harold Hassall pulled out through injury.

"We did not get a very good press," Wilshaw recalls, "and one reporter wrote that Wilshaw should be banned from international football. I think it was George Follows in the News Chronicle."

Wilshaw's father, Tom, suffering with the illness which would eventually take his life early in the New Year, was still able to get to Cardiff to see his son win his first cap and wrote to the Pressman in question. "He was in a lot of pain but nothing would keep him from that match," recalls Wilshaw, "but he was so incensed afterwards that he wrote to George Follows.

He did not get a very nice letter back, something along the lines of we were all entitled to our opinions." Sadly, Follows was one of the Pressmen killed in the Munich Air Crash of 1958.

Continues Wilshaw; "If I'd done that today – a left-footed player coming into the England side and scoring two goals – I'd probably be worth twenty-six million!"

The England side, with 20-year-old Albert Quixall also making his debut:
Merrick (Birmingham); Garrett (Blackpool), Eckersley (Blackburn); Wright, Johnston (Blackpool), Dickinson (Portsmouth); Finney (Preston), Quixall (Sheffield Wednesday), Lofthouse (Bolton), Wilshaw, Mullen.

Four days before the game in Cardiff, Wilshaw had played in the side Wolves sent to Gigg Lane to open Bury's new floodlights. Skippered by Bill Shorthouse Wolves lost 3-1 to a home side captained by former Molineux stalwart Angus McLean. Ron Stockin scored for Wolves who were level 1-1 at the break.

Wolves' line-up.
Sims; Clamp, Pritchard; Chatham, Shorthouse, Baxter, Hancocks, Broadbent, Swinbourne, Wilshaw, Stockin.

There was more floodlit action for Wolves before they could continue their push for league points. Scottish giants Celtic provided the opposition for Molineux's second game under lights and 41,820 fans were there on October 14 to see Wolves win 2-0 thanks to two goals in the last four minutes from Wilshaw.

The inside man may have had a point to prove as his two-goal debut for his country had counted for nothing, the selectors dropping him for the game against FIFA at Wembley. The Scots were not too happy with Wilshaw's first goal, claiming he had helped take the ball past their defence with the aid of his hand. While Celtic were still rattled Wilshaw hooked home a free kick to seal the win.

There were some top players in the Scottish side, notably, Bobby Evans, Bertie Peacock, Bobby Collins and Willie Fernie. Wolves were without Williams, Pritchard, Slater and Broadbent with a Tipton youngster, Bobby Mason, given his first team bow. Mason would later become a key man in Wolves' championship triumphs of 1957-8 and 1958-9.

21

Teams:

Wolves: Sims; Short, Guttridge; Baxter, Shorthouse, Wright; Hancocks, Mason, Swinbourne, Wilshaw, Mullen;

Celtic: Hunter; Haughney, Fallon; Evans, McIlroy, Peacock; Collins, Fernie, McPhail, Walsh, Mochan.

Two days after the Celtic clash there was another 40,000 crowd at Molineux, this time for the visit of Manchester United. Matt Busby's side were in a transitional stage as the old guard who had won the title in 1952 made way for some newer names. Bill Foulkes had settled in at right back while former Barnsley centre-forward Tommy Taylor was enjoying his first full season at Old Trafford. On their left wing was Harry McShane, father of actor Ian.

Taylor was on the mark after half an hour, cancelling out Johnny Hancocks's opener which had come from the penalty spot after United full-back Roger Byrne had needlessly handled. Taylor's goal came when he took advantage of a weak back pass by Bill Guttridge, deputising for the injured Roy Pritchard. The full-back had a difficult match trying to cope with England winger Johnny Berry. A Peter Broadbent header restored Wolves' lead and Roy Swinbourne made the game safe 18 minutes from time.

Arsenal's recent revival came to an abrupt end at Highbury where Burnley won 5-2, centre-forward Bill Holden grabbing three goals.

22

Albion still had a three-point lead at the top of the table, though, thanks to their 2-1 win at Sheffield United where the familiar duo of Johnny Nicholls and Ronnie Allen were on target. That lead would soon stretch to four points but first the spotlight turned from the title race to a little matter of England trying to keep the foreign invader at bay.

Unless you count the Republic of Ireland, who won at Goodison in 1949, no foreign foe had triumphed over England on English soil. All that would change with devastating effect in November, 1953, but first it was the multi-talented line-up assembled by FIFA, billed as 'The Rest of Europe' who would threaten England's home record at Wembley on Wednesday, October 21. The game was to celebrate the ninetieth anniversary of the founding of the FA.

As well as Blackpool's Stanley Mortensen coming in at the expense of Wilshaw, the England selectors – manager Walter Winterbottom did not have overall say in team choice, unlike his successor Alf Ramsey – recalled Mortensen's more famous right-wing partner Stanley Matthews after a two-year absence and gave a first cap to Charlton centre-half Derek Ufton. It was to prove his only one.

It was a tough match for Billy Wright's England who managed to scrape a 4-4 draw thanks to a last-kick penalty from ice-cool Ramsey. It was generally reckoned a lucky escape as the European stars showed, if it was not already appreciated, that English football no longer ruled the world. Jimmy Mullen could derive some satisfaction, though. He scored two of the goals. England had made a dreadful start, going behind in the first minute through a goal from the penalty spot by Ladislav Kubala after Bill Eckersley had brought down Vukas. It was 1-1 thanks to Mortensen but two goals from Italian winger Gianperto Boniperti put the Europeans 3-1 up only for Mullen to put the ball home after a mix-up in the Europeans' defence.

Mullen struck again in the second half shooting home after a typical dribble and centre from Matthews only for Kubala to make it 4-3. Then up stepped Ramsey to give England a reprieve. England: Merrick (Birmingham); Ramsey (Tottenham), Eckersley (Blackburn); Wright, Ufton (Charlton), Dickinson (Portsmouth); Matthews (Blackpool), Mortensen (Blackpool), Lofthouse (Bolton), Quixall (Sheffield Wednesday), Mullen.

Rest of Europe: Zeman (Austria), sub Beara (Yugoslavia); Navarro (Spain), Hanappi (Austria); Cajkovski (Yugoslavia), Posipal (West Germany), Ocwirk (Austria); Boniperti (Italy), Kubala (Spain), Nordahl (Sweden), Vukas (Yugoslavia), Zebec (Yugoslavia).

Wright was injured at Wembley and had to miss Wolves' trip to Bolton three days later. Bill Baxter deputised for him and Bill Shorthouse skippered a side in which Bill Guttridge was given another chance after his difficult game against Manchester United. A 1-1 draw was probably a fair reflection of a match in which the visiting forwards, Peter Broadbent apart, were below their best. Johnny Hancocks gave Wolves a 26th-minute lead which Willie Moir cancelled out a minute before half-time. Guttridge looked far steadier than against Manchester United and Bill Shorthouse had the measure of Nat Lofthouse virtually throughout though the England centre-forward did get in a flying header late in the match which brought an equally spectacular response from Bert Williams.

The point dropped cost Wolves second place as Huddersfield won 2-0 while Albion beat Chelsea 5-2 at home helped by three goals from Ronnie Allen. Albion's lead at the top was thus four points. They had 26 while Huddersfield and Wolves both had 22, the Yorkshiremen having a better goal average.

Sunderland remained at the bottom of the table after going down 6-2 to Preston at Deepdale, where centre-forward Charlie Wayman was a three-goal man.

That gap at the top was quickly narrowed to two points on Saturday, October 31, and Wolves, with a 1-0 home win over Preston, made sure it would be a two-horse race for the title from now on. While Huddersfield were being held 0-0 by Manchester United, Albion were suffering only their second defeat of the season – but an emphatic one at that, 4-1 against Blackpool at Bloomfield Road.

The Preston game was not an epic but it was significant for a first outing for Billy Wright as a left-back. Bill Baxter continued in the No 4 shirt but Ron Stockin got a rare game when an injury to Roy Swinbourne meant Dennis Wilshaw was switched to centre-forward. It was Wilshaw who got the goal after 55 minutes when a Jimmy Mulllen centre across the face of the goal was returned by Johnny Hancocks for Wilshaw to slot the ball home at the far post.

Preston, who had put six goals past Sunderland the week before, were without star right-winger

Tom Finney and gave a debut in his place to 18-year-old Les Campbell – all five feet two and a bit inches of him!

The Manchester United side at Huddersfield had a youthful look about it. Matt Busby had decided the time had come to let his talented youngsters have their chance. Dennis Viollet, Jackie Blanchflower and Duncan Edwards, still a few days short of his 17th birthday, were drafted into the team and would stay there for the rest of the season. The Busby Babes were on their way!

Wolves could have been without Slater for their next outing – the trip to Middlesbrough on Saturday, November 7. However, he decided to turn down the invitation to play in an England amateur trial game at Blackpool. This did not prevent the selectors naming him in their side for the match against France at Luton on the same day his club faced their first showdown with Albion – November 14. More of that later. Slater recalls: "I tried to avoid international games clashing with club games but the FA were very strict."

Although Wright was still at full-back, Swinbourne was back to lead the line, and Wolves had a more familiar look. However, Middlesbrough, bottom but one in the table, rose to the occasion even though Swinbourne and Johnny Hancocks beat Italian-born, Scottish-raised, goalkeeper Rolando Ugolini with two unstoppable long range shots in the first half.

In between came a reply from Albert Fitzsimons, Boro's Republic of Ireland international, and in the second half Ken McPherson and Jim Hartnett put the home side ahead. Then came yet another example of Wolves' never-say-die approach, Dennis Wilshaw netting four minutes from time from a Hancocks cross in similar fashion to his winner against Preston. Wolves were handicapped somewhat by an injury to Bill Baxter, who ended the match limping. Albion beat bottom-of-the table Sunderland 2-0 at The Hawthorns and now the scene was set for the meeting of the sides at Molineux – a 'four-pointer' if ever there was one:

	P	W	D	L	F	A	Pt
Albion	17	13	2	2	47	21	28
Wolves	17	10	5	2	44	26	25
Huddersfield	17	10	3	4	33	19	23

On the Monday before the big game there was another happy occasion for Eddie Stuart. He was chosen at left-half in the Anglo South African XI to play the touring South Africans at Highbury. The Wolves man managed to collect a goal, too, as the home-based Springboks triumphed 6-1.

Billy Wright and Jimmy Mullen also had a match to get through before the game all Wolves and Albion fans were eagerly awaiting. They were in the England side who beat Ireland 3-1 at Goodison Park, as was Stan Rickaby of the Baggies, winning his one and only full cap as deputy for Alf Ramsey. Goals from the Bolton pair Harold Hassall (two) and Nat Lofthouse, gave England their victory. The win ensured England would go to the World Cup finals in Switzerland as the top two sides in the Home International Championship were guaranteed places. It was not one of England's better displays but Wright did lay on the second goal, for Hassall, and Mullen the last one for Lofthouse.

Teams:
England: Merrick (Birmingham); Rickaby, Eckersley (Blackburn); Wright, Johnston (Blackpool), Dickinson (Portsmouth); Matthews (Blackpool), Quixall (Sheffield Wednesday), Lofthouse, Hassall, Mullen.
Northern Ireland: Smyth (Distillery); Graham (Doncaster), McMichael (Newcastle); D Blanchflower (Aston Villa), Dickson (Arsenal), Cush (Glenavon); Bingham (Sunderland), McIlroy (Burnley), Simpson (Rangers), McMorran (Doncaster), Lockhart (Aston Villa).

Wright, Mullen and Rickaby came through the game unscathed for the big Molineux showdown between the Black Country title rivals but Peter Broadbent had not recovered from an injury picked up at Middlesbrough. Ron Stockin deputised against a full-strength visiting side.

If any of the 56,590 who packed out the old ground were late arriving they may have missed the only goal of the game. Mullen scored it after only four minutes and there followed a typical derby game between contrasting rivals, Wolves preferring to keep things simple while the Baggies tended to rely on their short passing game.

25

There were escapes at both ends and Bert Williams had plenty of chances to distinguish himself though he had some luck when a flying header from Ronnie Allen hit an upright and rebounded into his arms. Albion ought to have heeded the fact that their nearest to a goal had come from a two-man build-up – Rickaby to Jimmy Dudley and then Dudley's cross into the middle for Allen.

Mullen's goal had an element of luck about it. He put in a centre-cum-shot, after Johnny Hancocks had robbed a hesitant Rickaby, and goalkeeper Norman Heath misjudged the flight of the ball.

Dennis Wilshaw recalls the derby encounters with much affection. "I always thought that the Wolves-West Brom were classic games. Two very different styles but both high class. I was also never aware of any hate between Wolves and West Brom fans. This has come about in recent times – if there was any animosity in those days it was against Villa."

While all eyes were on Molineux, Huddersfield kept in contention with a 2-0 home win over Sheffield Wednesday – that man Jimmy Glazzard collected two more goals – while Manchester United were 6-1 away winners over Cardiff, 20-year-old Dennis Viollet scoring twice. This is how the top of the table looked on November 14

	P	W	D	L	F	A	Pt
Albion	18	13	2	3	47	22	28
Wolves	18	11	5	2	45	26	27
Huddersfield	18	11	3	4	35	19	25

CHAPTER THREE

MAGYAR MAGIC

Albion bounced back in style from their Molineux defeat at the hands of Wolves as they, like Manchester United, gave Cardiff a 6-1 beating, with Ronnie Allen hitting four goals in the Hawthorns romp on Saturday, November 21. Wolves kept in touch, however, with another fine display in London, this time beating Charlton 2-0 as Roy Pritchard and Peter Broadbent returned after their injuries and Bill Slater after his amateur international outing. Broadbent, with members of his family in town to see how much he had progressed, opened the scoring when he took advantage of a slip by Athletic's left-half Cyril Hammond. Highlight of the game, however, was the second goal – a Johnny Hancocks special after 54 minutes. After racing on to a through ball from full-back Jack Short, he hit the ball from a narrow angle on the right so hard that goalkeeper Sam Bartram, still a first choice in his fortieth year, hardly had time to move. Roy Swinbourne and Dennis Wilshaw also went close, the latter seeing a shot skim the bar. Swinbourne once got past Bartram only for centre-half Ufton to race back to prevent a goal.

Four days later the neck-and-neck race for the championship was forgotten. November 25, 1953, a foggy day in London town, saw the banishing of any remaining doubts about the standing of the nation who invented Association Football. One scoreline says it all – England 3 Hungary 6. The legend of the Magical Magyars was born that day and Wolves' Billy Wright could only chase shadows like the rest of his team as Wembley staged one of its greatest matches. Grosics, Bozsik, Hidegkuti, Puskas and Kocsis suddenly became household names and, with his innate ability to treat triumph and disaster the same, Wright would often laugh in later years at the way Ferenc Puskas made a fool of him to score his side's third goal. Wright came steaming in to dispossess the tubby Magyar skipper with a tackle that 99 times out of a hundred would have been successful. This was No 100, however, as Puskas rolled the ball back with the sole of his left boot – he only used his right leg for standing on! – before firing home. It was a moment of genius the hazy film of which has been played many times since.

Wright would also smile when he recalled his remark to a team-mate as the players walked out on to the pitch. He had noticed the Hungarians were wearing lightweight boots cut away at the ankle. "We should be all right here," said Wright, "they have not got the proper kit." Equally memorable was the quip by a fan when forty years later, Puskas's old club side Honved provided the opposition for Wolves at the match to mark the completion of the new Molineux. Puskas, who by then had gone from portly in his playing days to absolutely massive, made the trip, too, and stood arm in arm with Wright, by then a Wolves director, surveying the impressive facilities from the players' tunnel. It was then a Wolves wag yelled: "Billy, that's the closest you ever got to him!"

Back in 1953, there was not much laughing among English football followers. The inquests were long and hard. The Hungarians had shown us how far we had fallen behind. The teams:

England: Merrick (Birmingham); Ramsey (Tottenham), Eckersley (Blackburn), Wright, Johnston (Blackpool), Dickinson (Portsmouth), Matthews (Blackpool), Taylor Blackpool), Mortensen (Blackpool), Sewell (Sheffield Wednesday), Robb (Tottenham).
Hungary: Grosics (Honved); Buzansky (Dorogi), Lantos (MTK); Bozsik (Honved), Zakarias (MTK), Budai (Honved), Hidegkuti (MTK), Puskas (Honved), Czibor (Honved), Sub: Geller (MTK) for Grosics.

It's hard for younger fans to realise that in those days Blackpool were a power in English football. Little Ernie Taylor was given his first, and only, cap that day as the Seasiders provided four men to the home line-up. Tottenham's George Robb also won his first, and only, cap in preference to Jimmy Mullen. A former amateur international Robb at least knew just how good the Hungarians were. He had seen them in action a year earlier in Finland where they became Olympic champions.

Another player who knew all about the Hungarians was Wolves' own Bill Slater. He had also played in the 1952 Olympics. "I stayed on after we got knocked out and saw Hungary beat Yugoslavia in the final in Helsinki," Slater recalls. "When I came back I spoke to Walter Winterbottom (England's manager) and he said 'Why not write something about it?' So I wrote an article for the FA's own periodical, I think it was called the FA News.

"I said they were really impressive and the way they played was marvellous and that there were features to their game that we should take note of – but nobody took any notice of what I wrote. There was no reaction whatsoever. Then they came to Wembley and people really opened their eyes. They were a bit special, it was not lucky, they utterly outplayed England."

Young Ron Flowers, still in the reserves at that time, was in the RAF and watched the game on TV at RAF Cosford. "The Hungarians were skilful players, there's no doubt about that," recalls Flowers. "It was something new, a different pattern of play and we just could not cope with it. They played at a different tempo across the ninety minutes. It made us stop and think. People were saying we were way behind – not just in tactics, everything."

Dennis Wilshaw has good reason to be thankful to the Hungarians – "those results helped get me back into the England side," he says with a smile, adding: "They did make a tremendous impression on me in many ways. We had never seen anything like Puskas. Billy Wright would always tell that story about a report of the game in which they said he was moving in to tackle when Puskas dragged the ball back and fired it into the net – and Wright was still moving in to tackle when the ball hit the back of the net."

Another report described that incident as Wright being like a fire engine arriving too late to put out the fire.

Wilshaw, who watched the game on television, adds "I thought Stan Cullis was an idiot when he arranged for us to play Honved who had half a dozen of the team that had beaten England. Yet we beat them and we did so playing the English way with long passing and using our wingers. It was no good trying to play tip-tap-toe against them. That was not the way we played in England. Only Tottenham were playing tip-tap-toe football in those days."

Eddie Stuart was at Wembley for the game. "I had never been there before, I was so excited," he says. "It was the first international I had seen and it still remains the best I have ever seen. The one I felt sorry for was Gil Merrick in goal. There was little he could do. Hungary were that good. You can imagine how we felt when we beat Honved a year later. I don't think I slept a wink all night, just thinking about what we had achieved."

Wolves goalkeeper Bert Williams was also at Wembley for the Hungary match – on the England substitutes' bench. "We did not usually have substitutes in those days but the Hungarians insisted on it," recalls Williams. "So I was on the bench, stripped and ready to go. Two or three players were injured at one stage in the game and Billy Wright was down injured near to us. So I went on the pitch to see if he was all right but apparently the commentator, Kenneth Wolstenholme, said on TV 'Oh, Ted Ditchburn (the Tottenham goalkeeper) is on the pitch' Well, Ted wasn't event in the squad."

Adds Williams: "They were an exceptional team. They had a star in every position, they were the best team I've ever seen – and they went out to score goals. The Brazilians were good to watch but they went in for intricate passing, the Hungarians were very direct."

A final verdict from Billy Wright on that epic England game is found in that excellent biography by Norman Giller (Billy Wright a Hero for All Seasons – Robson Books). "There was a mist over Wembley that afternoon and I felt as if we were lost in a fog as the Hungarians completely outplayed us. It was not that England played badly. Hungary were just in a different class and playing a style of football that was, well, foreign to us. It was a defeat which started a revolution in our game. We knew from that day on that we needed to get into the modern world. They were playing a different game from us."

It was back to league fare for Wright three days later and a 4-1 home win over Sheffield Wednesday but only after Wolves had been rocked by a goal from Dennis Woodhead after six minutes. On a fine mild afternoon, in stark contrast to misty Wembley, Wright and half-back colleague Bill Slater were key figures in turning things round as the side's unbeaten run was stretched to 17 games. Star of the show, however, was Johnny Hancocks. He was in dazzling form and set up goals for Dennis Wilshaw and Roy Swinbourne (two). The wee man hit the other goal from the penalty spot five minutes before half-time to put Wolves 2-1 up. Many thought at the time that it was Hancocks's second of the match. It was only afterwards confirmed that Wednesday keeper Bryan Ryalls had fumbled Hancocks's shot from the wing with Dennis Wilshaw putting the final touch for the first Wolves goal. At that stage of the season the inside forward was joint top scorer for the club with Swinbourne on 14 goals, while Hancocks had 12.

29

Albion's 3-2 win at Manchester City and Huddersfield's 3-1 home win over Burnley maintained the status quo at the top of the table but only for a week. Portsmouth, then in 19th place, went to The Hawthorns on Saturday, December 5, and gained an unexpected 3-2 win, inside-forward Johnny Gordon scoring twice. On the same day Wolves roared to a win at Tottenham by the same score and thus sat proudly at the top of the First Division. Hancocks picked up where he had left off against Sheffield Wednesday and won the match 12 minutes from time with a memorable goal. He won the ball near the byeline to the right of goal and as full-back Charlie Withers raced in to tackle brought the ball back to his left foot and fired a shot between goalkeeper Ted Ditchburn and the near post.

Wolves had again gone a goal down when Les Bennett put Spurs in front on 26 minutes. Headers from Dennis Wilshaw and Peter Broadbent in the space of a minute early in the second half turned the game round only for home centre forward Len Duquemin to level with a goal which had a distinct look of off-side about it.

Wilshaw remembers well his goal that day. "Jimmy Mullen centred the ball and it came across just a few inches above the ground and this stupid idiot – me – threw himself at the ball. Now Alf Ramsey was standing on the line with his right foot held back and if he had gone through with his kick he would have done me a lot of damage. I would have been hurt, it would have been my own fault and I would not have scored – but he kept his foot withdrawn and I shall always remember that. There were a few full-backs around who would not have done that."

With the season at the halfway stage, Wolves could look back with some satisfaction. They had put together an 18-match unbeaten run and had three times given the London scribes something to wax lyrical about. Broadbent and Hancocks had been scorers in each of those capital wins – at Arsenal, Charlton and Tottenham. The top of the table read:

	P	W	D	L	F	A	Pt
Wolves	21	14	5	2	54	29	33
Albion	21	15	2	4	58	28	32
Huddersfield	21	12	4	5	38	21	28
Burnley	21	13	0	8	48	38	26

If Wolves could match their first-half-of-the-season points haul in the second they would equal the then record First Division points total of 66 set by Arsenal. That was perhaps asking quite a lot. However, they were top of the table and could rightly be proud. Pride, of course, comes before a fall and that fall followed a week later.

Burnley came to Molineux on December 12 and completed a league double with goals that came right out of the Wolves textbook. Centre-forward Bill Holden twice raced on to long balls down the middle of the field to score in the 32nd and 54th minutes. Hancocks hit a consolation six minutes from time. Burnley, who thus became the only side to take four points off Wolves, were no friend of the pools punters as at that stage in the season they had yet to register a draw. Neither Albion nor Huddersfield took full advantage of the unexpected Wolves slip, the Baggies being held 2-2 away to Arsenal, to go top on goal average only, and Huddersfield sharing four goals at home to Preston. Burnley's win kept them fourth in the table, the top of which then read:

	P	W	D	L	F	A	P
Albion	22	15	3	4	60	30	33
Wolves	22	14	5	3	55	31	33
Huddersfield	22	12	5	5	40	23	29
Burnley	22	14	0	8	50	39	28

Manchester City were next to visit Molineux on the last Saturday before Christmas and they came not bearing gifts but a surprise in the shape of a 26th-minute opening goal from inside-left Gordon Davies. It was not part of the script as City were at the opposite end of the table and very much involved in the relegation struggle. City's centre-forward Jimmy Meadows was an interesting character. A versatile player he would switch to full-back the following season to such good effect that he won an England cap against Scotland in 1955, the day Wolves' Dennis Wilshaw hit four goals in a 7-2 win. Alas, Meadows broke his leg in the FA Cup final against Newcastle just a few days after that Wembley epic and would never play again.

He did not figure too prominently at Molineux back on that sunny December day in 1954. The match developed into a duel between Johnny Hancocks and City's German goalkeeper Bert Trautmann. The little winger fired in a succession of his famous cannonball shots but the keeper was equal to almost everything, though occasionally more by luck than judgement.

Hancocks did not beat Trautmann from open play until the last minute but he had cancelled out Davies's goal in the 36th from the penalty spot. Wolves took the lead through Wilshaw's goal after 62 minutes on a day when the half-backs of either side were the most dominant players. Revie and Paul ensured Peter Broadbent and Wilshaw were kept relatively quiet while Bill Slater and Billy Wright had a similar effect on the City midfielders, with Wright rated the outstanding player on the field. Hancocks's goals meant he had scored in five successive games and stood level with Wilshaw as the club's leading scorer on 16 goals.

To keep the see-saw title race going, Albion could not make it a Lancashire double for the Midland pair, losing 2-1 at Bolton. So Wolves were back on top and this time with a two-point lead:

	P	W	D	L	F	A	P
Wolves	23	15	5	3	58	33	35
Albion	23	15	3	5	61	32	33
Huddersfield	23	12	6	5	42	25	30

Then came a great chance for Wolves to stretch their lead and put more pressure on Albion. With the Baggies at home on December 25 – yes, matches were still played on Christmas Day in those days – Wolves' home clash with Villa was staged on Christmas Eve, a Thursday.

Some 40,000 fans put football before Christmas shopping but only those sporting claret and blue favours would be in a festive mood afterwards. It was a happy return to Molineux for Bill Baxter who had been transferred to Villa a month earlier. He was given the captaincy to mark the occasion and led his side to a 2-1 win despite Wolves having the majority of possession.

Everything had seemed to be going the home side's way at first as Dennis Wilshaw headed in a Hancocks centre after 22 minutes as goalkeeper Nigel Sims, deputising for Bert Williams, injured in the game against Manchester City, had virtually a spectator's role. Then Villa's veteran right-back Harry Parkes was injured and reduced to limping his way through the rest of the game – some 52 minutes – as a token right-winger. Yet Parkes's nuisance value helped Villa win possession in the 55th minute for Johnny Dixon to fire the ball home through a sea of legs. Parkes was not finished either. He sensibly booted the ball out as close to the Wolves corner flag as possible as his side hung on for a point. Villa quickly won a second throw-in and Tommy

Thompson put the ball across goal for an unmarked Peter McParland to score easily. It was the 19-year-old's first goal for the club in only his second appearance. He would go on to take his goals total to 120 – including those which gave Villa a 2-1 FA Cup final victory over Manchester United in 1957 – before being signed by Wolves in January 1962.

Villa paraded another noted Irishman in their ranks that day. Danny Blanchflower was switched from his usual half-back role to inside-right. Less than a year later he would move on to Tottenham where he went on to skipper the famous Double-winning side of 1961.

Wolves would get their revenge on Boxing Day but by that time Albion had taken over at the top of table on goal average after a 5-2 Christmas Day defeat of bottom-of-the table Liverpool at The Hawthorns. It was the third game running that Liverpool had let in five goals as they slumped to the bottom of the table. Albion were three up in fourteen minutes. Johnny Nicholls scored on two minutes, Ray Barlow on six and then Frank Griffin made it three. Goals either side of half-time saw Liverpool reduce the lead to a goal but Ronnie Allen and Griffin added further goals in the last six minutes. Christmas Day also saw Manchester United's Tommy Taylor score three goals in a 5-2 home win over Sheffield Wednesday.

Against Wolves at Villa Park, before a crowd of 48,000, Villa, with Stan Lynn deputising for Parkes, took the lead on 28 minutes, Thompson scoring after a solo run. Wolves, with Sims again in goal, were a far more determined outfit than they had been on Christmas Eve. They got back on level terms within three minutes as a Johnny Hancocks shot took a deflection off Baxter to leave keeper Keith Jones sprawling. In contrast to the first meeting the Wolves forwards were far more willing to try shots on goal, Roy Swinbourne hitting the bar and Dennis Wilshaw, Peter Broadbent and Jimmy Mullen all sending shots just over. Wilshaw, denied a goal earlier when Broadbent was given off-side, had the last word with two minutes to go when he headed the winner.

Wolves' playing their first Christmas game on December 24 had been something of a bonus as often sides were asked to play two games in two days. As Dennis Wilshaw recalls: "If I remember anything from those days, it's the stupidity of the Football League in asking us to play Christmas Day and Boxing Day or Easter Monday and Tuesday. It was just silly, you had no time to recover from any knocks."

In fairness to the League, perhaps it should be pointed out that before floodlighting came in, there had to be a cramming-in of games to accommodate a 42-match season.

To complete a happy Boxing Day, 1953, for Wolves there came news that lowly Liverpool had held Albion to a goalless draw at Anfield so that Wolves, on 37 points led the table again – by a point.

That's the way it stayed as 1954 arrived with games on Saturday, January 2 for the Black Country rivals. Wolves won 3-1 at Cardiff despite the presence in the home side of Trevor Ford, the rugged Welsh international centre-forward. Ford, signed from Sunderland a month earlier, did not get much change out of Bill Shorthouse.

The Welsh side's off-side trap was sprung a couple of times for Roy Swinbourne and Dennis Wilshaw to put the visitors two up before Cliff Nugent pulled one back for Cardiff only for Johnny Hancocks to make the game safe with eight minutes left. With Jack Short injured, Billy Wright got his second right-back outing of the season, Ron Flowers coming in at left-half.

Over at The Hawthorns Albion were beating Preston 3-2, which, had they but known it, was a score that would be repeated in the FA Cup final in May. Ronnie Allen scored twice, just as he would do at Wembley. A week later the Baggies were setting out on their Cup adventure with a 1-0 win over Chelsea but Wolves made an early exit at the hands of Birmingham City at Molineux.

With Short fit again and Wright back in his familiar left-half spot, Wolves led through Wilshaw after 12 minutes only for inside-left Ken Rowley, a one-time Wolves reserve, to level within two minutes. It was an unhappy first-ever Cup-tie for Sims who was beaten by Jimmy Murphy midway through the second half in what was Wolves' first home third-round tie since their Cup-winning season of 1949. There could be no excuses for the defeat, not even a late injury to Bill Shorthouse. Blues deserved their win and achieved it without their strapping 17-year-old centre-half Trevor Smith and tenacious left-half Roy Warhurst. A few years later Smith looked the obvious successor to Billy Wright in the England side. When Billy finally called it a day in 1959, Smith was given his chance by the selectors. However, after just two games he was banished to the international wilderness.

League action resumed a week later – Saturday, January 16 – and things went from bad to worse for Stan Cullis's men. While Albion were winning 1-0 at Tottenham thanks to a Ronnie Allen goal, Wolves were being beaten for the fourth time in five home games. The other half of the North London duo, Arsenal, did the damage with a 2-0 success – the only occasion during the season that Wolves failed to score at home.

Flowers was again drafted into the side as Billy Wright switched to centre-half, Shorthouse not having recovered from his injury in the Cup match. Flowers was one of three Wolves players to see shots hit the bar in the first half – Roy Swinbourne (twice) and Johnny Hancocks were the others. By that time, Arsenal were hanging on to the lead given them after nine minutes by little Scottish maestro Jimmy Logie. All other Wolves efforts to get on the scoresheet were countered by the Gunners' Welsh international goalkeeper Jack Kelsey in top form. Hancocks was in the wars but returned to the field after having three stitches put in a burst eyebrow. When Don Roper's centre was met with a flicked header by former Walsall inside-forward Doug Lishman with five minutes left the Gunners' smash and grab raid was complete and Albion were once again top of the table which read:

	P	W	D	L	F	A	P
Albion	27	18	4	5	70	36	40
Wolves	27	17	5	5	64	38	39
Huddersfield	27	13	8	6	47	32	34

One of Wolves' successes of the season had been Peter Broadbent. He had enjoyed extended

33

runs in the first team in both the previous seasons but now he was starting to show the sort of form that would win him a special place in the affections of fans who followed the team in the Fabulous Fifties. The biased among us would call him a genius – but he certainly had a special talent.

Broadbent's progress had not escaped the England selectors and when they embarked on a new venture – an under-23 side – he was given his first international recognition. It was not a happy match, however, on a snow-covered pitch in Bologna on Wednesday, January 20, the Italian under-23 side running out 3-1 winners after being a goal up at half-time. Skippered by Arsenal centre-half Bill Dodgin, the England line-up also included 17-year-old Duncan Edwards, the Dudley lad who was to lose his life as a result of injuries received in the 1958 Munich Air Crash.

The England side in Italy:
Wood (Manchester United), Gunter (Portsmouth), Ellis (Charlton); Whitefoot (Manchester United), Dodgin (Arsenal), Edwards (Manchester United); Finney (Sheffield Wednesday), Broadbent (Wolves), Leary (Charlton), Nicholls (Albion), Blunstone (Chelsea).

Three days later Broadbent was in action against Portsmouth at Fratton Park where Wolves were beaten 2-0 – the only time in the season, they would lose successive matches. Stan Cullis had decided to keep Ron Flowers in the side even though Bill Shorthouse was fit again. So rather than resume his familiar left-half spot, Billy Wright moved to left-back with Roy Pritchard dropped. Dennis Wilshaw missed the game as his father had been seriously ill for some weeks. He died the day after the game. Norman Deeley was drafted in at inside-right, Broadbent moving to the left.

It soon became clear it was not Wolves' day. England wing-half Jimmy Dickinson scored with a harmless looking lob early on. Bert Williams was unsighted as the ball bounced into the net. A lob by Johnny Hancocks also appeared to have found the net before the ball was cleared. Wolves players on the spot felt it had crossed the line, too. Then the referee decided to award a bounce-up rather than a foul on Shorthouse and the move that followed ended with a goal for Duggie Reid in the 63rd minute.

Wright had had his hands full with speedy right-winger Peter Harris but Wolves at anything like their best form ought to have avoided what was their first away defeat since August 26. Albion failed to take full advantage, being held 0-0 at home by Burnley, the first time the Lancashire side had drawn in 28 games since the start of the season.

CHAPTER FOUR

FLUCTUATING FEBRUARY

Albion had a two-point lead as January, 1954, came to an end with their fans daring to dream of the Double after a comfortable 4-0 FA Cup fourth-round home victory over Rotherham. That possibility would look even more likely by the time February ended even though the month began with a fillip for Wolves.

On his 30th birthday – February 6 – Billy Wright, back at left-half with Roy Pritchard recalled at left-back, led his team to an impressive 4-1 home win over Blackpool. Wolves dropped Peter Broadbent, Ron Flowers getting the inside-right spot, but Blackpool were missing no fewer than five England internationals – Stanley Matthews, Ernie Taylor and Stan Mortensen from the forward line and Harry Johnston and Tommy Garrett from their defence.

Wright and fellow wing-half Bill Slater called the tune while Roy Swinbourne took the goal honours. He hit three in the second half. Johnny Hancocks had given Wolves an early lead and Swinbourne made it two early in the second half, from a Flowers pass, before a reply from Mortensen's deputy Les Stephenson who cashed in when the bouncing ball eluded Bill Shorthouse, the centre-half's only blemish on a typically rousing display. With five minutes to go Swinbourne scored twice in a minute, the second one, a fierce left-foot drive, being the best goal of the game.

It was a busy time for Blackpool, who had by then given up hope of making an impact in the league and were concentrating on trying to retain the FA Cup they had won so dramatically at Wembley the previous May. Three days before their Molineux trip, the Seasiders had beaten West Ham 3-1 at Bloomfield Road in a fourth-round replay. Blackpool must have had hopes of making that Wembley return when the fifth round draw took them to Third Division North leaders Port Vale. However, it did not prove a happy return to his native Potteries for Matthews as he and his star-studded side were beaten 2-0. Vale had won at Cardiff in the fourth round and only bowed out of the Cup at the semi-final stage – to Albion.

Four days after the Blackpool game, Wright was joined by the Albion defensive trio of Stan Rickaby, Jimmy Dugdale and Ray Barlow in the Football League side who strolled to a 9-1 victory over the League of Ireland before 18,208 fans at Maine Road, Manchester. Don Revie and Jackie Sewell scored three goals each with others coming from Johnny Berry (two) and Nat Lofthouse.

Team:
Merrick (Birmingham); Rickaby, Byrne (Manchester United), Wright, Dugdale, Barlow; Berry (Manchester United), Revie (Manchester City), Lofthouse (Bolton), Sewell (Sheffield Wednesday), Metcalfe (Huddersfield).

The Albion contingent had more to celebrate on Saturday, February 13, when they beat Sheffield Wednesday 4-2, full-back Stan Rickaby scoring a rare goal for the Baggies, while Wolves were losing by the same score at Stamford Bridge, Chelsea gaining some revenge for that club record mauling at Molineux earlier in the season. With Flowers continuing at inside-right and Broadbent in the reserves, Wolves, before a gate of 60,276, were hampered when Bill Shorthouse went off after getting a kick in the side in the seventh minute. He returned about

20 minutes later but was restricted to shuffling around in the forward line, Wright switching to centre-half, where he turned in an impressive display, and Flowers to left-half.

By the time Shorthouse returned, Wolves were 2-1 down. Roy Bentley had scored in the first minute and winger Eric Parsons in the ninth before Roy Swinbourne gave Wolves some hope. Les Stubbs made it 3-1 on 62 minutes, with Dennis Wilshaw quickly replying and the gallant Shorthouse saw a flashing header cleared from the goalmouth. It proved a costly miss as Bentley struck again in the 69th minute. Given recent form the result was no great surprise.

Chelsea came into the match unbeaten in 12 games while Wolves had lost three of their previous four. Bolton, who had briefly gone third in the table, failed to get within a two points of Wolves when they were beaten 2-0 at home by Preston. Huddersfield took advantage with a 3-0 win at struggling Middlesbrough to regain third spot.

	P	W	D	L	F	A	Pt
Albion	30	19	6	5	75	39	44
Wolves	30	18	5	7	70	45	41
Huddersfield	30	14	10	6	54	35	38
Bolton	30	14	9	7	56	41	37
Burnley	30	17	2	11	62	48	36

Shorthouse's injury meant Wright stayed at centre-half and Flowers at left-half for the visit to Molineux of Sheffield United on Saturday, February 20. Peter Broadbent was recalled but a more significant change saw manager Stan Cullis decide to see whether Eddie Stuart had the makings of a right-back. The South African would grab his chance admirably and stay in the team for the rest of the season.

Wolves' form matched the brilliantly sunny weather as the Blades were swept aside 6-1. Two up at half-time, Wolves owed their win to goals from Roy Swinbourne (two), Johnny Hancocks (two), Broadbent and Dennis Wilshaw. The goal from Wilshaw in the final minute was probably the pick – a 25-yard shot which he would probably be first to admit was not a speciality of his.

It meant that at that stage, he, Swinbourne and Hancocks were the club's leading scorers, each with 21 goals. Hancocks ought to have taken his total to 22 but, with only goalkeeper Ted Burgin to beat, blazed the ball on to the Bushbury End stand. However, he had bettered his record of 19 for most League goals in a season by a Wolves winger.

The Blades' Jimmy Hagan was one of the greatest inside-forwards of his day but soon found Stuart was no respecter of reputations when the young full-back put in a hard tackle early in the game. "Hagan turned on me and called me a Zulu," recalls Stuart. "He added: 'What do they feed you on? Raw meat?'"

Stuart was not the only one enjoying a 'first' – it was also the first game as a paid player for Bill

Slater. He had signed professional forms two days earlier. The England amateur side's loss undoubtedly proved Wolves' gain.

While Wolves were enjoying their goal spree Albion were reaching the last eight of the FA Cup courtesy of a 3-2 home win over Newcastle and a Ronnie Allen hat-trick. It seemed odds-on the Baggies would restore their three-point lead over Wolves when the following Wednesday they played their game in hand at Ayresome Park against bottom-but-one Middlesbrough, who had lost their previous four games. Boro, however, ignored the form book and a frustrated Albion were held 1-1, the home goal coming from a penalty by Jamaican-born winger Lindy Delapenha.

Wolves' final game of February was an incident packed 3-2 home win over Newcastle for which Bill Shorthouse returned – but at left back in place of Roy Pritchard. That left Wright to show once again his potential as a centre-half and he had an outstanding game, especially as he was up against one of the country's most feared strikers, Jackie Milburn.

A match which ended with a flurry of snow also ended with a flurry of action. It had begun with a fine goal from Peter Broadbent who ran half the length of the field before scoring in the fourth minute. England international inside forward Ivor Broadis wasted a couple of good Newcastle chances before Dennis Wilshaw hit the second on 20 minutes and Wolves looked in command.

Then Milburn pulled a goal back on 80 minutes followed, four minutes later, by an equaliser from Broadis. That was the cue for Bill Slater to grab his first goal as a professional and it was one he would not remember – he knocked himself out as he sent home a rocket-like header for the winner. Albion, meanwhile, had virtually put paid to Huddersfield's bid to get in on the title race by winning 2-0 at Leeds Road.

The victory over Newcastle had come at a cost for Wolves as centre-forward Roy Swinbourne took several knocks and was unfit for the trip to Old Trafford on Saturday, March 6. Stan Cullis made the bold move of playing Ron Flowers at centre-forward. Alas, Flowers was guilty of a missed chance when Wolves were on top in the second half. He was not alone in failing to take his chances as Peter Broadbent also wasted one, as did Johnny Hancocks.

Wolves paid the price with six minutes to go and had only themselves to blame. They halted momentarily, expecting an off-side decision but none came as Johnny Berry waltzed through to hit the only goal of the game. United were starting to take on a youthful look with Duncan Edwards, Jackie Blanchflower and Dennis Viollet in their side and the win took them to fifth in the table. Wolves gave a youngster of their own his first team baptism, Eddie Clamp coming in at left-half.

Albion ought to have taken advantage but Sheffield United showed far more fight at The Hawthorns than they had done at Molineux the previous month and came from two goals down in the second half to earn a 2-2 draw. The point, however, still put Albion three points clear once more. Little did they know it but they would win only two of their remaining nine league games.

	P	W	D	L	F	A	Pt
Albion	33	20	8	5	80	42	48
Wolves	33	20	5	8	79	49	45
Huddersfield	33	15	11	7	59	41	41
Burnley	33	19	2	12	68	52	40
Man United	33	14	11	8	58	45	39
Bolton	33	15	9	9	61	48	39

There was an interesting diversion for Wolves fans before the championship battle resumed. Racing Club of Buenos Aires came to town for the latest Molineux floodlit spectacular. A crowd of 37,122 came to take a look at the Argentinians whose short-passing game was in stark contrast to the more direct play of Wolves.

Reserve Doug Taylor was given a rare outing at centre-forward and he opened the scoring when he tapped the ball home after a downward header from Dennis Wilshaw with 16 minutes gone. Within a minute the Argentinians were level when veteran international Mendez sent Pizzuti through.

That was a rare direct move from the tourists whose over-elaboration played right into Wolves' hands. Goalkeeper Dominguez had plenty of opportunity to show his paces as Wolves' methods paid off but he was powerless to stop a screaming 25-yard drive from Norman Deeley, playing at left-half, on the hour, or a Jimmy Mullen cross shot 11 minutes later. Deeley made the most of his rare outing but Wright, again at centre-half, was outstanding.

Saturday, March 13, saw Albion reach the FA Cup semi-final with a 3-0 home sixth-round win over Spurs, Johnny Nicholls scoring twice but four days later there was an almighty setback to their double hopes. They suffered their biggest defeat of the season – 5-0 at the hands of Chelsea at Stamford Bridge. That meant their lead at the top stayed at three points but now Wolves had a game in hand.

Albion would probably have denied that the Cup run was proving a distraction but there was no hiding the fact that Wolves' next opponents, Preston, had a day out at Wembley as their No1 priority. Three days before their March 20 Deepdale clash with Wolves, North End had been held 2-2 at home by Leicester in a sixth-round replay. The second replay was due the following Monday and so they rested three key men, Bobby Foster, Charlie Wayman and former Wolves man Willie Forbes, while star forward Tom Finney was sidelined with a pulled muscle.

Not surprisingly, Wolves, with Deeley keeping his place at left-half and Roy Swinbourne back to lead the line duly got their two points – but only just. Dennis Wilshaw hit the only goal ten minutes from time when his 25-yard shot hit a post and screwed along the line before breaking back into the net. Johnny Hancocks ought to have scored, too, but managed to put the ball wide from a pinpoint centre by Leslie Smith. Deputising for Jimmy Mullen, injured in training, Smith was the visitors' most effective forward.

Albion got back to winning ways with a 2-1 home win over Blackpool on the same day but four days later Wolves had the chance to narrow the gap to a point when Bolton came to Molineux for a Wednesday afternoon game, which attracted only 19,617.

The match did little to warm the fans who braved a cold day as Bolton frustrated the home side in a 1-1 draw. The kick-off time meant schoolteacher Dennis Wilshaw was not available so Eddie Clamp was brought in at inside-left to partner Leslie Smith. It was hardly his fault that he looked somewhat lost and the general view after the final whistle was that Wolves would have done far better if he had been switched to his more accustomed half-back spot with either Bill Slater or Norman Deeley, no strangers to inside-forward play, moving up front.

Peter Broadbent was one Wolves forward who looked lively and hit a 30-yard goal on 42 minutes to wipe out the lead given Bolton in the tenth by England centre-forward Nat Lofthouse. The leading positions:

	P	W	D	L	F	A	Pt
Albion	35	21	8	6	82	48	50
Wolves	35	21	6	8	81	50	48
Huddersfield	35	16	11	8	63	46	43
Burnley	35	20	2	13	71	54	42
Man United	35	15	12	8	63	48	42
Bolton	35	16	10	9	65	49	42

39

With Albion otherwise engaged on Saturday, March 20 – a little matter of the FA Cup semi-final against giantkillers Port Vale at Villa Park – Wolves could have gone back to top of the table on goal average if they could pile on the goals against struggling Middlesbrough at Molineux, especially with Dennis Wilshaw and Jimmy Mullen available to put the home forward line at full-strength against a team still bottom but one in the First Division.

Middlesbrough had drawn their previous five games but they did have a tradition of doing well at Molineux – four wins in their previous seven league visits since the War. In the end, tradition got the better of current form and Boro won 4-2 inspired by a vintage display from former England inside- forward Wilf Mannion. The little maestro may have been 35 and playing what proved to be his last season with Boro, but on this day he was too big a handful for Wolves.

It was Mannion's neat flick that put Tom Watkin in for a third-minute goal. Nine minutes later Les McPherson hooked home goal No2 and it was three after 34 minutes when Lindy Delapenha fired home a penalty, awarded somewhat harshly against Billy Wright for a tackle on right-winger Sam Lawrie.

Peter Broadbent revived Wolves' hopes with a cross shot from Swinbourne's pass and then a header to a Mullen corner. There was still time to salvage something. Instead it was Boro who scored again. A long clearance from goalkeeper Rolando Ugolini, who had played his part in frustrating Wolves, was latched on to by McPherson to score two minutes from the end.
So now the ball was in Albion's court – two points ahead, with a game in hand and in the FA Cup final after beating Port Vale 2-1. The Double beckoned.

However, fortune was to give Albion a raw deal. They were without full-backs Stan Rickaby and Len Millard, injured in the semi-final, as well as strike duo Ronnie Allen and Johnny Nicholls, when they visited Roker Park to play that game in hand. Not only did they lose 2-1 to the 20th-placed Sunderland but had goalkeeper Norman Heath injured at a crucial time in the match. There were no substitutes in those days and sadly the injury proved to be serious. It was feared at one stage that Heath would be paralysed. Happily he was not but his football career was over.

Neither Albion nor Wolves therefore were in the best of spirits for their next game – between the two of them at The Hawthorns on Saturday, April 3. It ought to have been the showpiece of the season, but injuries apart there was the little matter of the Scotland-England match taking place the same day at Hampden Park. This was also a showpiece game in those days and the England selectors had called upon Billy Wright and Jimmy Mullen from Wolves and Allen and Nicholls from their opponents. Imagine today if Manchester United had to face Arsenal on the same day as an international. It just would not be allowed to happen.

Albion still had Rickaby, as well as wingers George Lee and Frank Griffin sidelined so both sides had an unfamiliar look when they trotted out before a crowd of nearly 50,000. Albion's troubles increased when half-back Ray Barlow, playing as a makeshift centre-forward, was injured after only eight minutes in a tackle with Bill Shorthouse and handicapped for the rest of the game. If it was a bad day for the Baggies, it was a great one for Wolves who won with the only goal of the match when Roy Swinbourne swivelled and hooked the ball home at waist height after 58 minutes. Wolves, who had switched Johnny Hancocks to outside left and brought in Leslie Smith on the right to make up for Mullen's absence while recalling Roy Pritchard at left back, were now level on points with Albion and second only on goal average.

	P	W	D	L	F	A	P
Albion	37	21	8	8	83	51	50
Wolves	37	22	6	9	84	54	50
Huddersfield	37	18	11	8	71	48	47
Bolton	37	17	10	10	70	53	44

Shorthouse still takes some ribbing from Albion fans over the Barlow injury but insists it was just one of those things. "I was a hard player but I always played fair," says Shorthouse. "Ray was one of those players who was good at shielding the ball and he was always trying to do that. When this ball was played up towards him I just put my foot out and he just went down. I was going for the ball. Even now when I see Ray he always says something. He looks at me and says: 'You were the one!'

"I did not mind playing against Ray, it was Ronnie Allen who used to get to me. In those days you gave knocks and you took knocks and just got on with it. But Ronnie was always moaning. Mind you, he was good player though."

Making a rare appearance at outside-left for Albion at The Hawthorns was Reg Cutler. He made only five League appearances during his time with the Baggies but Wolves would have good cause to remember his name three years later when he was a key man in Bournemouth's 1957 FA Cup giantkilling run. Cutler not only scored the goal which gave the Cherries a shock 1-0 away win, he also succeeded in snapping one of the Molineux goalposts after colliding with the side netting.

Up at Hampden, England beat Scotland 4-2, with three of the Hawthorns absentees on the mark – Allen, Nicholls and Mullen. Ivor Broadis had scored England's first goal on a day Spurs centre-half Harry Clarke won what proved to be his only England cap. Full-backs Ron Staniforth and Roger Byrne were also making their international bow.

Scotland: Farm (Blackpool); Haughney (Celtic), Cox (Rangers), Evans (Celtic), Brennan (Newcastle), Aitken (Sunderland); McKenzie (Partick Thistle), Johnstone (Hibernian), Henderson (Portsmouth), Brown (Blackpool), Ormond (Hibernian).
England: Merrick (Birmingham); Staniforth (Huddersfield), Byrne (Manchester United); Wright, Clarke (Tottenham), Dickinson (Portsmouth); Finney (Preston), Broadis (Newcastle), Allen, Nicholls, Mullen.

Without doubt the momentum in the title race had switched to Wolves and a week later, on Saturday, April 10, they swept to the top of the table as they brushed aside Charlton 5-0 at Molineux while Albion were losing their third game in a row – 2-0 at Cardiff.

Wright, back from England duty, lined up at left-back and that's where he stayed until the end of the season with Flowers retained at left-half. Stars of the win over Charlton were wingers Johnny Hancocks, who had celebrated his 35th birthday two days earlier, and Jimmy Mullen. They each scored twice. Dennis Wilshaw was the other scorer as Wolves led 2-0 at the break. Hancocks could even afford to miss a penalty – he fired the ball wide – two minutes after he'd made it 5-0.

The little winger had sent a right-foot cannonball shot past Sam Bartram in the seventh minute before centring for Wilshaw to head home five minutes later. Hancocks also set up Mullen's goals while he had Peter Broadbent to thank for his own second. Not only had Wolves taken over at the top with a lead of two points, they also now had a better goal average than Albion – 1.648 compared with 1.57.

On the same day, there was a painful end to the long career of Joe Mercer. The Arsenal skipper broke his leg in a collision with his own full-back, Joe Wade, during the 3-0 win over Liverpool at Highbury. Mercer left the field on a stretcher and would never play again. Like Wolves boss Stan Cullis, he was born in Ellesmere Port. They were contemporaries as schoolboys, played together for England before the outbreak of the second World War and both skippered their country in wartime internationals. While Mercer won First Division championship and FA Cup medals as a player, Cullis just missed out.

As a manager Mercer saw service with Sheffield United and Villa but it was at Manchester City, in partnership with the flamboyant Malcolm Allison, that he would have his greatest successes as a boss.

While one Arsenal career was ending, another was just starting that day. Welsh inside-forward Derek Tapscott, signed by Tom Whittaker from Barry Town earlier in the season, marked his debut with two goals, helped by the promptings of veteran Tommy Lawton. Word of Tapscott's display got back to the Welsh selectors who promptly named him in their side to meet Austria in Vienna in May. He had won his first cap on the strength of just one match. To celebrate he scored twice in the Gunners' next game, a 3-0 Good Friday home win over Portsmouth.

An unchanged Wolves side dramatically lost the goal touch almost as quickly as they had rediscovered it when they were held 0-0 by Sheffield Wednesday at Hillsborough on Saturday, April 17. There were chances a-plenty for Wolves but they just could not cash in and even had to survive a brief spell of Wednesday pressure with Billy Wright diverting an Albert Quixall shot around the post. Earlier, Roy Swinbourne, Bill Slater, Dennis Wilshaw and Peter Broadbent had all gone close. There was another let-off for the visitors when Wednesday inside left Redfern Froggatt ballooned a chance over the bar.

At Anfield, Liverpool were beaten 1-0 at home by Cardiff thanks to a Tommy Northcott goal and so the Reds' relegation, just four years after they had reached the FA Cup final was made certain. To add to the misery, Everton ended the season promoted as Second Division runners-up.

42   Albion won 1-0 at home to Manchester City, thanks to a Ronnie Allen penalty, so they had 52 points compared with Wolves' 53 as they went into their Easter games. As was traditional at that time each side met the same opposition home and away over two days. For Albion it was a local derby double with Villa while Wolves looked to have the slightly easier task with home and away tussles against Huddersfield, whose outside title chance had by then as good as gone.

The wing wonders Hancocks and Mullen were again in fine fettle for Huddersfield's visit to Molineux on Easter Monday, April 19. Mullen opened the scoring after two minutes. A Hancocks power drive across goal was deflected to Mullen who fired home. Then, for the second successive home game, Hancocks contrived to miss from the penalty spot. Obviously 12 yards was too close for Hancocks and he promptly atoned by thumping home a free kick from all of 30 yards.

With Peter Broadbent in dazzling form, Wolves amazingly did not add to their tally until the last four minutes by which time Huddersfield had been reduced to ten men. Jack Wheeler, their goalkeeper, who had lost his place for most of the season to Harry Mills, was injured after 75 minutes and the division's top scorer, Jimmy Glazzard had to don the green jersey. He was beaten first by Broadbent and then by Dennis Wilshaw. It was not therefore an entirely happy return to Molineux for Town full-back Laurie Kelly, the man so dramatically dropped from Wolves side just before the 1949 FA Cup final. Kelly did have the consolation of getting a warm reception from the Molineux fans when he led his side out as captain for the day.

At The Hawthorns, Albion were held 1-1 by Villa but an almighty shock was awaiting the Cup finalists in the return game the following day. They were beaten 6-1 at Villa Park and obviously realising the Cup was now their lone objective Albion took off Ronnie Allen when he strained a groin muscle and dispatched him back to West Bromwich for injections.

It hardly mattered that Wolves were beaten 2-1 at Leeds Road, where Bill McGarry hit a 63rd-minute winner after a surging run by Bill Slater had enabled Dennis Wilshaw to cancel out Glazzard's second-minute strike. The title was as good as at Wolverhampton. Such was the goal average now in Wolves' favour that they could have lost their final match 4-0 and Albion would have needed to win theirs 9-0! Even so, the Football League would not allow the trophy to be at Molineux for presentation on the final Saturday of the season. With a match left, this is how the top of the table looked:

	P	W	D	L	F	A	P
Wolves	41	24	7	10	94	56	55
Albion	41	22	9	10	86	60	53
Huddersfield	41	19	11	11	76	60	49
Bolton	41	18	12	11	74	58	48

As it turned out there was never any question, in their final outings on April 24, of Wolves losing heavily or Albion going rampant. Wolves duly made certain of the championship by beating Tottenham 2-0 at Molineux while Albion's woeful end-of-season slump saw them lose 3-0 at Portsmouth. Roy Swinbourne scored Wolves' goals heading home on 18 and 68 minutes, each time from Jimmy Mullen crosses.

43

A crowd of 44,055 were there to see the climax of Wolves' years of striving to become England's top team. The memories of those near misses were forgotten, fans invaded the pitch and called for the players to take a bow which they duly did.

Skipper Wright addressed the throng and thanked his team-mates as well as boss Stan Cullis. The manager in turn thanked his captain and team. So Wolves fans went home happy – so happy they may even have been wishing Albion all the best in the Cup Final against Preston the following Saturday.

FINAL VERDICT

Albion duly completed the Black Country Double by beating Preston 3-2 in the FA Cup final, coming from behind to win with a late goal from right-winger Frank Griffin. It was time to celebrate. The town of Wolverhampton did just that on Monday, May 10, when a banquet was staged at the Civic Hall, attended by 500 guests, including Albion chairman Major Wilson Keys and director Horace Thursfield. The Hawthorns pair were able to acknowledge congratulations on their club's Cup triumph from Wolves director Arthur Oakley, Stan Cullis, Billy Wright and the town's mayor Alderman Mrs A A Braybrook.

The Wolves players had made their entrance via the Civic Hall stage to the musical accompaniment of the band of the 1st Battalion the South Staffordshire Regiment before making their way to the table of honour decorated in gold and black ribbons as was the Football League trophy itself.

Liverpool's Will Harrop, vice president of the Football League, was there to make the official presentations and also explained why the trophy had not been at Molineux on the final day of the season. Apparently the League had learned their lesson in 1947 when they brought it to the ground on the famous occasion when Wolves, on the day Cullis announced his retirement as a player, needed to win their final game – against Liverpool – to be Division One champions. Wolves lost and when Stoke failed to win their remaining game, the title duly went to Anfield. The League president and secretary had taken the trophy to Molineux on that day of drama only to have to take it back to their Preston headquarters.

Harrop's explanation why the trophy had not been at Molineux for the Tottenham game seemed somewhat thin for 1954's situation hardly compared to that of 1947. Only Wolves or Albion could be champions and such was the weight of goals that Wolves would need to concede and Albion would need to score on that final Saturday that the issue was beyond question.

However, it was not a night to quibble. The trophy was at last in Wolverhampton and each player was presented with a replica of it. Cullis told the assembled dignitaries and guests that the team who had won it were as good as any Wolves side he had known during his time with the club. Cullis also paid tribute to his able lieutenant, trainer Joe Gardiner. "Joe has had it hard for a long time. First he had to suffer me as a player and now he has to suffer me alongside him on the trainer's bench." Oakley, deputising for club chairman James Baker, who was ill, was also able to announce that Wright and Jimmy Mullen had been selected for the England team to meet Yugoslavia the following Sunday.

On the day of the Tottenham match, the Express & Star's Saturday night football paper, the Sporting Star had carried quotes on its front page from Wright and Cullis under the headline "How it feels to be on top of the football world."

Said Wright: "First duty on one of the proudest days of my life is to pay a tribute to the lads for the way they have played throughout the season, from start to finish, despite the fact that we lost two of the first three games. They have rallied round splendidly. Success, I think, has come because everybody in the team has pulled his weight all the time. We now realise what a

45

tremendously hard job it is to win the title – but we also know that the effort was well worth while. Adding interest to the season was our rivalry with the Albion. We wish them the best of luck in their effort to take the FA Cup next Saturday."

Cullis commented: "Let me put the credit where it rightly belongs – on the players, who have won this championship because they have given of their best from start to finish. Naturally, I am proud to be their manager and to have seen them win the Cup and the League in the course of six seasons, but I could have accomplished nothing without the players' loyalty. Without wishing to single out individuals, I feel I must pay a tribute to the captain, Billy Wright. I have had to make many demands on him this season but he has answered them all without question."

Inside the "Pink", as the paper is always fondly known, were many tributes from local and national figures in English football.

Eric Houghton (Villa manager)
"Congratulations, Wolves, from all of us at Villa Park. We all know the championship takes more winning than any other competition. You have thoroughly deserved your new title by giving good all-round performances and we wish you every success in the future."

F W Burgess (chairman of Port Vale)
"Wolves' championship success tops off a great season for Staffordshire football. Port Vale, as champions of the Northern section of the Third Division, send warm congratulations to their southern neighbours, who completed Staffordshire's 'league' double."

Arthur Drewry (president of the Football League)
"It has been a splendid all-Midlands finish. The favourites Albion, after a gruelling and in some respects unfortunate last lap, have been overhauled, and congratulations go both to winners and runners-up. Wolves are champions and, one willingly concedes, handsome champions. They are an ornament to the Football League. During an illustrious career, they have both taken and deserved the major honours in cup and league football."

Stanley Rous (secretary of the Football Association)
"Wolves' consistently good showing over recent years has received its full flowering. Congratulations to Billy Wright and his doughty band of players, to Mr Stanley Cullis and all the other officials, and to all the supporters whose cheers have helped Wolves gain their well-merited success."

Major H Wilson Keys (Albion chairman)
"It has been a great race. We have enjoyed every minute of it. Though we are sorry we have not come out on top we congratulate Wolves on a splendid achievement."

Len Millard (Albion skipper)
"It has been a great fight. As we have not been able to win the championship ourselves, I would rather it have gone to Wolves than anyone else, being virtually a Wolverhampton man myself."

46

Bob Brocklebank (Birmingham City manager)
"To win the championship shows consistently good play throughout the season and no one can deny that you are worthy winners. You have had to contend with the very good play of Albion, who have been near the top of the table for the greater part of the season, and to come back at the end, as you have, makes you highly deserving of the title 'League Champions.' Well done!"

Frank Taylor (Stoke manager)
"Congratulations! As a former Wolves player I am delighted my former team have landed the honour they have so long deserved."

Sammy Crooks (Shrewsbury Town manager)
"On average I would choose Wolves as the best post-War soccer team. Much of their strength has lain in having such powerful reserve sides. Heartiest congratulations on a wonderful performance and your first championship. It was long overdue, in my opinion, and only luck has stopped you before. It has been a great fight this season and we neighbouring clubs have been very proud of the the two Midlands clubs who have been fighting for the championship."

Billy Hartill (Wolves' centre-forward when they won promotion to the First Division in 1931-2)
"Wolves have done something we old scrubbers couldn't do – and they did it when everybody was running them down. Wolverhampton people are really lucky; they've had good sides to watch for many years."

47

Billy Wright and Jimmy Mullen were in action for the Football League side four days after the Tottenham game – April 28 – when the Scottish League were beaten 4-0 at Stamford Bridge. Mullen's partner at inside left was Fulham's rising star Johnny Haynes and the man who would skipper England in the 1962 World Cup finals was impressed by the Wolves outside left. He wrote in his autobiography It's All In The Game (Sportsman's Book Club): "Mullen was one of the best wingers I have ever played with; orthodox but good and always easy to find." Haynes was a a scorer that night as was his Fulham colleague Bedford Jezzard, who hit two goals, and Sheffield Wednesday's Jackie Sewell. Team:

Merrick (Birmingham); Ball (Bolton), Willemse (Chelsea); Wright Owen (Luton), Bell (Bolton); Harris (Portsmouth), Sewell, Jezzard, Haynes, Mullen.

There was a representative honour, too, for Wolves' reserve goalkeeper Nigel Sims. He was chosen for a newly-inaugurated game to be played on the eve of the Cup final – Old England v Young England or over-30s v under-30s. Sims was in the under-30s side who lost 2-1 at Highbury on Friday, April 30, before a gate of 43,554. Teams:

Over-30s: Bartram (Charlton); Mozley (Derby), Smith (Arsenal); Johnston (Blackpool), Leuty (Notts County), Cockburn (Manchester United); Matthews (Blackpool), Mannion (Middlesbrough), Lawton (Arsenal), Shackleton (Sunderland), Langton (Blackburn).
Under-30s: Sims; P Sillett (Chelsea), Byrne (Manchester United); Anderson (Sunderland), Smith (Birmingham), Edwards (Manchester United); Hooper (West Ham), Quixall (Sheffield Wednesday), Hines (Leicester), Viollet (Manchester United), Pilkington (Burnley).

Wilf Mannion and Tommy Lawton scored for the winners, Derek Hines, replying for the under-30s.

That England game against Yugoslavia, on May 16, was lost 1-0 in Belgrade thanks to a goal from Mitic three minutes from the end. Earlier Mullen had been denied what looked like a certain goal when Yugoslav keeper Beara tipped over his header. Still searching for a centre-half, the selectors had given Luton's Syd Owen a first cap at the age of 32. England's team:

Merrick; Staniforth, Byrne, Wright, Owen, Dickinson, Finney, Broadis, Allen, Nicholls, Mullen.

A week later came the return meeting with Hungary in Budapest. Wright retained his place but left-winger Mullen made way for Peter Harris the Portsmouth right winger, with Tom Finney, the Footballer of the Year, switching from right wing to left. Albion's Allen and Nicholls were also dropped from the side who faced Yugoslavia, losing their places to Jezzard and Sewell. Jezzard was winning his first cap but he and the rest of the England team were reduced to virtual spectators as Hungary again proved different class, this time inflicting upon England the biggest defeat in their history – 7-1 and it could have been more. Teams:

Hungary: Grosics (Honved), sub Geller (MTK); Buzansky (Dorogi), Lantos (MTK); Bozsik (Honved), Lorant (Honved), Zakarias (MTK); J Toth (Csepel), Kocsis (Honved), Hidegkuti (MTK), Puskas (Honved), Czibor (Honved)
England: Merrick; Staniforth (Huddersfield), Byrne (Manchester United), Wright, Owen, Dickinson; Harris, Sewell, Jezzard, Broadis (Newcastle), Finney.

The day before the Hungary debacle Dennis Wilshaw played in the England B side beaten 2-0 by Switzerland B in Basle. The selectors gave an unexpected chance to goalkeeper Ray King who had been a key figure in the Port Vale defence who had conceded just 21 goals in winning the Third Division North title. Team:

King, sub Thompson (Preston) HT; Green (Birmingham), Willemse (Chelsea); McGarry (Huddersfield), Dugdale (Albion), Edwards (Manchester United); Hooper (West Ham), Quixall (Sheffield Wednesday), Allen (Albion), sub Nicholls (Albion) HT, Wilshaw, Robb (Tottenham).

The season was still not done for Wolves players as Wright and Mullen were joined by Wilshaw in England's squad of 17 players to travel to the World Cup finals in Switzerland. Another five men were named as stand-by reserves – Allenby Chilton (Manchester United), Ken Armstrong (Chelsea), Haynes, Jezzard and Harry Hooper of West Ham, who would in 1956 be signed by Stan Cullis as the successor to Johnny Hancocks. Of the 17 men in the finals squad, nine were aged 30 or over. The selectors decided the deputy goalkeeper to Birmingham's Gil Merrick would be Sheffield United's uncapped Ted Burgin. Bert Williams was the obvious choice but the Wolves keeper recalls: "I was injured, that's why I did not get picked. I think I had broken my finger in training, stopping a ball. I'd also been named for the squad to play Hungary in Budapest." The World Cup squad:

Merrick, Burgin, Staniforth, Byrne , Ken Green (Birmingham), Wright, Owen, Dickinson, Bill McGarry (Huddersfield), Stanley Matthews (Blackpool), Broadis, Nat Lofthouse (Bolton), Tommy Taylor (Manchester United), Finney, Albert Quixall (Sheffield Wednesday), Wilshaw and Mullen.

It seems strange, given the season they had had, that neither Allen nor Nicholls figured among players selected. Though, given the whims of the England selectors at that time, perhaps it was not so strange.

After their rude awakening in the matches against Hungary, England were not given much chance, the most that could be hoped for being that at least the team would put up a good show, which they just about did in a competition, somewhat bizarrely configured. It was decided the 16 finalists would be split into four groups with two 'seeded' teams in each. However, the seeded teams would play only the other two teams in their group and not each other.

So England found themselves seeded with Italy in Pool 4 along with Belgium and hosts Switzerland. Another strange decision by FIFA was that should any of the group games end level at 90 minutes then extra time would be played. That's what happened to England in their opening game, against Belgium in Basle. Goals from Lofthouse (two) and Broadis saw England 3-1 up in the second half but they surrendered the lead and the score was 3-3 when normal time ended. Lofthouse restored England's advantage in extra time only for a Dickinson own goal to give the Belgians a point.

49

That match was on June 17 and on Sunday, June 20, England met the Swiss in Berne. Matthews had suffered a knock against Belgium so Finney switched to the right-wing, allowing Mullen to come in on the other wing. Lofthouse was also out, with Taylor moving from inside left to centre-forward giving Wilshaw a chance to partner his club colleague. More significant was a switch in defence, where Billy Wright replaced Syd Owen. The Luton man had taken a minor knock in the game against Belgium, a hasty reshuffle seeing Wright play the closing minutes of the match at centre-half. The Wolves man took to the role as if to the manner born – he had appeared there a few times for his club – and would retain the England No 5 shirt for the next five years as he went on to become the first footballer in the world to appear in one hundred internationals. As for Owen, he never played for England again though he was voted Footballer of the Year in 1959.

Both Wilshaw and Mullen got their names on the scoresheet as England beat the Swiss 2-0 – a far happier day than Mullen's last World Cup finals outing, the 1-0 defeat at the hands of the USA in Brazil in the 1950 tournament.

Wright's switch in Berne saw future Molineux boss Bill McGarry given his debut. It was McGarry who set up Wilshaw for England's second goal.

The win brought England a quarter-final date with world champions Uruguay in Basle on June 26 with Taylor and Mullen making way for the fit-again Lofthouse and Matthews. England gave a good account of themselves, fighting back from 3-1 down to 3-2 before finally bowing out

4-2. Lofthouse and Finney scored the goals and the general opinion was that the scoreline did not do justice to England, for whom Wilshaw was one of several impressive performers. He had set up Lofthouse's goal and had gone close to scoring himself, seeming to get a sly shove from a Uruguayan just as he was about to shoot. England's teams in the World Cup finals:

v Belgium: Merrick; Staniforth, Byrne; Wright, Owen, Dickinson; Matthews, Broadis, Lofthouse, T Taylor, Finney.

v Switzerland: Merrick; Staniforth, Byrne; McGarry, Wright, Dickinson; Finney, Broadis, T Taylor, Wilshaw, Finney.

v Uruguay: Merrick; Staniforth, Byrne; McGarry, Wright, Dickinson; Matthews, Broadis, Lofthouse, Wilshaw, Finney.

Despite the gutsy World Cup showing the selectors wielded the axe for the opening international of the 1954-5 season with no fewer than seven new caps named for the game against Northern Ireland. Wilshaw was among those dropped but his day would come in April 1955 when he became the only man ever to score four goals in an England-Scotland game as the Scots were trounced 7-2.

Bert Williams, too, would earn a recall before that season was out and there would be first caps for team-mates Bill Slater and Ron Flowers. All of which added confirmation to the view Cullis had expressed that night at the Civic Hall – the team of 1953-4 were as good as any Wolverhampton Wanderers side that had gone before.

It is a view that would appear to be shared by Jimmy Greaves, the former Chelsea, Spurs and England man who was without doubt a goal poacher with few equals. In his book, Taking Sides (Sidgwick and Jackson) which he co-wrote with Norman Giller and which was published in 1984, Greaves chose his top ten English sides since the Second World War and put the Wolves of 1953-4 among them.

"They were the team that conquered all-comers in a trail-blazer for European inter-club competition." wrote Greaves, and it is interesting to hear his verdict on some of the key figures at Molineux.

Stan Cullis
His flattened nose gave him the look of an ex-boxer and he was as tough as he looked. But while he was a demanding and unforgiving martinet of a manager, he was always a scrupulously honest, highly principled, and fair-minded man who treated everybody on an equal footing and would give his full support and encouragement to anybody – star or novice – who was prepared to give him and his beloved club 100 per cent effort and endeavour.

Bert Williams
He had great physical presence and was like a gymnast at the back of the Wolves and England defences. Bert would be in anybody's top ten of all-time great British goalkeepers.

Bill Slater
A superior mind was at work when Bill Slater was in action for Wolves and England, but while he brought brain to the game he was quite capable of adding considerable brawn and was a firm and authoritative player. He had great strength and stamina to go with his skill.

Billy Wright
England has never had a greater or more loyal servant and his exploits with Wolves lit a torch for many young players.

Johnny Hancocks
I have schoolboy memories of seeing little Johnny Hancocks bringing instant excitement to games with his sudden sprints down the right wing and surprisingly violent shots. He was an important cog in the Wolves machine, not only for his goalscoring touch but also because he could cross the ball accurately with either foot.

Peter Broadbent
Peter was a polished player with good vision and the ability to hit his target with long passes from either foot. I rated him in the Johnny Haynes class as a schemer. I cannot give him higher praise than that.

Dennis Wilshaw
An extremely versatile forward who could score goals from virtually any position. He played for England at inside left and on the left-wing and was a thrusting player who liked to shoot on sight with his favourite left foot.

Jimmy Mullen
Hancocks and Mullen went together like bacon and eggs. Mullen was the perfect foil for the more intricate play of Hancocks and his direct runs down left turned matches into nightmares for many right-backs.

It is probably the Hancocks and Mullen partnership that earns the 1953-4 team a special place in the hearts of older Wolves fans because it was something very special. The FA Yearbook of 1954-5 endorsed that view. Looking back at the previous campaign the annual reflected: "Probably no two wingers are closer in touch with one another during a game than Hancocks and Mullen; their wing to wing movements, combined with long diagonal passes that quickly change the point of attack, have throughout constituted a dangerous threat to opponents."

The yearbook also said "The current Wolves team is based firmly on experience and football craft blended with new blood brought in at the right moment."

If one can level criticism at the team it would be that they should have won the First Division title more than once. However, it was no easy task in those days. As Dennis Wilshaw rightly points out: "There were a lot of good teams in the First Division. You could not do as Arsenal and Manchester United can now and say we will be the top two. Any team was capable of beating the others."

It was left to the Wolves side at the end of the 1950s to add to the title haul. They were twice champions, once runners-up and Cup-winners in the space of three seasons, starting in 1957-8. Stalwarts like Williams, Shorthouse, Pritchard, Hancocks, Swinbourne and Wilshaw had been replaced by players of equal talent, men like Ron Flowers and Peter Broadbent were in full bloom and the league goals flowed at 100-per-season for four successive campaigns, yet the class of 1953-4 still seem to have a special magic all of their own.

They were the last to wear the famous old gold shirts – and who would argue they were not the best?

CHAPTER SIX

THE MATCHES

BURNLEY 4
Shannon 62, 86
Holden 64
Pilkington 70

WOLVES 1
Swinbourne 2

Wednesday, August 19, 1953

After a superb start to the season, with a goal in the second minute, Wolves faded badly and ended up well beaten at Turf Moor, where the home side hit four second-half goals in 24 minutes. Wolves did not translate their superiority into goals, although they had just as many chances to do so as Burnley, and that was the primary cause why the game finished with a defeat instead of a victory or, at worst, a high-scoring draw.

The second reason was the failure of the inside forwards to maintain the eager seeking for the ball with which they had begun. The inside forwards did not do their job completely, the ball being constantly thrown back at their defence, and they eventually found it more than they could take – with the inevitable result.

The climax followed two minutes of panic. In the 62nd minute a shot from Les Shannon was deflected the wrong way past Nigel Sims by a defender's foot and in the 64th minute, with the defence running both ways, Bill Holden drove home a great cross shot.

That was the beginning of the end which came six minutes later to provide something near mortification for Bill Shorthouse who up to that time, and indeed afterwards, played a gallant part. This time he made the mistake of hesitating to clear when challenged by Holden. He lost control, Holden took the ball and whipped it across goal to young Brian Pilkington who slammed it into the net.

The last came only four minutes from the end, when the Wolves defence, who had been tempted into playing square because Shannon was running into an off-side trap, were hoist with their own petard. Shannon went through a gap to chase a pass from Billy Gray. This time he was not off-side and the result was the fourth and last goal to make the transformation scene all too disappointingly complete. There were bright signs such as the effervescence of Billy Wright and the stalwart work of Shorthouse and Bill Slater who became the overburdened men as soon as Dennis Wilshaw and Ron Stockin faded out of the picture.

There was also some competent goalkeeping by Sims and, when Wolves were on top, a stout look about the defence generally. With Jimmy Mullen in his brightest mood and Johnny Hancocks placing the ball accurately, the opening work of the forwards was something good to see on the rain-soaked, slippery surface, but these things were no more sufficient in themselves than was Swinbourne's goal in one minute fifty seconds after a Mullen-Hancocks movement.

WOLVES: Sims, Short, Pritchard; Slater, Shorthouse, Wright; Hancocks, Stockin, Swinbourne, Wilshaw, Mullen.
BURNLEY: Thompson; Aird, Winton; Adamson, Cummings, Rudman; Gray, McIlroy, Holden, Shannon, Pilkington.
Referee: A Holland (Barnsley). Attendance: 32,822.

MAN CITY 0   **WOLVES 4**   *Saturday, August 22, 1953*
                         Wilshaw 18, Slater 36,
                         Swinbourne 56, 83

Unchanged Wolves made a return visit to Lancashire and this time it was a totally different story. City were outplayed for long periods as Wolves totally dominated the game from the start. In fact, they should have won by a bigger margin.

Manager Cullis must have driven home some hard messages after the defeat at Turf Moor and the players responded by forcing City back into their own half from the first whistle. Dennis Wilshaw drilled in the first shot which flew inches wide. Soon afterwards Roy Swinbourne tested City's German goalkeeper Bert Trautmann after some smart work down the left flank by Jimmy Mullen. Wolves had an early let-off when John Williamson, looking off side, was allowed to run on but his point-blank shot was saved by Nigel Sims. Wolves went ahead on 18 minutes. Short passed to Johnny Hancocks and his centre saw Wilshaw head into the roof of the neat.

In the 36th minute it was two thanks to the alert Bill Slater. Players hesitated thinking the referee would award a free kick but Slater spotted he had given a throw-in and motioned Ron Stockin to take it quickly. The ball went to Slater and he went through on his own before letting fly with a right-foot cross shot. The ball was blocked but came back to him and he steered it just inside the far post. Almost immediately Wilshaw could have added a third. City finally got in a worthwhile shot three minutes from the interval, Johnny Hart setting up Ivor Broadis, whose effort was easily saved by Sims.

Eleven minutes after the break, Roy Swinbourne pounced to net the third. A chipped pass from Wilshaw put Mullen in to send over a low pass and Swinbourne ran in to power the ball home. Trautmann got his hands to the ball but it went over the line before Stockin made sure. Wolves were by then playing some delightful football with wingers Hancocks and Mullen having field days against Ken Branagan and Jack Hannaway.

With Wolves stroking the ball around with precision, Billy Wright and Wilshaw had what looked like good goals disallowed before Swinbourne completed the scoring with seven minutes to go. Stockin sent Hancocks away and his centre was sidefooted home by the centre-forward.

Comments:"The Wolves wingers Hancocks and Mullen were quite brilliant." – Ivor Broadis (Man City)
"It was the fact that Wolves got the ball into the net four times in the second half that emphasised just how determined were their efforts to keep up the cracking pace they had set themselves." – Commentator (Express & Star).

MAN CITY: Trautmann; Branagan, Hannaway; Revie, Ewing, Paul; Anders, Hart, Williamson, Broadis, Clarke.
WOLVES: Sims; Short, Pritchard; Slater, Shorthouse, Wright; Hancocks, Stockin, Swinbourne, Wilshaw, Mullen.
Referee: A Murdoch (Sheffield). Attendance: 22,729.

54

SUNDERLAND 3   **WOLVES 2**   *Wednesday, August 26, 1953*
T Wright 18   *Hancocks 63 (pen)*
Shackleton 26   *Wilshaw 81*
Ford 52

Wolves, in their third successive away game, were unlucky losers, before a large crowd, in an end-to-end match, that could have gone either way after the visitors had pulled back from 3-0 down with some fine attacking football.

Sunderland's expensive line-up were businesslike from the start and after a couple of near misses took the lead on 18 minutes through Tommy Wright, who deflected an Arthur Wright shot past Nigel Sims.

Before the goal Wolves' Ron Stockin had failed to take advantage of a weak back pass by Ray Daniel. Dennis Wilshaw came close to an equaliser before Len Shackleton netted a second on 26 minutes after a tidy build-up, his shot taking a slight deflection before squirting past Sims.

Wolves did not deserve to be two down and after Roy Swinbourne and Jimmy Mullen had both gone close and Stockin had ballooned the ball over the bar from a narrow angle, Sunderland scored a third, against the run of play on 52 minutes. Harry Kirtley raced down the right wing and crossed for Trevor Ford to score with a terrific first-time drive.

Within five minutes Wolves had reduced the lead. Wilshaw was going clean through when he was brought down in the penalty area and Hancocks scored from the spot.

From that point it was nearly all Wolves. A fierce drive from Jimmy Mullen skimmed the bar, an overhead hook from Roy Swinbourne did the same before, nine minutes from the end, Wilshaw scored from close in after Swinbourne had headed down to his feet a lob from Billy Wright.

Wolves then kept up almost incessant pressure but despite whirlwind efforts from Johnny Hancocks, Swinbourne (twice) and Wilshaw, they could not get the consolation for their earlier missed chances.

Comments "Ford was just as tough as he had been when he played against me for Aston Villa."
– Billy Wright.
"The football-mad Roker Park crowd saw their expensive darlings pushed back as soon as the business began." – Express & Star.

SUNDERLAND: Cowan; Stelling, Hedley; Aitken, Daniel, A Wright; T Wright, Kirtley, Ford, Shackleton, McSeveney.
WOLVES: Sims, Short, Pritchard; Slater, Shorthouse, Wright; Hancocks, Stockin, Swinbourne, Wilshaw, Mullen.
Referee: T L Wood (Bury). Attendance: 57,135.

55

WOLVES 3   **CARDIFF CITY 1**   *Saturday, August 29, 1953*
Wilshaw 34, Mullen 38   *Grant 13*
Hancocks 39 (pen)

Peter Broadbent, absent for 16 games, was recalled to the Wolves side for the first home game of the season and turned in a fine performance. Wolves carried on from where they left off against Sunderland with some precise attacks down either flank.

Yet Cardiff might have saved a point. Wilf Grant was clear of the defence but allowed himself to be robbed and Ken Chisholm was presented with a golden opportunity but shot wide. City, after an opening spell of Wolves pressure, had taken the lead through Grant. Goalkeeper Ron Howells collected a Mullen centre and his long clearance saw Grant outpace Bill Shorthouse and beat Nigel Sims from the edge of the penalty area.

There was a let-off for City when a Hancocks shot struck Howells's foot as he fell and bounced away. Mullen then missed a chance but atoned by laying on the equaliser for Dennis Wilshaw on 34 minutes. Mullen chased a Peter Broadbent pass almost to the line before sending a centre skidding across goal. The ball beat Roy Swinbourne but Wilshaw, racing in, stuck out a foot and guided the ball past Howells. It was the first of three goals in a five-minute spell.

56

On 38 minutes Mullen made it 2-1 when he met Johnny Hancocks's right-wing cross and ninety seconds later Hancocks scored from the penalty spot even though he slipped and fell as he shot. The kick was awarded for a foul by Derrick Sullivan on Broadbent.

Cardiff defended well after the break as Wolves drove forward, producing plenty of shots and headers, none of which found a way past the in-form Howells, who made two fine saves from Dennis Wilshaw and Broadbent. Full-back Alf Sherwood was on hand to clear two more shots off the line. The win extended Wolves' unbeaten home run to eight matches.

Comments
"Full-backs Jack Short and Roy Pritchard played exceptionally well for Wolves. They never put a foot wrong. Our wingers, Williams and McLoughlin, hardly got a look in." – Alf Sherwood (Cardiff City).
"How City survived the second-half onslaught was a complete mystery."– South Wales Echo.

WOLVES: Sims, Short, Pritchard; Slater, Shorthouse, Wright; Hancocks, Broadbent, Swinbourne, Wilshaw, Mullen.
CARDIFF CITY: Howells; Frowen, Sherwood; Hollyman, Montgomery, Sullivan; Williams, Harrington, Grant, Chisholm, McLoughlin.
Referee: W H Clapton (London). Attendance: 33,221

WOLVES 3   **SUNDERLAND 1**   *Monday, August 31, 1953*
Wilshaw 35   *T Wright 2*
Mullen 68
Swinbourne 70

Quite a few of the Bank Holiday fans may have missed the opening goal as Tommy Wright, deputising at centre-forward for Trevor Ford, raced through the home defence to give Sunderland a shock lead. Following that surprise start, Wolves settled down to bombard the visitors' goal.

Jimmy Mullen had a point-blank shot saved by Sunderland goalkeeper Jimmy Cowan. Johnny Hancocks shot wide from 18 yards, Mullen and Roy Swinbourne saw headers go wide before the equaliser finally came after 35 minutes. Peter Broadbent pushed the ball past Ray Daniel, he and Cowan got in a tangle and the chasing Wilshaw coolly turned the ball into the net.

In the second half, after a couple of close calls at either end, Wolves won the game in the space of two minutes. In the 68th, Cowan could only palm the ball out and the waiting Mullen drove it home. Two minutes later Broadbent delivered a pinpoint pass to the feet of Swinbourne who turned to score from a few yards out.

Wolves came close to more goals on at least four more occasions and with better finishing could have run rampant.

Comments
"It was a good job our goalkeeper Jimmy Cowan was in good form or we would have conceded six at least." – Billy Bingham (Sunderland)
"I found myself, for the fourth match in succession, watching a Wolves team who looked at least six goals better than the opposition." – Commentator (Express & Star).

57

WOLVES: Sims; Short, Pritchard; Slater, Shorthouse, Wright; Hancocks, Broadbent, Swinbourne, Wilshaw, Mullen.
SUNDERLAND: Cowan; Hedley, Hudgell; Anderson, Daniel, A Wright; Bingham, Kirtley, T Wright, Shackleton, McSeveney.
Referee: T L Wood (Bury). Attendance: 41,442.

ARSENAL 2   **WOLVES 3**   *Saturday, September 5, 1953*
Roper 25   *Broadbent 22*
Holton 41   *Wilshaw 33, Hancocks 88*

This win, clinched by Johnny Hancocks's header with just two minutes to go, bridged a 20-year gap. It was Wolves' first League win at Highbury since a 2-1 win there in March, 1933. Playing in front of more than 60,000 spectators, Wolves should have clinched the points sooner, having led 1-0 and 2-1, only to squander chances. Arsenal may have been bottom of the table but retained one familiar characteristic – their ability to cover the goal-line.

Dennis Wilshaw, Peter Broadbent, Jimmy Mullen (twice) and Johnny Hancocks were all denied as bodies and legs came between shots and goals, aided by some fine goalkeeping by Jack Kelsey.

It was a quiet, start, however, with both goalkeepers restricted to dealing with crosses before Broadbent struck with a cool finish on 22 minutes Two defenders hesitated as Roy Swinbourne put the ball through, Broadbent took it on before beating Jack Kelsey with an accurately placed low drive.

After Wilshaw and Swinbourne had missed chances to make it two, Don Roper equalised on 25 minutes. Cliff Holton's centre from the right was pushed out to Roper who, from the inside-left position, sent a low cross shot past Bert Williams. Wolves restored their lead eight minutes later. Bill Slater's pass to Mullen saw the winger put the ball low across goal for Wilshaw to dive forward and head home. Wolves missed a couple more chances before Cliff Holton levelled four minutes before half-time. A breakaway saw Roper's centre pushed by Doug Lishman to Holton who hit home a cross shot.

It was Wolves who were on top early in the second half then Arsenal hit back. Kelsey was generally busier than Bert Williams but the Wolves man excelled with some fine leaps and catches. Back in the side after injury, Williams had been a little nervous at the start but a fine diving catch to deny Roper set him up for the rest of the game.

The winner came when Bill Slater sent Mullen away down the left-wing to cross for Hancocks, racing in from the other wing, to score with a flying header that would have done credit to Nat Lofthouse.

58

Comments
"I heard my bones crack following one mighty shoulder charge by Bill Shorthouse." – Doug Lishman (Arsenal).
"Wolves might have won this game much sooner, so superior were they to Arsenal." – Islington Gazette

ARSENAL: Kelsey; Wade, Evans; Forbes, Dodgin, Bowen; Roper, Logie, Holton, Lishman, Marden.
WOLVES: Williams; Short, Pritchard; Slater, Shorthouse, Wright; Hancocks, Broadbent, Swinbourne, Wilshaw, Mullen.
Referee: G Gibson (Urmston). Attendance: 60,460.

WOLVES 2   **LIVERPOOL 1**   *Monday, September 7, 1953*
Swinbourne 44   *Jackson 87*
Broadbent 88

A game that was drifting towards a 1-0 Wolves win came alive in the final three minutes as the visitors equalised only for Wolves to snatch a dramatic winner. Wolves failed to recapture the form they had shown at Highbury though they were hampered by an injury to full-back Jack Short. He was hurt after 23 minutes and finished the first half out on the right wing. He did not return for the start of the second half but came on in the 53rd minute to operate at centre-forward as nuisance value. Short, who it later turned out had torn a thigh muscle, almost got on the scoresheet with a header.

A rearranged Wolves side saw Billy Wright move to right-back, Dennis Wilshaw drop back to right-half, with Bill Slater moving over to the left, while Roy Swinbourne operated at inside-right. In a drab first half there were few chances. Wilshaw and Jimmy Mullen, with a cross-cum-shot, came closest for Wolves while Billy Liddell and Louis Bimpson had the best chances for Liverpool, Bert Williams saving well from the latter.

Wolves took the lead a minute before half-time. A body feint by Peter Broadbent allowed Johnny Hancocks to get over a centre which Roy Swinbourne headed past Russell Crossley. Liverpool came more into the game in the second half and Wright, in his emergency role, twice thwarted dangerous raids by the pacy Alan A'Court on Liverpool's left-wing. Bert Williams saved well from Liddell and Crossley denied Wilshaw before the late drama.

Right-winger Brian Jackson, playing his first game since national service, raced on to a long pass from Bimpson to send a scorching shot past Williams and it looked as though Liverpool had grabbed a point.

However, the gallant Short was still battling and set up the winner ninety seconds later. A poor header enabled him to push the ball through a gap in front of Swinbourne and Peter Broadbent. Brushing his team-mate aside, Broadbent fired the ball home from just inside the penalty area.

Comments
"Wolves are championship material. They have a wonderful side, full of quality players. Some of them are quite exceptional." – Billy Liddell (Liverpool).
"Short ought to be cited for an outstanding display of club spirit." – Commentator, Express & Star.

WOLVES: Williams; Short, Pritchard; Slater, Shorthouse, Wright, Hancocks, Broadbent, Swinbourne, Wilshaw, Mullen.
LIVERPOOL: Crossley; Lambert, Spicer; Saunders, Hughes, Maloney; Jackson, Liddell, Bimpson, W Jones, A'Court.
Referee: K A Collinge (Sale). Attendance: 35,701.

WOLVES 4   **PORTSMOUTH 3**   *Saturday, September 12, 1953*
Wilshaw 2, 3, 37   *Gordon 7, 48*
Swinbourne 86   *Harris 44*

Despite two goals in the first three minutes, Wolves led only 3-2 at the interval and had to rely eventually on a late winner from Roy Swinbourne.

Wolves brought in Len Gibbons at right-back for the injured Jack Short and Norman Deeley at right-half for Bill Slater who was playing for England in the amateur international against Ireland. Deeley's service to winger Johnny Hancocks was one of the features of the match.

Dennis Wilshaw struck in the second and third minutes. Jimmy Mullen forced a corner and his kick went across goal to Hancocks whose attempted half volley only went to the feet of Wilshaw. The inside-left reacted quickly to sidefoot the ball into the net. Wilshaw's second was a solo effort after he had been put away by Billy Wright. Wilshaw raced away, beat Pompey centre-half Duggie Reid and then slipped the ball past the advancing Ted Platt. Rattled Pompey were lucky not to go four down as Roy Swinbourne and Hancocks were only denied by goalkeeper Platt.

With the game still only seven minutes old, Portsmouth broke away for Johnny Gordon to score with a snap shot from the edge of the penalty area, the ball deflecting off the head of Bill Shorthouse out of Bert Williams's reach. Soon afterwards Williams saved a Gordon header with his chest. Then Williams had to be alert to prevent Peter Harris and Albert Mundy from grabbing an equaliser.

Portsmouth grew in confidence as England left-half Jimmy Dickinson kept a close watch on Peter Broadbent. Yet it was Wolves who struck again when Wilshaw scored after 37 minutes to complete his first three-goal haul since his sensational debut against Newcastle in March, 1949. It came when Hancocks took a quick throw-in to Roy Swinbourne. The centre-forward returned the ball to Hancocks whose centre was headed home by Wilshaw.

A minute before the break Peter Harris pulled back a goal for Pompey. The right winger scored with a vicious cross shot from just inside the penalty area. Three minutes into the second half they were level. A long pass sent Harris clear and his centre was headed against the underside of the bar by Gordon, the ball bouncing down over the line.

60

There was plenty of excitement as the second half wore on and it was only a piece of fine keeping by Williams that stopped Charlie Vaughan giving Pompey the lead. With eight minutes left Bill Shorthouse slipped as he tried to clear and Vaughan had a clear run on goal. Williams advanced and, as Vaughan tried to round him, managed to grab the ball from the centre-forward's feet.

Wolves, thanks to a piece of bad luck for Pompey, finally edged home through Swinbourne's goal four minute form time. Reg Pickett passed the ball back to Platt but the goalkeeper fell and the ball ran free for the centre-forward to stab it home.

Comments
"Centre-half Duggie Reid is an awkward customer to get round. He didn't move far from the middle and with Jimmy Dickinson alongside him he looked pretty formidable." – Roy Swinbourne.
"One of the brighter features of this game was the excellent service Hancocks received from young Deeley, who coming into the first eleven for the first time for more than a season, showed that best of all football combinations, confidence without conceit." – Commentator (Express & Star).

WOLVES: Williams; Gibbons, Pritchard; Deeley, Shorthouse, Wright; Hancocks, Broadbent, Swinbourne, Wilshaw, Mullen.
PORTSMOUTH: Platt; Gunter, Mansell; Pickett, Reid, Dickinson; Harris, Gordon, Vaughan, Mundy, Henderson.
Referee: N C Taylor (Westbury). Attendance: 36,524.

LIVERPOOL 1   **WOLVES 1**   *Wednesday, September 16, 1953*
W Jones 69   *Wilshaw 40*

With Jack Short still sidelined, Billy Wright was named right-back, Norman Deeley keeping his place with Bill Slater returning to the side at left-half. In a game of contrasting styles, Liverpool, after a run of five defeats, hit back well to earn their share of the spoils.

Wolves led through a fine goal from Dennis Wilshaw five minutes before the break. Seizing on a half chance when the ball rebounded to him from a defender he tripped delicately past two opponents before slipping the ball past Russell Crossley in the home goal. That came just after Louis Bimpson had hit the Wolves bar.

Wolves were on top for the opening twenty minutes of the second half but could not press home their advantage because they made one move too many when they got within striking distance. Johnny Hancocks was an exception and stung Crossley's fingers with two searing shots and was then unluckily denied a goal after 58 minutes. A Mullen centre beat Crossley and eluded Roy Swinbourne, who fell on the goal-line. Hancocks ran in to push the ball into the net but Swinbourne was given off-side.

Liverpool made the most of their let-off and were rewarded on 69 minutes when Bill Jones got the ball past a mass of players' legs and bodies after a Brian Jackson centre had been headed back into the goalmouth by Alan A'Court.

Wilshaw and Peter Broadbent did sterling work in Wolves' approach play and had good support from Slater and Deeley. The wingers were getting the ball across with precision but Swinbourne could not get the better of centre-half Laurie Hughes.

Although not as busy as Crossley, Williams made several fine saves, a one-handed downward punch from Jones being one of his best. Bill Shorthouse was the strong man in defence. It was he and Roy Pritchard who did most to smother the efforts of Billy Liddell.

Comments
"A draw was a fair result but we should have won." – Alan A'Court.
"The strong man of Wolves defence was Shorthouse. He was exceptional." – Liverpool Daily Post.

LIVERPOOL: Crossley; Lambert, Spicer; Saunders, Hughes, Maloney; Jackson, Liddell, Bimpson, W Jones, A'Court.
WOLVES: Williams; Wright, Pritchard; Deeley, Shorthouse, Slater; Hancocks, Broadbent, Swinbourne, Wilshaw, Mullen.
Referee: K A Collinge (Sale) Attendance: 29,848.

BLACKPOOL 0   **WOLVES 0**   *Saturday, September 19, 1953.*

Wolves did well to earn a point from the Cup holders considering they were handicapped from two minutes before half-time by an injury to Dennis Wilshaw which saw him hobbling at centre-forward throughout the second half.

Stan Cullis chose to keep his players together after the Anfield game, staying a few days in Blackpool before the game at Bloomfield Road. However, he had to make changes as Norman Deeley was with the forces and Bill Slater on England amateur international duty. Ray Chatham and Bill Baxter were drafted into their places.

Wilshaw and Roy Swinbourne were both denied by Blackpool's Scottish international goalkeeper George Farm early in the game and Jackie Mudie went close for Blackpool from a Stanley Matthews cross. It took a spectacular dive by Williams to collect Mudie's header almost on the line. There was another let-off for Wolves when Stanley Mortensen put Bill Perry away but could not get his foot to the ball when the left-winger returned it across goal.

Johnny Hancocks and Jimmy Mullen gave home backs Eddie Shimwell and Tommy Garrett a busy afternoon but it was the defence, well-marshalled by Bill Shorthouse, who took the honours as they kept the star-studded Blackpool forward line under control.

Wilshaw even managed to get the ball into the net but was ruled off-side but Wolves had a final escape two minutes from time. Mudie fired high over the bar, after being put through by Mortensen.

Comments
"I thought Pritchard, the Wolves full-back, played very well. I had a tough time against him, that's why I hung back a lot and tried to get inside." – Stanley Matthews.
"It is a long time since I saw an entire Wolves defence tackle so relentlessly." – Commentator (Express & Star).

BLACKPOOL: Farm; Shimwell, Garrett; Fenton, Johnston, Kelly; Matthews, Taylor, Mortensen, Mudie, Perry.
WOLVES: Williams; Wright, Pritchard; Chatham, Shorthouse, Baxter; Hancocks, Broadbent, Swinbourne, Wilshaw, Mullen.
Referee: J V Sherlock (Sheffield). Attendance: 35,074.

WOLVES 8   **CHELSEA 1**   *Saturday, September 26, 1953.*
Hancocks 3 (pen) 31, 54   *Bentley 76*
Wilshaw 48
Swinbourne 61, 79
Broadbent 71
Mullen 86

This was Wolves' best win, in terms of goals scored, since they beat Leicester 10-1 in April 1938, as they at last did what they had threatened to do against Cardiff, Sunderland and Portsmouth and scored a a hatfull of goals. It was also only the sixth time in the club's history that all five forwards had scored in a League game.

With Jack Short fit again to return at right-back, Billy Wright was able to switch back to left-half, while Slater was back after his amateur international call-up.

Wolves were given an early gift, when Stan Willemse conceded a needless penalty after three minutes. The Chelsea back had plenty of time to clear a Mullen cross but brought the ball under control with his hand. Johnny Hancocks scored from the spot. It was only 2-0 at the break, Hancocks having collected his second just after the half-hour. Bill Robertson, well out of his goal, made a poor clearance straight to Hancocks who sent the ball home from 35 yards before the keeper could recover.

Dennis Wilshaw made it three early in the second half. Peter Broadbent began the move with a short pass to Hancocks whose centre was headed out by Chelsea centre-half Ron Greenwood to Jimmy Mullen. From the left-winger's lob, Wilshaw steered a header inside the far post. On 54 minutes Hancocks collected his third. A long centre from Mullen to the far post caught everybody napping and Hancocks nipped past Willemse to slot the ball home from close range.

Roy Swinbourne made it five on the hour. Bill Slater made a good run to the bye-line before pulling the ball back to the centre-forward who volleyed it home. Peter Broadbent weighed in with one on 71 minutes.

Mullen chased a long pass and sent over a cross which Robertson tried to gather only for Broadbent to beat him to the ball and deflect it into the net inside the far post. Five minutes later Chelsea got on the scoresheet when Bert Williams saved a Roy Bentley penalty only for the centre-forward to score from the rebound. The kick had been awarded for a tackle by Jack Short on left-winger Frank Blunstone. It was only brief respite as Swinbourne scored his second on 79 minutes. He headed the ball low past Robertson from a typical Mullen centre. Mullen made it eight four minutes from time when he headed home a Broadbent centre. It might have been nine but, after a sparkling run by Mullen, Hancocks twice saw shots blocked by the visiting defence.

63

Comments
"We got a right roasting. There's no getting away from that. Wolves were good, very good, at times." – Ron Greenwood (Chelsea).
"It was the wing superiority which Wolves have enjoyed in so many of their games which paved the way to such an encouraging result." – Commentator (Express & Star).

WOLVES: Williams; Short, Pritchard; Slater, Shorthouse, Wright; Hancocks, Broadbent, Swinbourne, Wilshaw, Mullen.
CHELSEA: Robertson; P Sillett, Willemse; Armstrong, Greenwood, Saunders; Bentley, J Smith, Lewis, McNichol, Blunstone.
Referee: J H Clough (Bolton). Attendance: 36,134.

SHEFFIELD UNITED 3 **WOLVES 3** *Saturday, October 3, 1953*
Ringstead 19, 48 *Hancocks 10, Wilshaw 31*
Bottom 27 *Swinbourne 84*

A goal by Roy Swinbourne, four minutes from time, extended Wolves' unbeaten run to nine games after they had twice trailed at Bramall Lane. They had chances a-plenty, thanks to the continued supply of crosses from Johnny Hancocks and Jimmy Mullen, but failed to take them. Wolves started off in the same mood in which they had ended the match against Chelsea but their early dominance brought only a goal from Hancocks on ten minutes.

Mullen beat Fred Furniss and sent over a centre which Hancocks fired home.

Goalkeeper Ted Burgin got his hands to the ball but could not stop it hitting the roof of the net. Hancocks and Dennis Wilshaw then both missed chances before Alf Ringstead equalised after 19 minutes. He drove the ball home from just inside the penalty area after a good left-wing run by Derek Hawksworth.

Eight minutes later, reserve centre-forward Arthur Bottom put the Blades ahead. A clearance up the right saw Bottom get the better of Bill Shorthouse. Bert Williams advanced and then retreated and Bottom got to the ball first to beat the keeper with a low cross shot which went in off the far post. The goal was cancelled out by Wilshaw within two minutes. Sheffield could not clear the ball after a Mullen corner and when the ball rebounded off Hancocks to Wilshaw's feet the inside-left found the net from a few yards out.

64

Wilshaw went close to putting Wolves in front once more after good approach play involving Peter Broadbent and Mullen. Roy Swinbourne was also out of luck when he ran on to a pass and put the ball into the net, only to be ruled off-side.

Three minutes after half-time, Ringstead struck again. Hagan lobbed the ball over to the right-winger who had moved in from his wing. He took the ball in the inside-left position before beating Williams with a cross shot. With inside-forwards Hagan and Harold Brook in form, United pushed for more goals and Hagan had an effort ruled out for off-side.

Hancocks was put clear by Bill Shorthouse but shot just wide before Swinbourne had the final say. A mistake by Bill Toner left the centre-forward with a clear run on goal and he beat Burgin as the keeper advanced to earn a point, much of the credit for which went to Shorthouse and Williams, ably supported by Roy Pritchard.

Comments
"We matched Wolves kick for kick, pass for pass and deserved a point." – Jimmy Hagan
"The game provided another telling lesson on how costly continued misses can become." – Commentator (Express & Star).

SHEFFIELD UNITED: Burgin; Furniss, G Shaw; J Shaw, Toner, Rawson; Ringstead, Hagan, Bottom, Brook, Hawksworth.
WOLVES: Williams; Short, Pritchard; Slater, Shorthouse, Wright; Hancocks, Broadbent, Swinbourne, Wilshaw, Mullen.
Referee: F S Fiander (Loudwater, Bucks). Attendance: 35,961.

NEWCASTLE UNITED 1   **WOLVES 2**   *Saturday, October 10, 1953.*
Mulgrew 7   *Smith 81, Swinbourne 88*

Another late goal brought Wolves an historic victory at St James' Park, their first on Tyneside since a 4-2 win in February 1903. The win, featuring an outstanding display by goalkeeper Bert Williams, was another example of reserves rising to the occasion as Billy Wright, Dennis Wilshaw and Jimmy Mullen were away on international duty helping England beat Wales 4-1 in Cardiff. In came Ron Flowers for Wright, while Ron Stockin and Les Smith formed the left-wing in a team captained by Bill Shorthouse.

Newcastle, with wingers Jackie Milburn and Bobby Mitchell in form, pegged Wolves back at the start and took the lead on seven minutes. A Frank Brennan clearance found Milburn who sent the ball down the middle where Tommy Mulgrew was racing through. The inside man beat Bill Shorthouse before firing past Williams. Roy Pritchard then had to clear a Mitchell lob off the line and then Williams tipped a 25-yard Tommy Casey drive over the bar.

Wolves managed only three efforts on goal in the first half, one each from Roy Swinbourne, Stockin and Johnny Hancocks. Williams, in doubt right up until kick-off because of a heavy cold, kept Wolves in the game with saves from Len White and Mitchell, while Roy Pritchard stopped Milburn in full flight with a fine tackle. Pritchard sustained a kick in the first half but played on.

65

Newcastle kept up the pressure after the interval with both Milburn and Len White scorning chances. Shorthouse was at the heart of the rearguard action while Roy Swinbourne gave Brennan a testing time at the other end.

With nine minutes to go Smith grabbed a shock equaliser. After a weak pass by Jimmy Scoular, he cut inside full-back Bobby Cowell and raced down the middle to beat Bobby Simpson with a fierce right-foot drive, the home goalkeeper's view possibly blocked by Scoular.

Wolves drove forward in search of a winner and Swinbourne fired wide but, with two minutes left, Stockin won a free kick 25 yards out. Hancocks walked back a few yards as if to have a crack at goal but fooled the home defence by playing a short pass to Swinbourne's feet. The centre-forward turned to drive the ball low past Simpson.

Comments
"It was a very pleasant trip home from the North East that evening." – Peter Broadbent.
"It was the sheer persistence of Les Smith that brought Wolves back into the game." – Northern Echo.

NEWCASTLE UNITED: Simpson; Cowell, Batty, Scoular, Brennan, Casey; Milburn, Mulgrew, White, Keery, Mitchell.
WOLVES: Williams; Short, Pritchard; Slater, Shorthouse, Flowers; Hancocks, Broadbent, Swinbourne, Stockin, Smith.
Referee: F Thurman (Preston). Attendance: 39,913.

WOLVES 3   **MANCHESTER UNITED 1**   *Saturday, October 17, 1953.*
Hancocks 16 (pen)   *Taylor 30*
Broadbent 43
Swinbourne 72

Wolves' biggest crowd of the season so far saw them chalk up their eleventh successive home win and extend their unbeaten run to eleven games though United may have halted the run if they had taken their chances. Roy Pritchard's injury at Newcastle meant a rare game for Bill Guttridge but Billy Wright, Dennis Wilshaw and Jimmy Mullen returned after their England date.

Wolves were given a gift lead on 16 minutes when United left-back Roger Byrne needlessly handled the ball inside the penalty area and Johnny Hancocks blasted home one of his typical spot kicks. It then took a point blank save by Bert Williams to stop Tommy Taylor levelling. After 28 minutes Johnny Berry hit the post from where the ball bounced against Williams's body and was then cleared.

United did draw level when Taylor took advantage of a defensive slip, as Guttridge hit a weak back pass, to score with ease. That sparked off a spell of United pressure but Wolves survived it and took the lead two minutes before the break. Roy Swinbourne twice beat centre-half Allenby Chilton but the centre-half deflected his shot for a corner. The kick saw goalkeeper Ray Wood stranded and as the ball bounced across the goalmouth, Peter Broadbent was there to lob it into the net.

66

Both sides had chances after half-time with Williams saving well from Taylor and Jack Rowley and Wilshaw's best effort bringing a good save from Wood.

The points were sewn up eighteen minutes from time by Roy Swinbourne. A Slater through pass saw the centre-forward draw Wood out and get the ball just inside the far post from the narrowest of angles. With Bill Shorthouse and Slater in dominant mood the home defence held out comfortably until the final whistle and almost added a fourth – Hancocks put the ball into the net from a Jimmy Mullen corner but the referee had blown for time before the ball crossed the line.

Comments
"We tried, in vain for most of the game, to penetrate a very solid defence." – Johnny Berry (United winger).
"United had a lot of the game but did not show the same commitment as Wolves." – Manchester Evening News.

WOLVES: Williams; Short, Guttridge; Slater, Shorthouse, Wright; Hancocks, Broadbent, Swinbourne, Wilshaw, Mullen.
MANCHESTER UNITED: Wood; Foulkes, Byrne; Whitefoot, Chilton, Cockburn; Berry, Pearson, Taylor, Rowley, McShane.
Referee: L A Brown (Middlesbrough). Attendance: 40,084.

BOLTON 1   **WOLVES 1**   *Saturday, October 24, 1953*
Moir 44   *Hancocks 26*

For the point they brought back from Burnden Park, Wolves had to thank an all-round do-or-die defensive display in the last quarter of an hour and a magnificent save by Bert Williams to a flying header by England centre-forward Nat Lofthouse five minutes from time.

With Billy Wright injured playing for England against FIFA at Wembley, Bill Baxter came into the half-back line and made a good job of shackling England inside-forward Harold Hassall.

Wolves began well and took the lead through Johnny Hancocks, helped by a refereeing decision after Jimmy Mullen found Hancocks who looked to be well off-side. However, when goalkeeper Stan Hanson put the ball out a corner was awarded. Mullen's kick was pushed out to Hancocks whose low drive went over Hanson's hands and was a yard over the line despite John Ball hooking it out with an overhead kick.

Willie Moir equalised a minute before the break. He managed to squeeze the ball past Williams with a low cross shot after Doug Holden had taken the ball down the wing and then cut in along the bye-line before pulling the ball back. Wolves held the upper hand for the first fifteen minutes of the second half when both Roy Swinbourne and Dennis Wilshaw went close. Peter Broadbent also saw a shot bounce on the bar. Bolton reasserted themselves and went near to snatching victory with that Lofthouse header. For most of the game, however, the England man was well held by Bill Shorthouse.

It took a bit of quick thinking by Williams to thwart Lofthouse earlier in the game. The keeper caught a Moir centre and managed to get rid of the ball just as the Bolton centre-forward charged him over the line.

Guttridge also did well after his harrowing game against Manchester United.

Comments
Asked about his run of form, Williams said: "Goalkeeping is easy when you play behind a defence like the one we have at Wolves. I'm sure I'll have a few more busy days as the weeks roll by but I enjoy being tested – it's part of the game."
"It was a terrific battle between Lofthouse and Shorhouse with honours even." – Bolton Evening News.

BOLTON: Hanson; Ball, T Banks; Wheeler, Barrass, Bell; Holden, Moir, Lofthouse, Hassall, Parry.
WOLVES: Williams; Short, Guttridge; Baxter, Shorthouse, Slater; Hancocks, Broadbent, Swinbourne, Wilshaw, Mullen.
Referee: W Ratcliffe (Leek). Attendance: 40,027.

WOLVES 1   **PRESTON 0**   *Saturday, October 31, 1953.*
Wilshaw 55

Not one of Wolves' better days as they made hard work of beating a Preston team minus England wing maestro Tom Finney. It was a pity the 'Preston Plumber' was out as there could have been an interesting duel between him and Billy Wright, who was named left-back for the first time as Roy Pritchard failed a late test on his injured leg. Roy Swinbourne was also injured so Dennis Wilshaw moved to centre-forward with Ron Stockin drafted in at inside-left.

In Finney's absence Preston gave a debut on the right-wing to 18-year-old Les Campbell, who saw his first cross safely gathered by Bert Williams. After the initial flourish, it was poor fare and both sets of forwards got little change out of the opposition defenders with centre-halves Bill Shorthouse of Wolves and Preston's Aussie Joe Marston dominant.

Wolves gradually got on top but their forwards had an off day, with the exception of Johnny Hancocks because he saw too little of the ball, and ran themselves into difficulty. There were only four worthwhile efforts on goal during the first half, two to each side, with Wilshaw going closest.

Wilshaw finally broke the deadlock ten minutes after half-time. A long pass down the wing by Wright found Jimmy Mullen wide open and his cross beat everybody in the goalmouth. The ball was retrieved by Hancocks near the bye-line and from his pinpoint centre Wilshaw rose to head down past George Thompson. After that, Preston centre forward Charlie Wayman and winger Angus Morrison missed the visitors' best chances while Wilshaw (twice) and Mullen had efforts on target for Wolves. There was an escape for Wolves when a Denis Hatsell shot was only partially saved by Bert Williams. Jack Short was on hand to clear as the ball rolled along the line.

Wilshaw was denied a second when he got clear and beat Thompson only for Harry Mattinson to race back and clear the ball just before it crossed the line. Wright's switch saw transfer-listed Bill Baxter brought in at right-half and at least he and left-half Bill Slater got in a few attempts on goal with their forwards apparently so unwilling to shoot.

Comments
"It's a good job Tom Finney wasn't playing. I don't think we would have won if he'd been on the pitch." – Bill Slater.
"The Wolves forwards had a most unhappy knack of running themselves into difficulties and making everything more laborious than it need have been." – Commentator, Express & Star.

WOLVES: Williams; Short, Wright; Baxter, Shorthouse, Slater; Hancocks, Broadbent, Wilshaw, Stockin, Mullen.
PRESTON: Thompson; Cunningham, Walton; Mattinson, Marston, Dunn; Campbell, Hatsell, Wayman, Baxter, Morrison.
Referee: A W Luty (Leeds). Attendance: 34,211.

MIDDLESBROUGH 3   **WOLVES 3**   *Saturday, November 7, 1953*
Fitzsimons 22   *Swinbourne 16*
McPherson 56, Hartnett 73   *Hancocks 43, Wilshaw 86*

Wolves took their unbeaten run to 14 games but not without a fright in a see-saw match. With five minutes left they trailed 3-2, having led 2-1 at half-time. Fortunately they conjured up yet another late goal. Bill Slater turned down the invitation to play in an England amateur trial match and was one of Wolves' successes at Ayresome Park, along with Peter Broadbent and Dennis Wilshaw. Roy Swinbourne was back to lead the line and put Wolves ahead on 16 minutes but only after home inside-left Arthur Fitzsimons had almost beaten Bert Williams with a low shot. Swinbourne's was a fine goal. Taking a pass from Wilshaw, he ran square and then let fly from 25 yards to leave keeper Rolando Ugolini stranded.

Boro, in the bottom three of the division, hit back through Fitzsimons six minutes later. A free kick saw the ball go to and fro across the penalty area before a poor Wolves header went to Fitzsimons who beat Bert Williams with a rising drive. Both goals were under threat after that, mainly through long range shots, before Johnny Hancocks beat Ugolini from 25 yards two minutes before the break. The winger moved into the inside-left position to take a pass from Slater and then tricked three opponents before letting fly. Hancocks should have struck again on 54 minutes when put clear by Bill Baxter's through ball but he shot well wide

Two minutes later it was 2-2. Bill Shorthouse and Slater failed to deal with a raid by Fitzsimons and Lindy Delapenha and the right-winger got the ball back from the bye-line for centre-forward Ken McPherson to turn the ball past Williams. Swinbourne missed a good chance to restore the visitors' lead and Wolves were punished when unmarked Dubliner Jimmy Hartnett put Boro 3-2 up in the 73rd minute. A long pass by Gordon Hepple was headed down by McPherson for Harnett to beat Williams with a fine volley. With Mannion calling the tune, the home side looked in control especially as Wolves wing-half Baxter was limping after taking a knock on his left ankle.

69

However, Wolves kept battling and were rewarded with just four minutes left. Hancocks and Jimmy Mullen worked a short corner routine on the right wing for Hancocks to put over a perfect centre which Wilshaw nodded home. There was still time left for Wilshaw almost to snatch on unlikely victory. A Mullen, Swinbourne Hancocks move saw the right-winger put over a centre but Hepple beat Wilshaw to the ball.

Comment
"I'm sure my England colleague Wilf Mannion made the ball talk sometimes – he was in superb form." – Billy Wright.

MIDDLESBROUGH: Ugolini; Bilcliff, Hepple; Bell, Robinson, Gordon; Delapenha, Mannion, McPherson, Fitzsimons, Hartnett.
WOLVES: Williams; Short, Wright; Baxter, Shorthouse, Slater; Hancocks, Broadbent, Swinbourne, Wilshaw, Mullen.
Referee: R P Hartley (Burnley). Attendance: 24,284.

WOLVES 1   **WEST BROMWICH ALBION 0**   *Saturday, November 14, 1953.*
Mullen 4

Wolves won the first of the key championship clashes with arch rivals Albion despite being without Bill Slater, selected for the England amateur side against France at Luton, and Peter Broadbent out with an injury sustained late on at Middlesbrough.

This was one Wolves had to win, otherwise they would trail leaders Albion by five points, and they did it with a goal after just four minutes through Jimmy Mullen who put in a half centre, half shot, which goalkeeper Norman Heath misjudged completely. Johnny Hancocks had set up the chance when Albion full-back Stan Rickaby failed to clear and the little winger found Mullen on the left.

Wolves, who had Roy Pritchard at left-back with Billy Wright taking Slater's left-half spot and Ron Stockin deputising for Broadbent, went close to a second when Dennis Wilshaw headed a Mullen cross over the bar. Then Bert Williams had to be alert to parry a Ronnie Allen piledriver before diving on the ball at the foot of his near post.

Albion continued to press up to half-time and into the second half with left-winger George Lee firing just wide after being put clear by Ray Barlow. Allen connected with a good header only to see the ball bounce back off the post. This followed one of Albion's best moves when they did with two passes what they had earlier been trying to do with six. A four-man move then opened up Wolves' defence once more only for Johnny Nicholls to be too slow to reach Frank Griffin's cross.

Wolves responded and Dennis Wilshaw saw an effort saved by Heath and then Stockin fired over from 20 yards. Wolves had kept the game wide open, in contrast to Albion, and long crossfield passes gave Hancocks and Mullen plenty of opportunity to shine.

The visitors were fortunate that centre-half Joe Kennedy was in the sort of form that had made him an England candidate. Albion did managed a final flourish but Wolves held out.

Comments
"Yes it was a lucky goal but I meant it." – Jimmy Mullen
"Albion persisted in playing the short passing game and constantly came to grief against the hard-tackling Wolves defenders." – Sports Argus.

WOLVES: Williams; Short, Pritchard; Baxter, Shorthouse, Wright; Hancocks, Stockin, Swinbourne, Wilshaw, Mullen.
ALBION: Heath; Rickaby, Millard; Dudley, Kennedy, Barlow; Griffin, Nicholls, Allen, Ryan, Lee.
Referee: F Cowen (Manchester) Attendance: 56,590.

CHARLTON 0   **WOLVES 2**   *Saturday, November 21, 1953.*
                     Broadbent 24
                     Hancocks 54

After weathering a difficult opening 20 minutes, Wolves took complete control and might have

70

won by more goals. Determined tackling by the visitors ensured Charlton's neat passing came to nothing in that opening spell but the highlight of the match was a memorable goal from Johnny Hancocks.

The turning point came after 24 minutes when home left-half Cyril Hammond fell when trying to clear and Peter Broadbent was able to race through and beat Sam Bartram from twelve yards. From then until half-time it was all Wolves with wingers Hancocks and Jimmy Mullen giving full-backs Frank Lock and Syd Ellis a torrid time. Roy Swinbourne, who proved a handful for new England centre-half Derek Ufton, missed a good chance and Dennis Wilshaw was also guilty of a miss.

Nine minutes into the second half, Hancocks sewed up the points after the ball was booted out of the Wolves penalty area to him. Bustling in from the right wing he beat Bartram from the narrowest of angles with a shot of such ferocity that the goalkeeper had no time to move. That even had the usually placid reporters in the Press box applauding.

Swinbourne nearly made it three when Bartram was stranded only for Ufton to get back to clear the centre-forward's goalbound shot. Wilshaw also went near with a 25-yard shot that skimmed the crossbar. Such was the superiority of Wolves' defence that Eddie Firmani and Sid O'Linn were the only Charlton players to get a sight of goal in the second half.

71

Comments
"I was right behind that Johnny Hancocks shot and even then I never saw the ball." – Dennis Wilshaw.
"Like the good lady who followed the van, Charlton dillied and dallied and the more they did so, the more they became victims of those tough defenders who, supplemented by some excellent goalkeeping by Williams, represented sheer frustration for the home side." – Commentator (Express & Star).

CHARLTON: Bartram; Lock, Ellis; Fenton, Ufton, Hammond; Hurst, O'Linn, Firmani, Evans, Kiernan.
WOLVES: Williams; Short, Pritchard; Slater, Shorthouse, Wright; Hancocks, Broadbent, Swinbourne, Wilshaw, Mullen.
Referee: A A Howlettt (Swindon, Wiltshire). Attendance: 35,595.

WOLVES 4　　　　**SHEFFIELD WEDNESDAY 1**　　*Saturday, November 28, 1953*
Wilshaw 12　　　　*Woodhead 6*
Hancocks 40 (pen)
Swinbourne 49 80

After going a goal down in six minutes, Wolves, with Johnny Hancocks at his impish best, hit back to register their 14th successive home win on a day when a critical eye was turned upon English football after the humiliating 6-3 defeat of the national side by Hungary in midweek. Billy Wright, who had led England at Wembley, tested Wednesday goalkeeper Brian Ryalls with a shot from 25 yards and Peter Broadbent and Hancocks had shots blocked. Yet it was the visitors who took the lead. Wright tackled Albert Quixall but the ball ran free to Jackie Sewell who fed outside-left Dennis Woodhead, whose low angled shot beat Bert Williams.

Wolves, driven on by Wright, Peter Broadbent and Bill Slater, hit back strongly and were level within six minutes. A cross field moved involving Broadbent, Slater and Hancocks saw the right winger shoot from the wing and goalkeeper Ryalls fumble the ball – Dennis Wilshaw was on the spot to put it over the line.

Wolves stayed on top, though Williams had to save efforts from Quixall and Sewell, and went ahead five minutes before half-time. Wilshaw took Broadbent's measured pass in his stride but was floored inside the penalty area and Hancocks smashed home the resultant spot kick.

Then good work by Slater and Broadbent enabled Hancocks to bend a shot narrowly wide.

Four minutes into the second half it was 3-1 when a ball from Hancocks passed over Wilshaw's head only for Swinbourne to take possession, move forward and beat Ryalls easily.

Wolves created several more good chances, while Williams had to make two more useful saves, before a Hancocks drive set up Wolves' fourth goal. Ryalls could only parry the ball and Swinbourne was on hand to slot it home. In the final minute, Broadbent headed Mullen's dropping centre wide from a few yards out.

Bill Shorthouse and Williams continued their recent good form in defence where full-backs Jack Short and Roy Pritchard were also on top of their game.

Comments
"It would not be a bad thing if England selected the entire Wolves team." – Albert Quixall
"On the programme, Hancocks figured officially at outside-right. On the field, at some time or another during the game, he gave a studied demonstration of the technique required for all five forward positions." – Commentator (Express & Star).

WOLVES: Williams; Short, Pritchard; Slater, Shorthouse, Wright; Hancocks, Broadbent, Swinbourne, Wilshaw, Mullen.
SHEFFIELD WEDNESDAY: Ryalls; Conwell, Curtis; Gannon, O'Donnell, Davies; Finney, Quixall, Jordan, Sewell, Woodhead.
Referee: J H Clough (Bolton). Attendance: 35,154.

TOTTENHAM 2	WOLVES 3	Saturday, December 5, 1953
Bennett 26	Wilshaw 53	
Duquemin 59	Broadbent 54, Hancocks 78	

Wolves had extra reason to celebrate after their first ever win at White Hart Lane. Albion's surprise 3-2 home defeat by Portsmouth meant Stan Cullis's men were the new leaders of the First Division. Unchanged Wolves left their scoring to the second half and nearly went a goal down after two minutes but Len Duquemin mis-hit his shot straight at Bert Williams.

Roy Swinbourne had the visitors' first shot on goal, followed by another from Dennis Wilshaw, while Les Bennett, Duquemin and Eddie Baily went close for Spurs, who eventually took the lead on 26 minutes. Bennett was the scorer, heading home after Baily had chased the ball to the byeline and then centred.

With 35 minutes gone Sid McClellan got clean through but Williams dived at his feet to save. Wolves hit back and Ted Ditchburn, in the home goal, was kept busy dealing with a succession of crosses from the flanks.

Eight minutes into the second half, Wolves were level when Wilshaw stooped to within 18 inches of the ground to head in a Jimmy Mullen centre. Within a minute Mullen supplied the cross again and Broadbent headed in from a yard in front of the far post to make it 2-1. The scoring burst continued as Duquemin, despite looking a couple of yards off-side, put Spurs level on 59 minutes. Baily's pass had put the centre-forward clear and though Williams came out he could not stop him from sliding the ball home.

Wolves' response was to go in search of a winner and they got it thanks to another Hancocks special. The winger raced to the bye-line to collect a diagonal pass that looked like going out of play. As full-back Charlie Withers raced in to tackle him, Hancocks switched the ball from his right foot to his left and hit a powerful shot between Ditchburn and the near post. Hancocks almost made it 4-2 before the end and Wilshaw was close with a header as the season reached its halfway stage with Wolves' unbeaten run now 18 games.

73

Comments
"Yes I was off-side all right but I was always taught to put the ball in the net and let the referee make the final decision." – Len Duquemin.
"Wolves deserved the spoils on account of their ability to maintain a pace at which many a side would have wilted. In a team who played magnificently, I give special marks to Short, continuing his steady improvement, and Broadbent, who had no superior, even including Baily, when it came to controlling the sometimes difficult ball." – Commentator (Express & Star).

TOTTENHAM: Ditchburn; Ramsey, Withers; Nicholson, Clarke, Burgess; Walters, Bennett, Duquemin, Baily, McClellan.
WOLVES: Williams; Short, Pritchard; Slater, Shorthouse, Wright; Hancocks, Broadbent, Swinbourne, Wilshaw, Mullen.
Referee: Rev S V Davis (Oxford). Attendance: 48,164.

WOLVES 1 **BURNLEY 2** *Saturday, December 12, 1953*
Hancocks 84 *Holden 32, 54*

Leaders Wolves were brought quickly down to earth – and into second place – as their 18-match unbeaten run was ended by Burnley, whose close marking and tackling was straight out of the Molineux handbook. Fielding the same side for a fourth week running, Wolves found Burnley in uncompromising mood and, after an even first half-hour it was the visitors who went ahead. Centre-forward Bill Holden held off the challenge of Bill Shorthouse to thump the ball home after a long clearance from centre-half Tommy Cummings into the Wolves half. Before half-time a flying Johnny Hancocks header to a centre by Jimmy Mullen saw the ball hit the post before going out.

Wolves could have equalised first through Roy Swinbourne and then Dennis Wilshaw but nine minutes into the second half they were two down. The ball was again fired downfield and Holden got the better of Shorthouse and Roy Pritchard to run on and beat Bert Williams.

Burnley defended in depth, often having nine players in their penalty area, but Hancocks fired in his 14th goal of the season on 84 minutes to give Wolves hope. A shot by Mullen was sent into the air by Thompson but Hancocks fired the ball home through a sea of legs.

Hancocks went close again before time ran out, as did Wilshaw, but Burnley hung on to become the only team to complete a double over Wolves all season.

Comments
"When we kicked off I had a feeling in my blood that we would not lose this game." – Jimmy Adamson (Burnley).
"Wolves played hard but Burnley played harder. Wolves were fast but Burnley were faster and, to everybody's surprise, Burnley stood the cracking pace as comfortably as their opponents." – Commentator (Express & Star).

WOLVES: Williams; Short, Pritchard; Slater, Shorthouse, Wright; Hancocks, Broadbent, Swinbourne, Wilshaw, Mullen.
BURNLEY: Thompson; Aird, Mather; Adamson, Cummings, Attwell; Gray, McIlroy, Holden, Shannon, Pilkington.
Referee: A Holland (Barnsley). Attendance: 35,043.

WOLVES 3   **MANCHESTER CITY 1**   *Saturday, December 19, 1953*
Hancocks 36 (pen) 89   *Davies 26*
Wilshaw 62

Having been victims of a league double defeat at the hands of Burnley, Wolves completed one of their own by coming from behind to gain a hard-earned win over City. With Albion losing 2-1 at Bolton, Wolves were back on top of the table with a two-point lead.

Roy Swinbourne (Wolves) and City left-winger Roy Clarke both had early chances before Bert Williams made a smart save to deny Joe Hayes. Then City's German goalkeeper Bert Trautmann had to make a two-handed save to keep out a Dennis Wilshaw hot shot.

City inside right Gordon Davies, playing only his second game of the season, finally broke the deadlock on 26 minutes. He received the ball from Clarke, who had beaten two players in a tricky run, and escaped the attentions of Bill Shorthouse to score from ten yards.

Wilshaw twice went close, as Wolves stepped up a gear, and Hancocks fired in his sixth penalty goal of the season to make it 1-1 nine minutes before half-time. Dennis Wilshaw had been going through only to be brought down by Dave Ewing and though Jimmy Mullen put the ball into the net, the kick had already been awarded. After that the game developed into a personal battle between the right-winger and Trautmann, who denied him on at least six occasions, sometimes with his legs and once with his shoulder.

The four half-backs, Wolves' Billy Wright and Bill Slater and City's Don Revie and Roy Paul, were outstanding, the visiting pair reducing the effectiveness of Wolves inside men. Revie even found time to test Williams with a long-range half-volley following a corner.

Wilshaw finally put Wolves ahead on 62 minutes. Mullen's run led to a melee in the visitors' goalmouth and, with Trautmann stranded off his line, Wilshaw, with his back to goal, brought the ball under control before turning to fire high into the net. A minute from time Hancocks at last got the better of Trautmann from open play, burying the ball in the corner of the net after a neat move involving several players ended with a Mullen centre.

Comments
"We weren't two goals better than them – maybe three. No, only kidding, it was a close contest." – Roy Pritchard.
"Wolves' overall display did not come up to the standard they have set themselves so far this season." – Commentator (Express & Star).

WOLVES: Williams; Short, Pritchard; Slater, Shorthouse, Wright; Hancocks, Broadbent, Swinbourne, Wilshaw, Mullen.
MANCHESTER CITY: Trautmann; Branagan, Little; Revie, Ewing, Paul; Hayes, Hart, Meadows, Davies, Clarke.
Referee: A Murdoch (Sheffield). Attendance: 27,606.

WOLVES 1 **ASTON VILLA 2** *Thursday, December 24, 1953.*
Wilshaw 22 *Dixon 55, McParland 80*

Villa, making eight changes, five of them positional, after two successive defeats, came from behind to spoil Wolves' Christmas, 19-year-old Peter McParland netting the winner ten minutes from time. On a heavy pitch, there were far too many fouls, several lengthy hold-ups and a lot of misdirected passing.

Bill Baxter, transferred to Villa Park a month earlier, was made captain for the day and was one of the few players to emerge with any credit.

Wolves took the lead after 22 minutes, somewhat against the run of play, when Dennis Wilshaw got his head to a Johnny Hancocks centre.

To help Wolves' cause, Villa right-back Harry Parkes was injured after 38 minutes and spent the rest of the match hobbling on the right wing, having switched with Gibson. It was Parkes's persistence which helped Villa equalise ten minutes into the second half, Johnny Dixon firing the ball through a ruck of players with Nigel Sims, deputising for Bert Williams, probably unable to see the ball until it was past him.

Parkes also had a part in the winning goal. With nobody to pass to he put the ball out as near to the Wolves corner flag as possible. When a second throw-in was not effectively cleared, Tommy Thompson hit the ball across goal for the unmarked McParland to score easily before being nearly mobbed by his team-mates.

Villa had the ball in the net with virtually the last kick but the effort was disallowed because of pushing by Dixon.

Comment
"The only Wolves forward for whom I felt sorry was Hancocks. He probably did more shooting than he should have done as an orthodox right-winger, but if he had not made these attempts there was nobody else likely to." – Commentator (Express & Star)

WOLVES: Sims; Short, Pritchard; Slater, Shorthouse, Wright; Hancocks, Broadbent, Swinbourne, Wilshaw, Mullen.
ASTON VILLA: Jones; Parkes, Vinall; Baxter, F Moss, A Moss; Gibson, Blanchflower, Dixon, Thompson, McParland.
Referee: J McCann (Preston). Attendance: 40,536.

ASTON VILLA 1 **WOLVES 2** *Thursday, December 24, 1953*
Thompson 28 *Hancocks 31, Wilshaw 88*

Albion, 5-2 winners over Liverpool on Christmas morning, were held 0-0 at Anfield so Wolves' revenge win over Villa took them back to the the top of the table. Wolves looked a far better side than they had done on Christmas Eve yet fell behind against the run of play on 28 minutes. Tommy Thompson latched on to a long clearance from Frank Moss, rounded a defender and went through on his own to beat the advancing Nigel Sims.

Wolves were level within three minutes when Johnny Hancocks claimed his 17th goal of the season. He got in a drive which was deflected by Bill Baxter and goalkeeper Keith Jones failed to hang on to the spinning ball.

For all Wolves' dominance, Villa always threatened to break away and score and first Johnny Dixon and then Thompson went close. Dennis Wilshaw had the ball in the Villa net but Peter Broadbent had strayed off-side, Roy Swinbourne saw his shot hit the bar, Wilshaw and Broadbent fired inches over and Hancocks sent two powerful shots narrowly wide. A goal just had to come and Wolves finally secured the win they deserved when the ball was lifted high into the Villa penalty area. Three players went for it and Wilshaw jumped highest to head home.

Comments
"With this professional display Wolves more than redeemed themselves for their shortcomings of Christams Eve." – Birmingham Gazette.

76

"Hancocks deserved the goal for he was on the warpath again and sometimes took the attention of several opponents." – Commentator (Express & Star)

ASTON VILLA: Jones; Lynn, Vinall; Baxter, Martin, A Moss; Gibson, Blanchflower, Dixon, Thompson, McParland.
WOLVES: Sims; Short, Pritchard; Slater, Shorthouse, Wright; Hancocks, Broadbent, Swinbourne, Wilshaw, Mullen.
Referee: J McCann (Preston). Attendance: 49,123.

CARDIFF CITY 1   **WOLVES 3**   *Saturday, January 2, 1954*
Nugent 59   *Swinbourne 20*
                     Wilshaw 37, Hancocks 82

With Billy Wright deputising for the injured Jack Short at right-back and Ron Flowers brought in at left-half, Wolves kept their one-point lead at the top despite being handicapped by a first-half injury to Bill Slater. Welsh international centre-forward Trevor Ford, who had joined City from Sunderland, got in a couple of early shots, one of them tipped over the bar by Nigel Sims, but after that was well policed by Bill Shorthouse.

Once Wolves settled they deservedly took the lead when Roy Swinbourne beat the home side's off-side trap to score after 20 minutes. A Jimmy Mullen cross reached Johnny Hancocks who sent Swinbourne away down the right. The centre-forward cut in and beat Ron Howells from a narrow angle. After a couple of chances had been missed, Dennis Wilshaw again beat the off-side trap to make it 2-0 eight minutes before half-time. Swinbourne made the goal. He fought for the ball near the right-hand corner flag and after beating Stan Montgomery lobbed the ball across for Wilshaw to head home.

Cardiff came back into it after the interval and reduced the lead just before the hour. Keith Thomas worked his way down the right, found space and whipped over a low cross which Ford knocked back for Cliff Nugent to fire hard and low past Sims from 12 yards.

Wolves were quickly on top once more and saw two efforts graze the woodwork before Johnny Hancocks made the game safe eight minutes from the end. He fired the ball home after a fine run and cross by Jimmy Mullen. There was still time for Sims to make a couple of useful saves.

Comments
Wolves played well, so did we, but they got the breaks, we didn't." – George Edwards (Cardiff). "Nigel Sims did an excellent job in the Wolves goal in the absence of Williams." – South Wales Echo.

CARDIFF CITY: Howells; Rutter, Stitfall; Baker, Montgomery, Sullivan; Thomas, Nugent, Ford, Northcott, Edwards.
WOLVES: Sims; Wright, Pritchard; Slater, Shorthouse, Flowers; Hancocks, Broadbent, Swinbourne, Wilshaw, Mullen.
Referee: W H Clapton (London). Attendance: 47,113.

WOLVES 0   **ARSENAL 2**   *Saturday, January 16, 1954*
Logie 9
Lishman 85

A week before the visit of Arsenal, Wolves had bowed out of the FA Cup, beaten 2-1 at home by Birmingham City so the Londoners' shock win was a fourth home defeat in five games.

With Bill Shorthouse out, injured in the Cup-tie, Billy Wright moved to centre-half and Ron Flowers was brought in at left-half, while Bert Williams returned after injury. Flowers had been omitted from the team against Birmingham as Jack Short returned at right-back, allowing Wright to wear the No 6 shirt.

A Molineux crowd of nearly 46,000 saw the Gunners go a goal up after nine minutes through Scottish inside-right Jimmy Logie though the build-up had seen right-winger Arthur Milton find Cliff Holton in what looked like an off-side position. Other than that, Holton was kept under tight control by Wright.

After the goal the game developed into Wolves versus Jack Kelsey and the Welsh goalkeeper chose this day to have one of the best games of his career, pulling off a string of fine saves plus a few fortunate ones. Arsenal, after their early goal, were content to try to block everything Wolves threw at them. Flowers had a shot hit the crossbar, Roy Swinbourne hit it twice and Johnny Hancocks rattled it as well.

Kelsey added to Wolves' frustration by making spectacular saves from Hancocks and Dennis Wilshaw and eventually the inevitable happened – Arsenal broke to score again. Both Arsenal wingmen had looked dangerous on occasions and it was left-winger Don Roper who made the second goal, moving to the right wing to get in a centre from which Doug Lishman scored with one of his trademark flick headers.

Hancocks was off the field for eight minutes in the second half having three stitches put in a burst eyebrow but returned to the action with no apparent ill effects as his side failed to score at home for the only time in the season. Wolves paid the price, slipping to second place as Albion won 1-0 at Tottenham.

Comments
"Wolves did everything but score in a game they dominated for long periods." – Evening Standard.
"Disappointing the result may have been but it was worth something to see the resurgence of the old fighting spirit." – Commentator (Express & Star)

WOLVES: Williams; Short, Pritchard; Slater, Wright, Flowers; Hancocks, Broadbent, Swinbourne, Wilshaw, Mullen.
ARSENAL: Kelsey; Wills, Wade; Dickson, Dodgin, Forbes; Milton, Logie, Holton, Lishman, Roper.
Referee: G Gibson (Manchester). Attendance: 45,974.

78

PORTSMOUTH 2   **WOLVES 0**   *Saturday, January 23, 1954*
Dickinson 8, Reid 63

Wolves' bad run continued at Fratton Park where they suffered their first away defeat since August 26 even though a rearranged side did enough to have earned a point. Wolves had to bring Norman Deeley into the forward line when Dennis Wilshaw was allowed to stand down because of his father's serious illness. Sadly, Tom Wilshaw died the following day.

Stan Cullis made a surprise decision before kick-off, leaving out Roy Pritchard and moving Billy Wright to left-back so Ron Flowers could stay in the team. Bill Shorthouse returned at centre-half.

Flowers and Deeley set up an early chance for Roy Swinbourne but he failed to take advantage and on eight minutes Portsmouth went ahead with a goal that had a touch of luck about it. England left-half Jimmy Dickinson lobbed the ball into the Wolves penalty area and it bounced past Bert Williams, unsighted as Pompey centre-forward Duggie Reid and Shorthouse ran across his path.

It was obviously not Wolves' day as Hancocks thought he had scored and several others felt his shot was well over the line before it was cleared. To make it worse the referee decided on a bounce-up when Wolves felt they should have been awarded a free kick for what looked like a foul on Shorthouse. From it, Pompey gained possession and set up a goal for Reid on 63 minutes and clinch their first home win over Wolves since 1949. Despite Deeley's grafting, Wilshaw was missed up front as Wolves lost successive league games for the only time in the season. Albion were held 0-0 at home by Burnley and so led Wolves by 41 points to 39.

79

Comments
"We were too feeble up front, their defenders seemed to have the edge." – Stan Cullis
"Wright did well enough against the electrifying Harris and Flowers was always determined but in this game I thought the captain might have been of greater use in his proper position, with an experienced man behind him." – Commentator (Express & Star).

PORTSMOUTH: Platt; Wilson, Mansell; Phillips, Rutter, Dickinson; Harris, Gordon, Reid, Barnard, Henderson.
WOLVES: Williams; Short, Wright; Slater, Shorthouse, Flowers; Hancocks, Deeley, Swinbourne, Broadbent, Mullen.
Referee: N C Taylor (Westbury, Wiltshire). Attendance: 35,312.

WOLVES 4   **BLACKPOOL 1**   *Saturday, February 6, 1954*
Hancocks 17   *Stephenson 69*
Swinbourne, 54, 84, 85

Thanks to three welcome goals from centre-forward Roy Swinbourne, Wolves got back to winning ways against a Blackpool side minus five internationals. Roy Pritchard was recalled at left-back and Billy Wright switched back to his familiar left-half spot but Ron Flowers kept his place in the team, being given a game at inside right with Peter Broadbent dropped. In a one-sided second half Wolves put in no fewer than 14 efforts on goal. They had taken the lead through Johnny Hancocks. Flowers fed Hancocks who reversed play by finding Jimmy Mullen on the left. He went past Eddie Shimwell and crossed into the goalmouth where Roy Swinbourne tried a back-heel. The ball seemed to be going out but Hancocks slammed it home from a narrow angle.

With half-backs Wright and Bill Slater calling the tune Wolves kept goalkeeper George Farm busy but it took a good save from Bert Williams to keep out a header from the Seasiders' South African left-winger Bill Perry. The goalkeeper had to leap backward to turn the ball over one-handed.

Swinbourne made it two, nine minutes into the second half. Flowers's fine run saw him beat centre-half John Crosland and then cross to give the centre-forward a simple chance.

Reserve centre-forward Len Stephenson halved the deficit when he latched on to the bouncing ball which had eluded Bill Shorthouse. Blackpool might have equalised but Williams turned an Allan Brown effort round the post.

There were more escapes before Swinbourne struck two late goals. The first came when good work by Johnny Hancocks and Jimmy Mullen saw the left-winger try a hard drive across goal for Swinbourne, as he fell, to deflect the ball past Farm. Swinbourne's third confirmed he had rediscovered his scoring touch after only one goal in his previous eight games. Moving to the left of goal he powered home a shot which was in the net almost before the keeper could move. Blackpool were without Stanley Matthews, Ernie Taylor, Stanley Mortensen, Harry Johnston and Tommy Garrett.

Comments
"I know we won, and won well, but it would have been a much closer contest had Blackpool been at full strength." – Bill Shorthouse
"Wolves did not spurn the opportunity of playing against a weakened side – they took it in their stride." – Blackpool Evening Gazette

WOLVES: Williams; Short, Pritchard; Slater, Shorthouse, Wright; Hancocks, Flowers, Swinbourne, Wilshaw, Mullen.
BLACKPOOL: Farm; Shimwell, Frith; Fenton, Crosland, Kelly; Harris, Mudie, Stephenson, Brown, Perry.
Referee: J V Sherlock (Sheffield). Attendance: 27,795.

CHELSEA 4	WOLVES 2	*Saturday, February 13, 1954*
Bentley 1, 69	*Swinbourne 19*	
Parsons 9, Stubbs 62	*Wilshaw 64*	

The side who had beaten Blackpool were given a second outing but came to grief at Stamford Bridge where they went two goals down in nine minutes by which time they were also down to ten fit men. Bill Shorthouse sustained a kick in the side after seven minutes and returned to the action 18 minutes later but could only limp along up front, Ron Flowers being forced to drop back into the half-back line.

Chelsea's first goal, in front of a massive crowd, came after 55 seconds when Roy Bentley struck. When a centre came over from the right he calmly lobbed the ball out of Bert Williams's reach. Then winger Eric Parsons made it two after latching on to a through pass by Bentley. Roy Swinbourne reduced the arrears on 19 minutes. Jimmy Mullen's corner kick was helped on by Bill Slater for Johnny Hancocks to get in a shot that was blocked by one-time Wolves man John Harris, Before the Chelsea defender could recover, however, Swinbourne nipped in to turn the ball home.

The efforts of Wright, by then playing at centre-half, and goalkeeper Bert Williams kept the Londoners at bay but Wolves went 3-1 down just after the hour, Parsons breaking clear before putting over a cross which Les Stubbs turned past Williams despite the efforts of Bill Slater. Within two minutes, Dennis Wilshaw had put Wolves back into the game. Swinbourne dummied centre-half Ron Greenwood and centred for Wilshaw to slot the ball in. The gallant Shorthouse almost made it 3-3 with a header that just skimmed the bar. Jimmy Mullen also went close with a cross-shot.

They proved costly misses as on 69 minutes Bentley struck again, popping up at the far post to head home a Ken Armstrong centre. It could have been worse as Bentley netted again with five minutes left but was judged to have fouled Williams. There was still time for the keeper to make fine saves from Stubbs and John McNichol.

Comments
"The injury to Bill Shorthouse affected our game, there's no doubting that. He has been as solid as a rock for weeks." – Roy Pritchard.
"The man who stood out was Wright, whose display at centre-half after Shorthouse had gone, was one of the highlights of the game." – Commentator (Express & Star).

CHELSEA: Thomson; Harris, Willemse; Armstrong, Greenwood, Saunders; Parsons, McNichol, Bentley, Stubbs, Blunstone.
WOLVES: Williams; Short, Pritchard; Slater, Shorthouse, Wright; Hancocks, Flowers, Swinbourne, Wilshaw, Mullen.
Referee: J H Clough (Bolton). Attendance: 60,289.

WOLVES 6 **SHEFFIELD UNITED 1** *Saturday, February 20, 1954*
Swinbourne 33, 44 *Cross 86*
Hancocks 46, 66
Broadbent 84
Wilshaw 89

This was a memorable day and not just because Wolves won well. Eddie Stuart was given his first league outing – at right-back – since April, 1952, Bill Slater played his first game as a professional and Johnny Hancocks's two goals took his total to 21, bettering by two the record he had previously set for most goals in a season by a Wolves winger.

United, without a win in nine matches, kept the home side out until 33 minutes, even though four good chances were created by Wolves. Roy Swinbourne broke the deadlock. A shot by Hancocks, who had been sent away by a long downfield clearance from Stuart, looked to be going wide but Swinbourne stuck out a foot to divert the ball into the net. A similar move a minute before the break brought Swinbourne his second. Stuart found Hancocks, whose cross was turned past Ted Burgin by the unmarked centre-forward.

A minute after the break Hancocks, who had caused trouble for both full-backs, Cecil Coldwell and Graham Shaw, collected his record-breaking goal. He met a Wilshaw centre and when Burgin could only parry the ball he followed up to tap it into the net. Soon afterwards Hancocks beat Graham Shaw but was denied by a Burgin save.

The Blades made only occasional breakaways and Peter Broadbent had a goal ruled out for offside before Hancocks made it four on 66 minutes. Jimmy Mullen created it, cutting in along the byeline before driving across goal. Burgin saved well but the ball ran to Hancocks who made no mistake.

82

The match ended with three goals in the last six minutes, Broadbent getting on the scoresheet, beating Burgin with a cross shot after a solo run by Wilshaw. Jack Cross scrambled a goal for the visitors from Jimmy Hagan's centre only for Wilshaw to hit the sixth goal with seconds to go, firing home a fine shot from 25 yards. It meant he, Hancocks and Swinbourne each had 21 league goals for the season. With Bill Shorthouse injured, Bill Wright was given another outing at centre-half.

Comments
"We played some of our best football today. It was a delight to watch the ball being pinged around the field." – Stan Cullis
"United were second best throughout the ninety minutes and were lucky not to have conceded more goals." – Sheffield Telegraph.

WOLVES: Williams; Stuart, Pritchard; Slater, Wright, Flowers; Hancocks, Broadbent, Swinbourne, Wilshaw, Mullen.
SHEFFIELD UNITED: Burgin; Coldwell, G Shaw; J Shaw, Johnson, Rawson; Ringstead, Hagan, Cross, Hawksworth, Grainger.
Referee: F S Fiander (Loudwater, Bucks). Attendance: 27,823.

WOLVES 3	NEWCASTLE UNITED 2	Saturday, February 27, 1954
Broadbent 4	Milburn 80	
Wilshaw 20, Slater 86	Broadis 84	

Bill Slater won the game for Wolves four minutes from time, knocking himself out in the process, after his side had let slip a two-goal lead.

Wolves, with Bill Shorthouse returning, though at left-back to the exclusion of Roy Pritchard, got off to a flying start, taking the lead after four minutes. Bert Williams threw the ball out to Johnny Hancocks on the right-wing; he sent it further forward to Peter Broadbent who collided with centre-half Frank Brennan as he controlled the pass. The Wolves man was quicker to react and fired in a fine goal from fully 20 yards, leaving goalkeeper Ronnie Simpson stranded.

Newcastle responded well but English international Ivor Broadis wasted a couple of good chances before Wolves scored again on 20 minutes. Jimmy Mullen drove a corner low across goal, Broadbent stepped over the ball and Dennis Wilshaw was there to drive it high into the net.

Slater took a knock eight minutes later and Newcastle came more into the game, twice testing Williams. Roy Swinbourne took a blow to the head and left the field just before the break but was able to start the second half even though still groggy.

After a flurry of snow Jackie Milburn scored from close range with ten minutes to go and Newcastle were back in it. Four minutes later Broadis scrambled an equaliser after Williams had failed to hold a point-blank shot by inside-left George Hannah following a free kick by Alf McMichael. For most of the game the menacing Milburn had been kept quiet by Billy Wright. Wolves were not done and four minutes from the end, Slater ran in to head home a corner by Johnny Hancocks for his first goal as a professional. With less than a minute to go Mullen got clear and though his shot beat Ronnie Simpson the ball rebounded off the post.

83

Comments
"After the game I asked Dennis Wilshaw what hit me on the head – was it a hammer?" – Roy Swinbourne.
"Slater may have stolen the climax, but for the rest of the game it was Wolves' all-round teamwork that made them worthy of the full reward." – Commentator (Express & Star).

WOLVES: Williams; Stuart, Shorthouse; Slater, Wright, Flowers; Hancocks, Broadbent, Swinbourne, Wilshaw, Mullen.
NEWCASTLE UNITED: Simpson; Cowell, McMichael; Stokoe, Brennan, Casey; Foulkes, Broadis, Milburn, Hannah, Mitchell.
Referee: F Thurman (Preston) Attendance: 38,592.

MANCHESTER UNITED 1   **WOLVES 0**   *Saturday, March 6, 1954*
Berry 84

Wolves paid the price of not playing to the whistle as Johnny Berry scored a late winner at Old Trafford, where Eddie Clamp was given his debut at left-half with Ron Flowers switched to centre-forward in place of the injured Roy Swinbourne.

Flowers found it hard going against the solid tackling of former England centre-half Allenby Chilton and the young Duncan Edwards while Clamp, though not overawed, was at times caught out by the home right-wing pairing of Berry and Jackie Blanchflower.

Defences were on top for long periods. United had slightly the better of a scrappy first half, with two or three more worthwhile attacks than Wolves, though chances were limited.

The best came on 33 minutes when Berry broke clear down the right. He raced into the penalty area but instead of passing to an unmarked Tommy Taylor chose to shoot and sent the ball into the side netting.

Early in the second half Wolves won a series of throw-ins and then a corner The pressure finally brought their best chance but Flowers spooned the ball over from almost beneath the bar. Wolves did create a couple more chances late on, Dennis Wilshaw and Johnny Hancocks both missing the target. United, with twin strikers Taylor and Dennis Viollet always a threat, made them pay six minutes from time.

Berry burst through the middle, a linesman appeared to raise his flag then lower it and Wolves' defenders relaxed. However, Berry continued and beat Bert Williams who, with the rest of his team-mates, was appealing to the referee to blow for off-side. There was still time for Wolves to create one more chance but Hancocks shot hastily wide. Albion were held 2-2 at home by Sheffield United so led Wolves at the top of the table by three points.

Comments

"The linesman looked as though he was addressing a train at Paddington Station – up down, up down." – Stan Cullis.
"The virile Taylor gave Wright his most difficult centre-half problem to date." – Commentator (Express & Star).

MANCHESTER UNITED: Wood; Foulkes, Byrne; Whitefoot, Chlton, Edwards; Berry, Blanchflower, Taylor, Viollet, Rowley.
WOLVES: Williams; Stuart, Shorthouse; Slater, Wright, Clamp; Hancocks, Broadbent, Flowers, Wilshaw, Mullen.
Referee: A Brown (Middlesbrough). Attendance: 40,774.

| PRESTON 0 | WOLVES 1 | *Saturday, March 20, 1954* |
| | *Wilshaw 80* | |

With Preston thinking about progress in the FA Cup, a Dennis Wilshaw goal ten minutes from time kept Wolves within three point of Albion at the top of the table. Roy Swinbourne's return after injury did not mean Ron Flowers regained the left-half spot – that went to Norman Deeley. There was also a change on the left-wing, Leslie Smith deputising for the injured Jimmy Mullen. Smith would prove to be Wolves' liveliest forward.

Preston, with only three defeats in their previous 12 League and Cup matches, were enjoying a useful run but had been held 2-2 at home in midweek by Leicester in an FA Cup sixth round replay. The sides were due to meet again in two days' time. While ace winger Tom Finney was injured, Preston rested Foster, Wayman and Forbes. Bill Shorthouse had complained of feeling under the weather before kick-off but still played and marked Finney's deputy, Les Campbell, tightly throughout a closely-contested game. It started at a frantic pace with home goalkeeper George Thompson having to fly-kick the ball to safety in the first minute.

Preston continued to look lively but centre-forward Dennis Hatsell and inside-left Eric Jones were wayward with their shooting or Wolves might have been trailing at the break.

In the second half home men Angus Morrison and Hatsell were guilty of more bad misses but Johnny Hancocks wasted the best chance up to that stage. He miscued his shot from just six yards out.

With ten minutes left the in-form Smith, who had put over a series of good crosses, finally created the only goal of the game. He whipped over a telling centre and Wilshaw eluded the challenge of right-half Tommy Docherty to beat Thompson with a left-foot shot from 25 yards, the ball hitting a post and then screwing along the line before breaking back into the net.

Before the goal, Hancocks had been on the end of another fine Smith centre but managed to push the ball wide from the easiest of positions.

Comments
"You can put that down as the worst miss ever." – Johnny Hancocks.
"We didn't play well but we won and that's what the game's all about – picking up points when you're having an off-day." – Leslie Smith.

85

PRESTON: Thompson; Cunningham, Walton; Docherty, Marston, Dunn; Campbell, Baxter, Hatsell, Jones, Morrison.
WOLVES: Williams; Stuart, Shorthouse; Slater, Wright, Deeley; Hancocks, Broadbent, Swinbourne, Wilshaw, Smith.
Referee: A W Luty (Leeds). Attendance: 28,857.

WOLVES 1   **BOLTON 1**   *Wednesday, March 24, 1954*
Broadbent 42   *Lofthouse 10*

Wolves could have narrowed the gap at the top to a point but their rejigged side never looked like beating Bolton in this rearranged midweek clash. With Jimmy Mullen injured and Dennis Wilshaw unable to get away from school duties, Wolves fielded a new-look left wing of Eddie Clamp and Leslie Smith, the former never looking comfortable in his unaccustomed position. The game, before a low crowd, often had the air of a nothing-at-stake end-of-season affair yet Wolves were after the title and Bolton chasing talent money.

Moments when it was lifted out of its rut were few. Among them were the duels between Billy Wright and Bolton's England centre-forward Nat Lofthouse. Honours between them ended even though Lofthouse got on the blind side of Wright to hit Bolton's goal after ten minutes.

Wolves replied and Clamp tested goalkeeper Stan Hanson from long range. Deeley tried to lift Wolves with some darting runs and Peter Broadbent went close with a snap shot before Roy

Swinbourne, eluding Malcolm Barrass for once, brought a low save from Hanson. Earlier, Harold Hassall and Ray Parry had both tested Bert Williams

Broadbent grabbed the equaliser three minutes before half-time with a shot from all of 30 yards. The second half produced a few goalmouth thrills but not much else. On one occasion the ball was headed back and forth across the Bolton goal before Swinbourne nodded it towards the net only for Bolton right-half Derek Hennin to scoop the ball away. Smith also saw a shot hit the bar.

Comments
"Not a good game, I admit, but we should have won. We were the better team." – Nat Lofthouse
"Don't blame Clamp. He has been back and half-back hitherto this season and, when called on to play as first-team inside-left, as part of an already weakened wing at that, the occasion proved too much." – Commentator (Express & Star).

WOLVES: Williams; Stuart, Shorthouse; Slater, Wright, Deeley; Hancocks, Broadbent, Swinbourne, Clamp, Smith.
BOLTON: Hanson; Ball, T Banks; Hennin, Barrass, Bell; Holden, Moir, Lofthouse, Hassall, Parry
Referee: W Ratcliffe (Leek). Attendance: 19,617.

WOLVES 2	MIDDLESBROUGH 4	*Saturday, March 27, 1954*
Broadbent 73, 78	*Watkin 3, McPherson 12, 88*	
	Delapenha 34 (pen)	

Just when they could have drawn level on points with Albion, Wolves were struck by the Middlesbrough jinx at Molineux. It was Boro's fifth win there in eight post-War visits. Former England international Wilf Mannion was the architect of the win as Boro went three goals up after 34 minutes. When Mannion was not carving open the home defence, Boro goalkeeper Rolando Ugolini was defying Wolves with a series of fine saves.

On three minutes, Mannion's flick set up winger Billy Watkin to hit the first goal from fourteen yards. Nine minutes later, Boro struck again when, from Watkin's lob, centre-forward Ken McPherson got in behind Bill Shorthouse and Billy Wright to finish a move begun by Mannion fifty yards from goal. Bert Williams got his fingers to the ball but could not prevent it crossing the line just inside the post.

Wolves hit back and Roy Swinbourne (twice), wingers Johnny Hancocks and Jimmy Mullen and Bill Shorthouse all missed chances before Lindy Delapenha made it 3-0 from the penalty spot on 34 minutes. It seemed a harsh decision against Wright who tangled with Sammy Lawrie as the right-winger was bearing down on goal after being put through by Delapenha.
It took a long time in the second half for Wolves at last to get on the scoresheet. Peter Broadbent volleyed in a cross shot from Swinbourne's pass on 73 minutes and five minutes later struck again when he headed home a Mullen corner.

Wolves searched for an equaliser but were rocked again when Ugolini's long clearance caught out Wright and bounced kindly for McPherson who ran on to beat Williams from just inside the penalty area. Deeley went close for Wolves before the end but his shot lacked power.

Comment
"Middlesbrough, inspired by the open-space-using Mannion, found a degree of form which they had not previously touched this season." – Commentator (Express & Star).

WOLVES: Williams; Stuart, Shorthouse; Slater, Wright, Deeley; Hancocks, Broadbent, Swinbourne, Wilshaw, Mullen.
MIDDLESBROUGH: Ugolini; Stonehouse, Corbett; Bell, Dicks, Harris; Lawrie, Mannion, McPherson, Delapenha, Watkin
Referee: R P Hartley (Burnley). Attendance: 29,145.

WEST BROMWICH ALBION 0 WOLVES 1   *Saturday, April 3, 1954*
Swinbourne 58

This was a championship decider all right but it was spoiled even before kick-off, being scheduled on the same day as the Scotland v England game at Hampden Park. That robbed the title showdown of four of its stars – Billy Wright and Jimmy Mullen of Wolves; Ronnie Allen and Johnny Nicholls of Albion.

Albion were also hard hit by injuries and the only regular member of the forward line available to them was inside-forward Paddy Ryan. Ray Barlow was moved up from left-half to lead the attack while Stan Rickaby was missing from their defence. Goalkeeper Norman Heath had been seriously injured in midweek when Albion crucially lost 2-1 at Sunderland and would never play again.

Very early in the match Barlow was injured in a tussle with Bill Shorthouse, who was dominant in a Wolves defence who allowed Albion little chance to shine. The home side's only chance in the first half fell to Ryan who shot weakly at Bert Williams. The goal came 13 minutes after half-time. Peter Broadbent, who was the game's outstanding player, headed on a Leslie Smith corner and Roy Swinbourne swivelled to hook a half-volley past Jim Sanders. Half-backs Jimmy Dudley and Joe Kennedy tried to drive Albion forward but made little impression and as the game warmed up Shorthouse and Roy Pritchard of Wolves and Ryan were spoken to by the referee. Good Wolves approach work ought to have brought more goals but Swinbourne, Dennis Wilshaw (twice) and Johnny Hancocks failed to put the finishing touches.

Comments
"Wolves did their homework and over the whole ninety minutes were the better organised side but injuries did not help us one little bit." – Ray Barlow
"Apart from the goalkeepers, who did their job well, there were five men who strove mightily to bring to the game the touch of class that it deserved. They were the four wing-halves and Broadbent, and the greatest of these, I thought, was Broadbent." – Commentator (Express & Star).

WEST BROMWICH: Sanders; S Williams, Millard; Dudley, Dugdale, Kennedy; Cox, Ryan, Barlow, Carter, Cutler.
WOLVES: Williams; Stuart, Pritchard; Slater, Shorthouse, Flowers; Smith, Broadbent, Swinbourne, Wilshaw, Hancocks.
Referee: F Cowen (Manchester). Attendance: 49,669.

WOLVES 5   CHARLTON ATHLETIC 0   *Saturday, April 10, 1954*

Hancocks 7, 70
Wilshaw 12
Mullen 53, 59

With Albion losing at Cardiff, this emphatic win at Molineux put Wolves top of the First Division for the first time since January 2. Billy Wright and Jimmy Mullen were back after England duty but Wright was given the left-back spot in preference to Roy Pritchard as the Slater-Shorthouse-Flowers half-back line which had done so well against Albion, was retained. Charlton gave debuts to Ron White and Pat Terry.

Star of the win was Johnny Hancocks and he rounded off an impressive Wolves opening by putting them ahead after seven minutes. Wright started the move with a quick through pass to Wilshaw whose centre was headed on to Hancocks beyond the far post. Although the ball was almost chest height, the winger hit it with such force that Sam Bartram could only push it into the net.

Five minutes later Hancocks returned the compliment after he was sent down the wing by Eddie Stuart and sent over a cross which Wilshaw nodded past Bartram, who was making his 500th League appearance for Charlton. Charlton relied mainly on breakaways but caused few problems for Wolves and Roy Swinbourne saw a header cleared off the line by Eddie Firmani.

Eight minutes into the second half, Hancocks set up Mullen for his first goal since mid-November. The left-winger turned inside full-back Jock Campbell and then rolled the ball past Bartram who could only watch it trickle inside a post.

On 59 minutes the duo did it again. Hancocks beat Firmani near the corner flag whipped over a centre from the right and, when the ball was headed out, Mullen, with his back to goal, brought the ball down, swivelled and drove it into the corner of the net.

Peter Broadbent set up Hancocks's second goal on 70 minutes when he beat two men out on the right before crossing for Hancocks to net through a crowded penalty area from ten yards. The little winger should have taken his tally to three two minutes later. Full-back Firmani, who had been given a difficult afternoon by Hancocks, handled inside the penalty area only for his tormentor to fire a yard wide from the spot kick.

Comments
"We simply couldn't hold 'em. They played some wonderful football. I'm glad we don't meet Wolves every week." – John Hewie (Cahrlton).

"Charlton were second best from first to last whistle. Wolves should have scored more goals." – Kentish Times.

WOLVES: Williams; Stuart, Wright; Slater, Shorthouse, Flowers; Hancocks, Broadbent, Swinbourne, Wilshaw, Mullen.
CHARLTON: Bartram; Campbell, Firmani; Hewie, Chamberlain, Hammond; Hurst, Ayre, Terry, White, Kiernan.
Referee: A A Howlett (Swindon). Attendance: 35,028.

SHEFFIELD WEDNESDAY 0   WOLVES 0   *Saturday, April 17, 1954*

Despite creating a host of chances Wolves had to settle for a point at Hillsborough where Wednesday goalkeeper Dave McIntosh made a succession of good saves and had luck on his side on the rare occasions he was found wanting.

In the first half Roy Swinbourne twice saw shots hit the outside of a post, Bill Slater, Dennis Wilshaw and Peter Broadbent all shot wide when well-placed and McIntosh saved one of Hancocks's specials.

In a rare Wednesday attack Redfern Froggatt blazed high and wide form six yards. The home side did have a spell of pressure and Bert Williams had to save on the line while Billy Wright turned just wide of the near upright an Albert Quixall shot that was aimed for the far corner. As Wolves continued to scorn chances, they nearly paid late on but Jack Marriott's shot was deflected wide by Wright. Bill Shorthouse twice had to receive treatment and was off the field for a few minutes after his second knock.

Comments
"We were nervous travelling up to Sheffield, nervous in the dressing room and nervous on the pitch – but we scraped a point, just." – Johnny Hancocks.
"Slater, Flowers and Shorthouse were magnificent and never spared themselves from first to last." Commentator (Express & Star)

SHEFFIELD WEDNESDAY: McIntosh; Kenny, Curtis; Gannon, O'Donnell, Davies; Marriott, Quixall, Shaw, Froggatt, Woodhead.
WOLVES: Williams; Stuart, Wright; Slater, Shorthouse, Flowers; Hancocks, Broadbent, Swinbourne, Wilshaw, Mullen.
Referee: J H Clough (Bolton). Attendance: 40,707.

WOLVES 4   HUDDERSFIELD TOWN 0   *Monday, April 19, 1954*
Mullen 2, Hancocks 34
Broadbent 86, Wilshaw 89

Leaders Wolves tore into Huddersfield to give their goal average a boost and could even afford the luxury of Johnny Hancocks missing a penalty for the second home game running. Huddersfield, skippered by former Wolves full-back Laurie Kelly, were a goal down in two

89

minutes. Johnny Hancocks drove across goal and a deflection took the ball to Jimmy Mullen who moved inside his full-back before striking the ball low past goalkeeper Jack Wheeler.

Town hit back well and Billy Wright had to clear the ball off his own goal-line while centre-forward Jimmy Glazzard was close with a smart right-foot shot.

In the 27th minute Dennis Wilshaw was brought down as he burst into the penalty area but Hancocks blazed the ball wide from the spot. The winger made quick amends in spectacular style when seven minutes later he fired home a free kick from 30 yards. It had such pace that Wheeler had no chance.

Town continued to battle, with Bill McGarry the driving force at right-half, and there was brief scare when Bill Slater left the field after being injured in a heading duel with Glazzard. The Wolves man returned holding a sponge.

There was another burst of Huddersfield attacking at the start of the second half before Mullen saw a shot roll along the goal-line Then Ron Flowers fired wide from 25 yards and Dennis Wilshaw put another chance wide.

With fifteen minutes left, the visitors were reduced to ten men when Wheeler was injured, Glazzard going in goal. Before Wolves could take advantage it took a good tackle by Billy Wright to stop right-winger Gerry Burrell as he burst through the centre. Deputy 'keeper Glazzard did his best but was beaten by the bounce of the ball from a Peter Broadbent header to a Jimmy Mullen corner with four minutes to go. Then he could not hold a Wilshaw drive in the final minute.

Comments
"Broadbent waltzed his way through the game to become the designer of most of Wolves' attacks and, if I sometimes wished he had remembered his recently demonstrated shooting power, nothing could detract from the excellence of his ball control." – Commentator (Express & Star).
"What a great win! We knew we couldn't lose this one. It was so important not only to us the players but also to the supporters." – Billy Wright.

WOLVES: Williams; Stuart, Wright; Slater, Shorthouse, Flowers; Hancocks, Broadbent, Swinbourne, Wilshaw, Mullen.
HUDDERSFIELD TOWN: Wheeler; Staniforth, Kelly; McGarry, McEvoy, Battye; Burrell, Cavanagh, Glazzard, Watson, Frear.
Referee: W J Gaiger (Manchester). Attendance: 42,862.

HUDDERSFIELD TOWN 2   **WOLVES 1**   *Tuesday, April 20, 1954*
Glazzard 4, McGarry 63   *Wilshaw 43*

Despite losing at Leeds Road, Wolves and their 8,000 travelling support travelled home happy knowing the title was virtually sealed as Albion had been trounced 6-1 at Villa Park.

Town took a shock lead in the fourth minute when John Battye banged a long clearance down the middle. The ball bounced over the head of Bill Shorthouse, leaving Jimmy Glazzard with a clear run to beat Bert Williams with a low right-foot drive from the edge of the penalty area. Wolves still played well enough to have won but were off form in front of goal. Roy Swinbourne missed a couple of chances and Dennis Wilshaw another when his shot was headed against an upright by Laurie Kelly. From the rebound Wilshaw had his shot blocked and then it ran to Jimmy Mullen who drove wide.

Wilshaw made no mistake two minutes from half-time, however, after Bill Slater had bored his way through the home defence to set up the chance.

Swinbourne, Wilshaw and Hancocks missed more chances in the second half and Wolves paid the price when McGarry ran on to a cross pass from Battye to power home a 25-yard shot which flew past Bert Williams. This happened while Shorthouse was out of the middle. He had gone off for treatment after getting a knock on the head when he blocked a shot by Gerry Burrell. Shorthouse first returned to play on the right wing before resuming his normal position.

Wolves should have won but also had a couple of decisions go against them. Wilshaw had the ball in the net on 74 minutes when Peter Broadbent pushed the ball low across goal, only to have what looked like a good goal disallowed on a linesman's decision. With nine minutes left home full-back Ron Staniforth was lucky not to concede a penalty. In a tussle with Jimmy Mullen, Staniforth fell over and seemed to grab the ball goalkeeper fashion but got away with it.

Comments
"Wolves made their openings but just could not take them; they tried the net-breaking shot when the soft tap might have served them better." – Commentator (Express & Star).
"Wolves were far too anxious in front of goal." – Huddersfield Examiner.

HUDDERSFIELD TOWN: Mills; Staniforth, Kelly; McGarry, McEvoy, Battye; Burrell, Cavanagh, Glazzard, Davie, Frear.
WOLVES: Williams; Stuart, Wright; Slater, Shorthouse, Flowers; Hancocks, Broadbent, Swinbourne, Wilshaw, Mullen.
Referee: W J Gaiger (Manchester). Attendance: 35,814.

WOLVES 2   **TOTTENHAM 0**   *Saturday, April 24, 1954*
Swinbourne 18 68

With the title virtually assured before the match, Wolves made sure by taking the game to Spurs right from the start and England goalkeeper Ted Ditchburn, who was to have a fine match, was soon in action saving from Roy Swinbourne.

Spurs' resistance was finally broken on 18 minutes when Swinbourne beat England centre-half Harry Clarke in the air to head home a pinpoint Jimmy Mullen cross. Ditchburn kept out another effort from Dennis Wilshaw and then Bill Slater's drive flew to safety off a defender's

91

leg. At the start of the second half the visitors came more into the game and Bert Williams had to save well from Eddie Baily and Dave Dunmore.

The points were secured on 68 minutes, however. Mullen took a quick throw-in to Wilshaw who returned the ball for the winger to dash down his wing and centre for Swinbourne to leap and head firmly into the net.

Eddie Stuart almost got in on the scoring act on 73 minutes when he drove wide after a goalmouth melee. Swinbourne might have completed a hat-trick but was denied by the acrobatic Ditchburn.

WOLVES: Williams; Stuart, Wright; Slater, Shorthouse, Flowers; Hancocks, Broadbent, Swinbourne, Wilshaw, Mullen.
TOTTENHAM: Ditchburn; Baker, Willis; Nicholson, Clarke, Wetton; Walters, Bennett, Dunmore, Baily, McClellan.
Referee: Rev S V Davis (Oxford). Attendance: 44,055.

CHAPTER SEVEN

THE TITLE BRINGERS

JOHNNY HANCOCKS
Born: Oakengates, April 8, 1919
1953-4 appearances 42 Goals 24

Signed by Walsall from Oakengates Town in 1938, he played 38 League and Cup games for the Saddlers, scoring 10 goals. He signed for Wolves in May, 1946, for a fee of £4,000. Despite his short stature, he packed a powerful shot and became the club's penalty expert.

He was unlucky to be playing at the same time as great right-wingers Stanley Matthews and Tom Finney but still won three England caps, the first two at outside-left. He scored two goals on his England debut in a 6-0 win over Switzerland at Highbury in December, 1948. Both goals came from Matthews crosses. A key member of the 1949 FA Cup-winning side, Hancocks was chosen in the summer of 1950 to go on the FA's tour of Canada and the USA, where they were unbeaten in 11 games. In the final game of the tour, a Hancocks free kick proved the only goal of the match when an England XI beat the USA at Triborough Stadium, New York on June 19.

This also served as a warm-up game for the USA before they set off to the World Cup finals in Brazil. Little could Hancocks and Co have dreamed that ten days after that New York game, the Americans would rock the football world by beating England 1-0 in Belo Horizonte in one of the biggest shocks in World Cup history. Ten of the American team who had faced the England XI were in the side who won in Brazil. News of the defeat was received by the FA party as they sailed home across the Atlantic.

Hancocks was a notoriously bad traveller but apparently the sea trip was something he could cope with. When he arrived home, Hancocks created some stormy waters around Molineux. He refused to re-sign for Wolves and so they began the 1950-1 season without him. When the little man finally saw sense and at last signed up once more, he went on to score 19 goals, five of them penalties, to break a 35-year-old record for most goals in a season by a Wolves winger, beating the 18 by Sammy Brooks in 1914-15. His form in the games after his delayed start to the season won him his only cap in his recognised outside-right spot against Yugoslavia, also at Highbury in November, 1950. Though he was an impressive performer, according to reports, in the 2-2 draw it was to prove his last appearance for his country.

Hancocks's 24 goals in 1953-4 would take his club goals-from-the-wing record to new heights. It did not end there – in 1954-5 he scored 26 league goals, despite making only 32 appearances. Hancocks, lost his place for a spell of 15 games during the 1952-3 season, During that time, several clubs were reported to be interested in signing him including Sheffield Wednesday who, rumour had it, were willing to pay £20,000 – a substantial fee in those days. However, Hancocks regained his place before the end of that season and played in all the 1953-4 league games – the club's only ever present and joint second highest scorer.

What others said

Dennis Wilshaw: "He was a character – a brilliant player at home and a good one away! He was a one-off, being so small and having such a powerful shot. He was not a very good trainer, he didn't need it. Some of us would put on weight but not Johnny. He had no nerves which was probably why he was a penalty expert. His crossing was excellent as well."

Roy Swinbourne: "He was mercurial. Sometimes he had little spells when he didn't want to know – if the full-back was a bit rough. But playing one on one, he could be brilliant. I remember him playing against Walley Barnes of Arsenal, who was a Welsh international, and Johnny turned him inside out. To be fair to Barnsey, I remember when he'd been beaten by Johnny for the umpteenth time he just raised his hands as if to say 'What can I do?' When he had days like that, Johnny was just unstoppable.

"We had a good understanding Johnny and I. Whether he was going to centre to me at the near post or the far post, we just knew. We didn't have to signal or anything, it was instinctive. It just happened. Sometimes he'd come inside and I'd go out on the right wing. We just gelled. I couldn't do that with Jimmy Mullen because he always hugged the touchline. Johnny was so accurate as well. In training we'd put balls on the 18-yard line and he'd say 'left post', 'right post', 'cross bar' and he would hit them with his shots.

"It was a pity he would not fly because he would have won a few more caps, but he hated travelling. We'd even come back from somewhere like Manchester and I've seen him standing on the coach steps at the end of the journey being physically sick. He never liked travelling."

Norman Deeley: "I remember him doing that thing from the 18-yard line with me once in training. He said he'd hit the cross bar and he did it five times out of six. Amazing! He had a powerful shot and his free kicks were tremendous."

Ron Flowers: "Johnny was an enigma. He'd be shuffling along on his wing and then he'd suddenly drop his shoulder and he'd be off. He was explosive. He was not a flyer but he was good over a short distance and was a jinky sort of player. He could hit a ball, too. There may be players today who can shoot harder but in his time, with that heavy caseball, Johnny's was the hardest shot I ever saw."

Bill Slater: "Johnny was a legend – so small but a remarkable player. I had been brought up to pass the ball ahead of my winger so he could race on to it but Johnny liked it to his feet. Once that was sorted out we played well together when I was playing behind him. He always seemed to be available for a pass but even when he was tightly marked he could somehow wriggle his way clear with the ball when you thought it wasn't possible."

Nigel Sims: "You would not believe how good Johnny was. He was special and he could hit the ball so hard with both feet. I remember once when I was training, Joe Gardiner asked Johnny to stay behind and give me some shots to save. He just beat me every time, I never saw the ball – left-hand corner, right hand corner, the balls just kept flying past me. In the end, Joe told him to 'push off' and Joe took over, firing the ball at me so I could make a save or two."

Bill Shorthouse: "I remember once when Johnny was about to take a shot at goal from a free kick. Billy Wright said: 'Get on to him!' But I was too late. Johnny had picked up the ball, walked in that special way of his to place it – he used to walk with a sort of wobble – and before

I could do anything he had fired the ball into the top corner of the net. I said to Billy: 'Just let him get on with it in future!'"

Eddie Stuart: "I would go in goal sometimes when we practised and found out what it was like trying to stop his shots. For his size and weight, his shooting power was tremendous, with either foot. When I got into the team I used to protect him – if he got clobbered then I would sort them out, in the nicest possible way, of course!"

Bert Williams: "There'll never be another like Johnny Hancocks. If you ever saw his calf muscles! He had huge calf muscles, He had timing, style and a superb follow through. I remember him taking a free kick against Hanson the Bolton goalkeeper and the ball hit him on the head, he went in the back of the net and the ball did as well. He just could not get his hands up quickly enough. Goodness knows how fast his shots would be today with the lighter ball. Johnny and I played together at Walsall and it was funny how he got his chance. There was a young man named Wally Brown, an inside-forward, from Oakengates that they wanted to sign. He said he'd only come if he could bring his mate with him – Johnny. So they put them in digs together. Wally looked a better player than Johnny but then the War came. I saw him in Belgium during the War and he'd put on about three stone."

BILL SHORTHOUSE
Born: Bilston, May 27, 1922
1953-4 appearances 40

Having joined Wolves as an amateur in 1941, he was a soldier during the Second World War and was wounded in the D Day landings in Normandy. He made his debut for Wolves during the War, against Walsall on December 20, 1941. His Football League debut for the club was on the first day of the 1947-8 season at left-back but he soon switched to centre-half. He was a no-nonsense defender who came very close to winning an England cap.

He missed only two league games during the 1953-4 season but the following season switched once more to left-back as Billy Wright moved to centre-half to emulate his new England role. Shorthouse's only goal for the club was in 1955 against Charlton at Molineux. After a career which saw him never dropped once he had become a first team regular, he was a youth team coach for England, Birmingham and Villa.

Many thought Shorthouse was good enough to play for England and he must have been very close to winning a cap once Stoke's Neil Franklin was outlawed. Franklin was one of the players who rocked football by opting to go to the Bogota club in Colombia, a country not then a member of FIFA. In the days of a maximum wage in England, the Colombians were offering big salaries and many other perks. Franklin was acknowledged as the best centre-half in the country and had played in 27 successive internationals – every England game since the end of World War II – when he made his sensational move on the eve of the World Cup.

In searching for a successor, England's selectors tried many players – Laurie Hughes and Bill Jones of Liverpool, Allenby Chilton of Manchester United, Jack Taylor of Fulham, Malcolm

Barrass of Bolton – and none was able to make the position his own. They even capped Arsenal's Leslie Compton at the age of 38, England's oldest ever debutant. Yet all the time Shorthouse was turning in steady displays for Wolves but never got his chance.

Shorthouse, an amiable man of 81, still fit enough to enjoy a game of golf, is philosophical when he looks back on the cap that never was. "It would have been nice but it did not happen. I still had a great club career with a wonderful set of players. I know I was very close. I'm not being big-headed but I know I was better than some of those that did win caps."

Twice Shorthouse thought he had made it. "I remember a game against Bolton and as we came off the pitch Malcolm Barrass waited for me and shook my hand and said 'Well done Bill, you must be in now' but I didn't get picked. On another occasion Arthur Oakley (Wolves director and FA member) said I was going to be in when they announced the next England team but when it came out it was Malcolm Barrass who got in. I did get named as a reserve once for the Football League when we went across to play the Irish League but that was the nearest I got. I always thought it was a pity because Bert Williams went to the same school as me (St Martin's at Bradley in Bilston) and he always said it would have been wonderful if two lads from St Martin's had both won England caps."

It was playing for St Martin's Old Boys that helped Shorthouse in his football career. "They were good days. We used to have to carry the goalposts to the pitch and we'd strip for the match at a pub. One night the landlord asked my dad to come and see him and told him he had got me in for a trial at Molineux. I had started work by then at John Thompson's in Ettingshall, helping to make bomb carriers."

Shorthouse joined the club after his trial and played a few games before being called up to serve in the Army. "I went to Norton Barracks in Worcestershire for my training. The Express & Star sports editor George Gillott was a sergeant there. I then went to the South Staffs Regiment before being transferred to the Royal Engineers." It was with the engineers that he got involved in the D Day landings. "It was our job to clear the beaches of mines. We worked in groups of four and had to put matting down for the tanks to run on. It was while doing this I got wounded. I was fired at from about 70 yards away and the bullet went right through my left forearm. I was very lucky, really, it could have been much worse, though I could not use the arm for about twelve months."

Once he had recovered, Shorthouse was able to continue his football progress and was signed full-time for Wolves by manager Ted Vizard. He had played a few games for Burnley during the war. "I was up that way on a training course and Burnley gave me a few matches – not in the first team – and I scored a few goals. There was no chance I would have joined them after the War, though. It was always Wolves for me."

It was not easy being a centre-half in the late 1940s and early 1950s. "There were some good centre-forwards about. "Jackie Milburn was always the toughest. He was so fast. Nat Lofthouse was tough and John Spuhler at Middlesbrough could be a handful. We played Newcastle in the 1952 semi-final and Milburn said to me before the kick-off 'If we get to the final I'll get you

Wolves team in the early part of the campaign. Back (left - right): Slater, Wright, Williams, Shorthouse, Short, Pritchard; Front: Hancocks, Broadbent, Swinbourne, Wilshaw, Muller

The skipper - Billy Wright

The boss - Stan Cullis

Full-back - Jack Short

Goalkeeper - Bert Williams

Full-back - Roy Pritchard

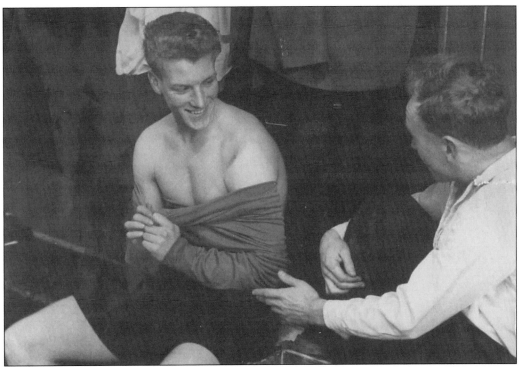

Getting ready for action - Ron Flowers and Billy Wright in the dressing room

Bill Slater - turned professional during the season

Bill Shorthouse - a stalwart centre-half

Jimmy Mullen in action against Newcastle

Right-winger - Johnny Hancocks

Wolves wing maestro - Jimmy Mullen

The Mighty Atom - Johnny Hancocks practises one of his cannon-ball shots

Manager Stan Cullis and trainer Joe Gardiner talk to inside-forward Peter Broadbent

Dennis Wilshaw - top scorer with 26 goals in 1953-4

England Skipper - Billy Wright in his International kit

Action man - Roy Swinbourne, the centre-forward who hit 24 goals

Wolves official autograph sheet for 1953-4

three tickets if you'll do the same if you win.' Well they won and he kept his word and got me the tickets."

Shorthouse has very fond memories of the men of 1953-4. "They were a great set of lads. We all seemed to get on well. We had reserves who did not get many first team games but they would not ask for a transfer. It was just a happy place to be – Molineux. I enjoyed the atmosphere and I enjoyed the training and made many lasting friendships."

"I'm not saying the training wasn't tough, though. We would be taken to Cannock Chase and dropped off near Brocton and had to run up and down hills. But it paid off. Our fitness was one of our biggest assets."

What others said

Dennis Wilshaw: "Bill was a helluva a good player. As a centre-half he was worth a cap. He also did well when he went to full-back. He did not think so but he was a good full-back – except, perhaps, when he played against Tom Finney."

Roy Swinbourne: "I play golf with Ray Barlow and Ray still talks about that game against us in 1953-4 when he had to play at centre-forward against Bill at The Hawthorns. He got injured very early on in a tackle with Bill and even now starts jumping up and down when we talk about it, but it was just one of those things. Bill was big and strong but he was always fair."

97

Norman Deeley: "He was always there in the thick of the action. He very rarely missed a tackle. Nine times out of ten he'd win the ball."

Ron Flowers: "Shorty was Mr Reliable. He was big and stocky but he could climb for a ball and was good in the air. He was a strong tackler who always let the opposition know he was around. He and Wrighty used to do most of the organising in defence and Bill was a good vice captain."

Bill Slater: "Tree trunk legs – not many got past Bill. He was very strong and his tackling was hard but fair and he always had plenty to say during a match."

Nigel Sims: "It was man's game in those days and that's the way Bill played it. He was a hard man and very dedicated."

Eddie Stuart: "Bill was a fine centre-half and a good club man and I'll never forget his gesture in standing down from the team so I could captain Wolves against South Africa in our first floodlit match."

Bert Williams: "Bill and I went to the same school and when we won the Cup we took it back to St Martin's to show the pupils. They loved it. Bill was a good player to play behind. He was straightforward, no frills, hard, a genuine club man who gave everything he'd got for Wolves. I think when he made his debut as a left-back he'd got flu and didn't do very well. He eventually came back in at centre-half for Gordon Brice. It wasn't very comfortable playing behind

Gordon, he did not read the game as well as Bill. With Bill, you knew exactly what he was going to do. He should have played for England and I remember that occasion when Arthur Oakley told him he was in the team. He said 'Lads, I want you to congratulate Billy Wright, Bert Williams and Bill Shorthouse. They've been selected to play for England.' I heard him say that. It was very rough on Bill."

ROY SWINBOURNE
Born: Denaby, August, 25, 1929
1953-4 appearances 40 Goals 24

A product of Wolves' Wath Wanderers nursery club in Yorkshire, Swinbourne came to Molineux in 1944. His league debut was at inside-right in a 1-1 home draw with Fulham in December, 1949. He kept his place for virtually the rest of the season, soon switching to centre-forward. He became a regular the following season and was top scorer with 22 league and cup goals. He lost his way a bit during 1951-2 and actually asked to be played in the reserves but was top scorer once more in 1952-3 with 21 goals and it was clear he would be first choice No 9 at the start of 1953-4. He missed only two games during the championship-winning campaign and was joint second highest scorer for the club on 24 goals. It seemed he was an England centre-forward in the making in 1955 as Nat Lofthouse's reign was coming to an end.

98

He scored three hat-tricks on successive Saturdays at the start of the 1955-6 season when he opened the campaign with 17 goals in 11 games to cement his claims for a cap. Alas, a knee injury at Preston proved to be the beginning of the end for his playing career. He had played for England B in March 1955 scoring his side's goal in the 1-1 draw with West Germany B at Hillsborough That team included Duncan Edwards, Johnny Haynes and Harry Hooper, who was destined to join Wolves in 1956. Swinbourne was a two-goal hero when Wolves came from 2-0 down to beat Hungarian aces Honved 3-2 in the famous floodlit encounter of December, 1954.

Swinbourne might have played for Major Buckley – but not when the Major was at Molineux. The Major had made a shock departure to Notts County in 1944 and ran the rule over the young Swinbourne with a view to taking him on the Meadow Lane ground staff. "I was an outside right in those days," said Swinbourne. "I was picked for the Sheffield and Hallamshire District trial match, the Possibles against the Probables. I had a good game there and a few scouts showed an interest and Major Buckley came to our house in Denaby Main, the mining village where I lived near Doncaster. My father did all the talking to him but decided I should stay at home and go to Huddersfield as an amateur. I was 14 at the time.

"When I played in this trial game I was one of the Possibles but the lad playing outside right in the Probables team had a great game. He was fast, he could catch pigeons. I was also outside right, in the Possibles, but at half-time I was told to take my shirt off and put on the No 8 in the Probables team. So I went inside right to this lad and we were selected for the team to play at Rotherham United's ground. That's when the scouts started knocking at our door again."
"Then I was approached to join Wath Wanderers, Wolves' nursery club. Mark Crook, who ran it, came to see my dad and we talked about it. Now Wolves in those days were packing them in

and Huddersfield were not getting exactly big gates and we decided I'd be better off at Wolves." Swinbourne's father, Tom, had been on Villa's books. "He was born in Birmingham and did not make the grade so went down to Worcester City. That's where he met mom, she was a Worcestershire girl, and then he was offered the managership of Denaby United in the Midland League. So he went up to Yorkshire which was where their sons were born – I was the youngest of five. So that's how we became Yorkshiremen." Swinbourne eventually moved down to Wolverhampton when he was 16.

What others said

Dennis Wilshaw: "He deserved an England cap. He was not just one of those blood and guts types of centre-forward. He had great ability. I have great regrets for Roy having to end his career through injury just when he was at his peak."

Norman Deeley: "I always remember he seemed to hang in the air when the went up to head the ball. For a big man, he had lovely control and could turn well. He was a class player."

Ron Flowers: "I first saw Roy when I was playing in the juniors. We played Newcastle in the morning and then went to watch Sunderland play Wolves in the afternoon. I remember thinking I would hate to play against him. He would not give a defender a minute's peace. He had got everything – good control, speed and good in the air."

Bill Slater: "What a shame he suffered that injury! He was just at his peak. He was not just a centre forward waiting in the goalmouth for others to make chances for him. He was very good at coming away from the opposing centre-half so if you were coming out of defence you could pass to him and he knew how to shield it from the player behind. He could make himself a target for you – he was a very good outlet."

Nigel Sims: "Sometimes I thought he needed a bit too much time to turn but his game improved and he certainly got a lot of goals."

Bill Shorthouse: "Roy was a good centre-forward – big and strong,"

Eddie Stuart: "I'd put Roy Swinbourne among the three best centre-forwards Wolves have ever had – along with Derek Dougan and Steve Bull. He could shoot with both feet, hold the ball up – he lacked nothing. He had all the qualities to be an England centre-forward."

Bert Williams: "Roy was the ideal centre-forward. He could control, could hold the ball up, was a good header of the ball and would give everything he'd got for Wolves."

BILL SLATER
Born: Clitheroe, April 29, 1927
1953-4 appearances 39 Goals 2

Slater was the last amateur to appear in the FA Cup final. He was inside-left for Blackpool when they lost 2-0 to Newcastle at Wembley in 1951. He also registered the quickest ever goal for the Seasiders when he scored after 11 seconds against Stoke on December 10, 1949, at Bloomfield Road.

He joined Brentford in December, 1951, and Wolves the following August. One of the highlights of his amateur career should have been in 1952 when he was in the Great Britain side for the Olympic Games. However, the team lost 5-3 to unfancied Luxembourg in extra time, Slater scoring one of the goals. The tournament was run on a knockout basis so that was the end of it! "There was a suspicion Luxembourg might have had some players in from other countries but we were all true blue amateurs," recalls Slater, who was still an amateur when the 1953-4 season started and added three caps to his England amateur collection before becoming a part-time professional. His first game as a paid player was the 6-1 home win over Sheffield United on February 20, 1954. His debut had come on October 4, 1952 as deputy to Billy Wright who was on international duty. Slater had an outstanding game that day at Molineux as Wolves came from 2-0 down to beat Manchester United 6-2. Yet he did not gain a regular place until the last two and a half months of the 1952-3 season. However, his displays, as he quickly adjusted to the pace of the professional game, clinched his first-team status.

Slater's impressive form during the championship season continued into 1954-5 and he won his first England cap against Wales in November, 1954, and then played against world champions West Germany. Both games were won 3-1 but Slater was promptly dropped for the following April's game against Scotland. He gained the third of his 12 full caps in 1958 when he took over the left-half spot following the death of Duncan Edwards as a result of injuries received in the Munich Air Crash which claimed the lives of seven other Manchester United players.

That same year, Slater formed an all-Wolves England half-back line with Eddie Clamp and Billy Wright for four games, three of them in the World Cup finals in Sweden. Against Brazil in Gothenburg, Slater did a fine man-marking job on star midfielder Didi as England became the only side during the tournament not to lose to the eventual winners, drawing 0-0.

Having also gained league championship medals in 1957-8 and 1958-9, Slater switched to centre-half in the autumn of his career, captaining Wolves in their FA Cup final victory over Blackburn at Wembley in 1960. Such was the success of his move that he was also named Footballer of the Year for 1959-60 and earned a recall to the England side – against Scotland at Hampden Park.

For a brief period, with Johnny Hancocks having lost his place, Slater became Wolves' penalty-taker, scoring four in four games towards the end of the 1955-6 season, including two against Tottenham in a 5-1 win on April 18, 1956, the first time Molineux had staged a floodlit League match. That evening, Slater scored from the spot in the final minute of each half. He also scored twice from the spot at the start of the 1956-7 season but had one saved when a John Charles-inspired Leeds came to Molineux and won 2-1 on the day goalkeeper Malcolm Finlayson made his Wolves debut. After that the penalty-taking role was given to right-winger Harry Hooper. Later the penalty duties were taken over by Eddie Clamp but with Clamp out of favour at the start of the 1958-9 season, Slater was again entrusted with the 12-yard duties. He was successful from the spot on the famous day Wolves lost 6-2 to Chelsea at Stamford Bridge when a teenage Jimmy Greaves collected five goals. Slater then lost the role after a bizarre piece of drama against Tottenham at White Hart Lane on September 27, 1958. When Peter Broadbent was brought down by Spurs' full-back Mel Hopkins, Slater promptly fired home the resultant penalty. However, York referee H Webb ruled a Wolves player had moved before the kick was taken and so Slater had to try again. This time home goalkeeper John Hollowbread saved Slater's kick only for the referee to order another retake, this time because a Spurs player had moved. Slater then decided it would not be third time lucky so Clamp, back in the team, was entrusted with the kick. He promptly took a 12-yard run to fire the ball unceremoniously into the net.

Slater explained how he had started playing for Brentford. "My fiancee was living in Ealing so I used to go to see her at weekends. When I came up to Birmingham University, Brentford gave me a letter of introduction which I took along to Stan Cullis. I said I was keen to play and did not mind which team I played in. That brought me a lecture – he did not want players unless their ambition was to play in the first team. Now, if I had gone along and said to him I wanted to play in the first team, I would have got another lecture, so I was in a no-win situation."

However, Slater's talent soon won him a first team place at the end of 1952-3 though he was still working as a PE lecturer at Birmingham University. "Turning part-time professional meant I could buy a small car so I could come across from Birmingham by car when the players reassembled in summer for training. It worked out well as it was still summer vacations for the students when training began so I could get in a full pre-season. After that I would train on my own though sometimes I'd come across on Wednesday mornings if we'd got a big game."

101

Slater is very modest about his role as a sports administrator. His daughter Barbara was a fine gymnast, competing in the 1976 Olympics."I was a keen gymnast myself so took a big interest and was eventually made president of the British Gymnastics Associations. I also sat on the British Olympics Association committee and served on one or two grant-giving bodies."

His service to sport over the years has seen him honoured with an OBE and then CBE.

What others said

Dennis Wilshaw: "Bill did not say much but he was a good wing-half. He was a tremendous player and a very nice guy."

Roy Swinbourne: "A classic player, Bill. He was still playing like an amateur when he arrived but he soon learned. We used to play five-a-side games on the car park at Molineux in those days and it got a bit rough and when Bill first started playing in those games he found it a bit hard with players like Bill Shorthouse and Bill Guttridge around. They toughened him up very quickly."

Norman Deeley: "Bill was a gentleman and a very good player. He would be thinking a game all through the 90 minutes. He could tackle well and could distribute the ball well."

Ron Flowers: "I reckon that in the season he was voted Footballer of the Year, 1959-60, he was a better player than Billy Wright, which is the highest praise I can give. Over the years, Billy probably just had the edge but in that one season Bill Slater was brilliant. Everything he did was immaculate. People always say he was a gentleman, which he was, but I don't think they realised how fit and strong he was. He could look after himself."

Nigel Sims: "Bill was class. He was a good player but he was hard as well. He was such a nice fella. You could always get on well with him."

Bill Shorthouse: "When he first came with us training you could never stop him running. Joe Gardiner used to say 'Steady down a bit, Bill.' He was a stylish player at times. He had good ball control and he could pass it well."

Eddie Stuart: "Bill had tremendous ability. I always looked on him as a great centre-half, better even than the great Billy Wright. He was perfection. As a captain, I was probably stricter and harder while Bill was quietly spoken and did things differently. He was also an absolute gentleman."

Bert Williams: "I liken Bill Slater to Tom Galley. They were two of the best wing-halves Wolves ever had. They were studious well-drilled players. Bill Slater was an intelligent, conscientious player, a helluva good lad, a helluva good person all round."

BILLY WRIGHT
Born: Ironbridge, February 6, 1924
1953-4 appearances 39

Has to be the greatest player in Wolves' history and one of football's all-time greats. His story has been told many times – how he was once informed by Wolves boss Major Frank Buckley that he was too small to make the grade but, given a second chance, went on to lead his club to an FA Cup triumph and three First Division titles as well as being voted Footballer of the Year in 1952. He almost collected the football writers' trophy again in 1959, in what proved to be his final season. He received 134 votes but Luton veteran Syd Owen pipped him with 137.

Wright captained his country 90 times, a record later equalled by Bobby Moore, and missed only three of the first 108 games played by England after the Second World War, including a run of 70 successive caps. Wright also played in four Victory Internationals in 1945-6 but these did not count as full caps. He switched to centre-half for England during the 1954 World Cup and Wolves moved him to that position permanently in 1954-5. During the 1953-4 campaign Wright showed his versatility and willingness to play out of position when asked. He was in his recognised left-half spot in only half of Wolves games but played at No 5 in seven matches as well as appearing 11 times at full-back. In his early years he had played mostly left-half for Wolves but right-half for his country. He began the championship-winning season with 51 caps to his name, already an England record. Few would have forecast that he would win another 54 before he retired, becoming the first man in the world to play in 100 full internationals. He reached that milestone against Scotland at Wembley in April, 1959, and there to see him was wife Joy who had recently presented him with his first child. His show business marriage – Joy and twins Teddy and Babs were the singing Beverley Sisters – made Billy and his wife almost the Beckhams of their day.

He led Wolves to their 1949 FA Cup final triumph over Leicester at Wembley and, as well as 1953-4, won championship medals in 1957-8 and 1958-9. He was appointed manager of the England youth side in 1960 and many thought the FA were grooming him to take over when England boss Walter Winterbottom retired. However in 1962, he accepted the post of manager of Arsenal and many say he laid the foundations for their Double-winning side of 1971. However, Wright was not really cut out for management and was sacked in 1966.

He became a TV presenter and later a TV executive in the Midlands before he retired. Much to his pride, he was made a director of Wolves when Sir Jack Hayward took over the club but he died aged 70 in 1994.

A key factor in Wolves' successes during the 1950s was the relationship between skipper and manager and there is no doubt Stan Cullis had the utmost respect for Wright. In his autobiography, All For The Wolves (Rupert Hart-Davis, 1960), Cullis wrote: "He managed to play anything between fifty-five and sixty hard matches every year and under every sort of condition without ever falling very far from his own impeccable standard of play. The reason for this tremendous consistency could be found in his approach to the game. I never met anybody who trained so hard and conscientiously and who concentrated his mind on his profession almost to the complete exclusion of other interests

"Apart from his tremendous qualities on the field, he was the perfect club man. He typified the spirit which every manager would like to find in his dressing-room – the spirit which was a vital factor in bringing to Wolves the success which came during his reign as captain of the club. I would say he did more than any other player, past or present, to raise the social status of the professional footballer."

What others said

Dennis Wilshaw: "People in the Potteries tend to say to me 'Was Billy Wright as good as Neil Franklin (centre-half for Stoke and England)?' but they were totally different players and of course Billy was 30 when he switched to centre half. He would never have tried to do what Neil did – trap a ball on his own six-yard line and try to beat his opponent. What Billy did, as a wing-half and centre-half, was reach a standard that was very high and he kept to that week after week. That was what made him such a great player to have in your side."

Roy Swinbourne: "What can you say about Billy? He has to be the best player I ever played with. The great thing about him was his anticipation. He'd be playing against someone like Nat Lofthouse and you'd see Billy move to the left and you'd think if Lofthouse turned the other way he'd be through, but he never did. That's the way it was – Billy always seemed to know what the other man was going to do. He read the game so well. As a captain he did not do a lot of shouting – Bill Shorthouse did all the shouting. He led by example with Bill as his right hand man.

"I don't think I ever saw Billy play a bad game"

Norman Deeley: "You had to be a very good player to win 105 caps. He helped me a lot the day I played my first game – against Arsenal. That was how he was, whether you were a first team regular or one of the youngsters."

Ron Flowers: "Over the years, I thought Billy was brilliant. He helped me a lot. I would often say at half-time in a game 'I'm in trouble against this fella' and Billy would advise me how to play him or what position to take up. He'd help me during a game as well. He was a big influence on me. Billy was very good in the air, considering his lack of real height, and a good clean tackler. He also had that ability to recover very quickly if he'd missed the first tackle and have another go at the player. Ray Wilson, the England full-back, was the best I've seen at doing that but Billy ran him very close."

Bill Slater: "What can I add to what's been said many times about him? He was a very fine player and also very good to me in particular. It could have been difficult, me being an amateur and not always there for training once the season was under way. In some cases, a player might not have been made welcome but it was never like that with me. They all made me very welcome and Billy, in particular, went out of his way to do so. You'd get the odd jibe now and then of course, me being an amateur, but never anything nasty."

104

Nigel Sims: "I must be the only one who could not see what all the fuss was about when he played at wing-half. I just saw him is a good player but when he switched to centre-half, that's when I think he became a really great player."

Bill Shorthouse: "I got on well with Bill, though when they switched me to left-back I thought I was still as good a centre-half as him. A lot of people agreed with me so that's quite a compliment because he was very good. He was a good header of the ball for his size and when he got the ball he did not waste it. He was a good captain. He was not one to get on to the players. I think I did more shouting. He would just have a quiet word."

Eddie Stuart: "No player gave more loyalty, support and dedication to a club than Billy. If he had two bad games in a season, that was all. As far as skills were concerned he was not a Stan Matthews but where he excelled was in his anticipation – and he was deadly in the tackle. Because of his timing he could outjump most of his opponents even though he was only about 5ft 9in and his reading of a game – nobody in world football was better at that. I was his vice captain for several years and he encouraged me and helped me. If there were things I was doing wrong, he would often come back in the afternoon so we could work on them."

Bert Williams: "You knew very well with Billy that he was going to cover more ground than two players. He was strong in the air and, like most of them at Molineux in my day, he was a genuine Wolves player. He sacrificed most of his personal life for Wolves. Billy was a real confidence booster in defence. Against a six-footer, he could jump and seem to hang in the air. And he never gave up running. We had never lost until the final whistle. I said to him once 'Wouldn't you have liked to have been playing today?' Billy said: 'No, I may not have been so lucky.' It's a lovely way of looking at things. He was a genuinely nice person, a down-to-earth person. "

DENNIS WILSHAW
Born: Stoke, March 11, 1926
1953-4 appearances 39 Goals 26

Although he signed for Wolves in 1943, Wilshaw was loaned out to Walsall for a couple of seasons and soon showed his talent for goalscoring. He had made his debut for Wolves in 1943-4 and played eleven games that season, scoring four goals. He also played two games in 1943-4. He made a sensational Football League debut debut for Wolves, at outside-left, scoring a hat-trick in a 3-0 win over Newcastle at Molineux in March 1949.

He was promptly dropped as Jimmy Mullen was the first choice and had helped Wolves to reached the semi-final stage of the FA Cup.

Wilshaw had a similar experience in the 1953-4 campaign. His fine displays for Wolves earned him his first England cap, against Wales on October 10, 1953, when original choice Harold Hassall (Bolton) had to pull out through injury. Wilshaw scored twice in a 4-1 win only to be omitted from the side for the next game. Blackpool's Stanley Mortensen got the vote against FIFA in the game to celebrate the FA's 90th anniversary. However, Wilshaw was named in the England squad for the 1954 World Cup finals. He scored in the 2-0 win over Switzerland as did his clubmate Jimmy Mullen. Wilshaw also played in the following match, the 4-2 quarter-final defeat at the hands of Uruguay.

His greatest day at international level came the following April when he became the first – and still only – man to score four goals in an England-Scotland match. A Stanley Matthews-inspired side beat Scotland 7-2 on the day an 18-year-old named Duncan Edwards won his first cap but Wilshaw's historic feat provided few cuttings for his scrapbook – there was a newspaper strike on in England at the time. In all, he scored ten goals in 12 full internationals. He left Wolves for Stoke in 1957 and was later a sports psychologist.

Wilshaw came to the attention of Wolves during the war. "I was playing for the village team Packmoor, a mining village where I was born, We beat Michelin in the North Staffs League 16-0 and I got ten, not knowing there was a Wolves scout watching. I think it was a guy from Crewe.

"A week later I was in the Wolves first team against West Brom. Major Buckley was always experimenting with young talent. I was a centre-forward with the village team but he played me at inside-left.

"When the war ended I suppose there was no room for me so they loaned me out to Walsall and Harry Hibbs (the former Birmingham and England goalkeeper who was manager at Fellows Park) turned me into an inside-left. Then they signed Dougie Lishman, who later moved to Arsenal, and Harry had the brainwave of playing me at outside left. So when I went back to Wolves it was as a reserve winger.

"One of the first things Stan Cullis did when he took over as manager was to bring me back from Walsall. Many's the time he wished he hadn't. At Walsall I'd applied to Loughborough College, one of the top PE colleges at the time, and got accepted. Stan never liked the fact that I was doing something other than football. I could guarantee to have a row with him every month. But all through, I had great respect for him.

"Although I was dropped after making my debut it was no surprise. It was difficult to break into Wolves' team in those days A little later Stan played me at inside-forward. It was a gamble on his part but I stayed there."

Wilshaw was teaching at Hanley High School during the 1950s, the school he attended as a youngster. He kept himself fit and only trained with his Molineux team-mates during holiday times. "That did not suit Stan," recalls Wilshaw, "and he would play some tricks like not playing me at the start of the season saying I was not fit until September came. Funny though, he thought I was fit enough to go on our pre-season tour to Russia in 1955."

He admits the situation was not easy. "I would never give up teaching for full-time football." Wilshaw taught PE and mathematics but was later put in charge of schools sport in Stoke-on Trent. "It was an experiment and I was responsible for all schools and youth clubs. We had never had a smell of the ESFA (English Schools Football Association) Trophy before but, happily, we won it twice during my time."

He later went to Keele University as Stoke were introducing a counselling service and it was from there he moved into psychology. He became a lecturer in psychology at Alsager College and was eventually made head of the Social and Community Studies department.

"Nineteen-fifty-four was an incredible year for me," says Wilshaw. "I scored more goals than anybody else for Wolves that season, we won the title and I played for England – but it was a mixture of joy and tragedy because I lost my father."

Tom Wilshaw, a haulage contractor, died aged 56, in January, 1954. Though ill, he had seen his son win his first international cap. "He had been everything to me," says Wilshaw. "He loved football, though he was never any good at it himself. I remember him taking me to watch Stoke in the days of Stanley Matthews and Freddie Steele. When I lost him it was the end of the world for me but he had lived to see my first international. He went to Wales and saw that match even though he was in pain. Nothing would keep him away."

Wilshaw does not recall too much detail of the World Cup quarter-final against Uruguay but says "I do recall that Gil Merrick had a shocker." The tournament completed a special season and Wilshaw speaks highly of the men who, along with him, brought the title to Molineux.
"I have the deepest respect for every player I played with. I had it then and I have it now. They were tremendous characters, tremendous guys and damn good players. Every chance I have to meet up again with them I'll always take."

What others said

Roy Swinbourne: "He was a great goalscorer. He did not score many from outside the box but he was always around. He once scored four against Scotland and that takes some doing. He would always be there if a chance fell. I'd often joke by showing a him a picture of a game afterwards and say 'Where were you in this goalmouth scramble, Dennis?' but when there was a chance, he'd pop up in the right place."

Norman Deeley: "He was a poacher of goals. What people did not realise was that he had to work very hard to be in the right place at the right time. That's why he scored a lot of goals."

Ron Flowers: "I think Dennis was a lot faster than people realised. He was not one of those who ran with his arms pumping and neck straining, he just seemed to glide. He was fast, all right, but he glided. He was a precise player and he could see chances before anyone else. In many respects, I'd call him a modern day player. I think he would fit into today's game very easily. He was that good."

Bill Slater: "Sometimes Dennis could seem to be on the fringe of things but he had that uncanny knack of coming into a game and scoring goals which is very difficult. It's not something you can teach. He was like Jimmy Greaves, always in the right place at the right time. He was very different from Peter Broadbent who would come back into our half to receive the ball and work it away. Dennis did do that, as well, of course, but what he was very good at was scoring goals because he was quick and fast and had good control."

107

Nigel Sims: "He was amazing, a real goaltaker like Jimmy Greaves. He would turn up in a dangerous spot and just slot the ball in. He was just a natural in the same way Greaves was."

Bill Shorthouse: "His dad was a lovely man, too. He was haulage contractor and when Dennis and I were in the reserves together he would follow the coach in his car. He watched a lot of our games and gave Dennis a lot of support."

Eddie Stuart: "My old pal from Stoke! He was another superb player. It would seem like he would touch the ball only six or seven times in a match and score two goals. He'd seem to be out of the game and suddenly he'd get a goal. He was definitely Jimmy Greaves-like in that respect."

JIMMY MULLEN
Born: Newcastle-on-Tyne, January 6, 1923
1953-4 appearances 38 Goals 7

The likeable Geordie was thrust into the limelight right at the start of his Wolves career. He became the club's youngest ever player in a league game when he faced Leeds on February 18, 1939 at the age of 16 years and 43 days. He also played in Wolves' 5-0 FA Cup semi-final victory over Grimsby at Old Trafford but was not chosen for the final. Like Billy Wright, he was a guest player for Leicester during World War II, having helped Wolves win the Wartime League (North) Cup.

The first of his 12 full caps for England came against Scotland at Wembley on April 12, 1947, when he partnered Middlesbrough legend Wilf Mannion. Mullen also played in a Wartime International against Wales at Anfield in September, 1944, and in a Victory International against Belgium at Wembley in January. 1946. .Mullen later made history by becoming England's first substitute, coming on for injured outside-right Jackie Milburn against Belgium in Brussels on May 18, 1950, scoring in a 4-1 win. He was chosen for the 1950 World Cup finals in Brazil and was in the side infamously beaten 1-0 by the USA. He also made the squad for the 1954 finals in Switzerland and scored in England's 2-0 win over the host nation.

Without doubt, Mullen and Hancocks were key members of the 1953-4 side as wingers who often switched the point of attack by long balls to the opposite wing. They differed greatly in style, Mullen being more elegant with a knack of pulling his centres back from the byeline just when it seemed he must run the ball out of play.

A 1949 FA Cup winner, he also won championship medals in 1957-8 and 1958-9 before retiring to concentrate on his sports outfitters business. It was his death in 1987 that prompted Wolves legends, who had met up at his funeral, to meet again under happier circumstances and found the Wolverhampton Wanderers Former Players' Association.

What others said

108

Dennis Wilshaw: "You could not get two greater wingers than Johnny Hancocks and Jimmy Mullen. They often used to say that when they picked the Wolves team it was Williams, Wright, Hancocks and Mullen and then choose seven others.

"Jimmy was quick but you had to give Jim the ball in front of him or over the full-back's head. He did not like the ball played to his feet whereas Johnny did. I gave Jimmy a right rollicking once at half-time. I'd passed to him and the ball was only about six inches behind him and he let it run into touch and then he gestured to the crowd as if to say it was my fault! The thing about Jimmy was that he could cross a ball from right on the dead-ball line which takes some doing."

Roy Swinbourne: "He used to like to stay on the touchline but what a player! What a great left foot! Very quick as well. He was a lovely fella as well, socially. In fact we all got on well together. After training in a morning we'd all go up to Lyons cafe in Queen Square and have cup of coffee and people would come up and chat. We were part of the town."

Norman Deeley: "He was a grand winger with a superb left foot and could centre the ball on the run. Jimmy did not score a lot of goals but he made a lot for other people."

Ron Flowers: "He was the first of the established players I met when I arrived at Molineux. Trainer Joe Gardiner introduced me to him and asked him to show me around. I didn't know whether to call him 'Mr Mullen' or what but he could not have made me more welcome.

He said 'Call me Jim' and introduced me to all the players. Like everyone else I remember how he could cross the ball just when you thought he must run it over the line. He was very quick and would often push the ball one side of the full-back and run past him on the other."

Bill Slater: "Jimmy might have been a bit one-footed but what he could do with that one foot! If I was coming out of defence on the right and the way was blocked Jimmy would make himself available so you could swing the ball across to him. He would always take up the correct position."

Nigel Sims: "I really rated Jimmy. Of course in my day we had wingers and the spectators loved it – to see players, like Jimmy, taking the ball down the wing to the deadball line and pulling back crosses. It was exciting and it was harder for goalkeepers. I reckon if Beckham had been playing in my day he would have been nothing. The fans used to love to see wingers but then Alf Ramsey came along and killed all that. Jimmy and Johnny Hancocks were very good to me. They used to help me practise a lot by testing me with crosses."

Bill Shorthouse: "Not many people could put over a ball like Jimmy. He was very fast and you were always thinking he was going to run the ball out but he would always get it back into the middle, would always put in good crosses."

Eddie Stuart: "Jimmy had a wonderful left foot, was fast and a beautiful crosser of the ball and the number of times those crosses would be met by Johnny Hancocks. Everybody liked, Jimmy. I never met a greater player or a greater person in football. He, Bert Williams and Billy Wright are three all-time greats."

109

Bert Williams: "Jimmy, they said, had only one good leg but it did not matter. He was a straightforward player, fast and could he cross a ball! He'd do it when it did not look possible. They say Major Buckley tried to teach him to use his right foot by putting the ball between a couple of bricks – but Jimmy just kept kicking the bricks."

PETER BROADBENT
Born: Dover, May 15, 1933
1953-4 appearances 36 Goals 12

A rarity in the 1953-4 side – he cost a big transfer fee. He was signed as a 17-year-old from Brentford, having made 16 league appearances for them. Son of a miner, Broadbent also worked in the coalmines for a year before pursuing football fame. His father was a Yorkshireman and his mother came from Northumberland.

Broadbent joined Wolves in February, 1951. His older brother, Jack, a goalkeeper, had a trial at Molineux but did not make the grade as a professional and became a policeman in Kent. A player of exceptional skill, Broadbent gained a regular place in the fourth game of the title-winning season, having made his debut at home to Portsmouth on March 17, 1951. He went on to be architect of the side who won the title again in 1957-8 and 1958-9 as well as the FA Cup in 1960.

His talents deserved more than seven England caps but he was unfortunate to be playing at a time when Johnny Haynes was regarded by the selectors as the country's main man in midfield. Broadbent won an England under-23 cap during the 1953-4 season but had to wait until 1958 for his first full cap, being brought into the side with Chelsea's Peter Brabrook to form the right-wing in the World Cup finals play-off game with Russia which England lost 1-0. He scored twice against Wales at Villa Park in November, 1958, and was still in the side against Scotland the following April when Billy Wright won his 100th cap.

Many regard Broadbent as being a scheming type of inside forward yet he scored a lot of goals – 127 in the League for Wolves – particularly in the four seasons up to and including 1959-60. He later played for Shrewsbury, Villa and Stockport and is still regarded by older Wolves fans as a footballing genius, the one man allowed by manager Stan Cullis to dwell on the ball and deviate from the club's direct style of play. A measure of his talent is the fact George Best became a firm admirer as he watched TV footage of Wolves games as a youngster in Belfast.

Broadbent's move to Molineux may well have been down to George Poyser, the former Port Vale full-back who was a coach with Wolves at the time. Poyser had been a player with Brentford, player-manager of Dover Town and also did some coaching for Brentford. "I think George had a lot to do with my move," recalls Broadbent.

"He may well have been the one who said I was worth having a look at. Whatever the case, I'm very glad Wolves decided to sign me because it was one of the best things that ever happened to me. I'd only been at Molineux a few weeks and we were off to tour South Africa. I'd never been abroad before.

"I had many wonderful years with Wolves. I can only repeat what other players have said – there was a great spirit at the club and some great players who would always help you. They were very special people and we had some very special years." Like so many football stars of his era, Broadbent honed his skills from a very early age. "There was a big wall at the side of our house and I used to spend hours, as a young lad, kicking a ball against that wall and learning how to control the ball. It must have paid off.

"A lot of people said I should have been given more caps but I don't know about that. I was just proud to get seven and I'll always remember playing in Billy Wright's hundredth international as well as those two goals against Wales at Villa Park. The second was a header and I did not score many with my head."

Broadbent was one of those talented sportsmen who had a good eye for the ball which made him useful at cricket, table tennis and golf. He once won the top amateur prize in the Staffordshire Open and his golfing ability seems to have been passed down the generations. His son Gary is teaching professional at Queslett Park while in 2003 his grandson, Andrew Smith, was completing a golf scholarship at university in Louisiana, USA, having already won the world boys title.

Broadbent's wife Shirley confirms George Best's admiration for him. "We were on holiday in Majorca many years ago and George was staying there, too. He made himself known to us

and made such a fuss. He said he really did think a lot of Peter and said he was so thrilled to meet him."
What others said

Dennis Wilshaw: "Peter was a star, a brilliant dribbler. His ball control was excellent, his transfer of the ball was excellent. He wasn't there as a goalscorer but I am surprised what a lot of goals he did get during his career. He played deep while I played up front."

Roy Swinbourne: "His great assets were his ball control and his bodyswerve. I remember Danny Blanchflower ending up on his backside after Peter had just gone up to him with the ball, shrugged his shoulders and gone past him. He was something else, Peter."

Norman Deeley: "He was my friend all through my career. It was great to play alongside him, he was such a very good player. I rated him better than Johnny Haynes. He could beat a man just by shrugging his shoulders and he was such a good ball player. I remember when we played together for England against Brazil in 1959 we could not believe how the others would not run for the ball. They wanted it to their feet all the time they weren't prepared to run on to it which seemed all wrong to us. Peter never really got the chance he deserved with England."

Ron Flowers: "Peter was one who could really turn it on. He could do his shuffles and his shimmies and they could not get near him. He was well respected by all they opposition. When he was on song he was very, very good – an entertainer."

Bill Slater: "He was one of the few of us who overlapped from that early part of the '50s to the latter part and he was a big influence all through. He had lovely ball control and that sort of hip-wiggle that could send players the wrong way."

Nigel Sims: "Peter was a natural. They talk about 'width' today but Peter knew how to use the the whole of the pitch and bring the wingers into play and how to make space for himself. He would sometimes go out on the wing, in fact he would turn up all over the place."

Bill Shorthouse: "Peter was as good as anybody in his day. He had such a quick brain and reacted to any situation easily. I think the first time I really talked to him was at the airport before we went on the South African tour. He was only a young lad. He celebrated his eighteenth birthday while we were in South Africa. He was only young but you could see he was going to be a good player."

Eddie Stuart: "Peter was born too early. If he'd been playing today he would have been worth tens of millions of pounds. He was the complete inside-forward. His ball control was phenomenal. People may not have appreciated his running off the ball as well. If a player is good at running off the ball and taking up positions it makes the game so simple and Peter could do that."

Bert Williams: "I would put him in the same class as Shackleton, Carter and Mannion – the really great inside-forwards. His ball control was uncanny. Beckham has not got the same skill

111

that Peter had. Johnny Haynes kept him out of the England team and he could use the ball really well but Peter could use the ball AND he could take on three people and beat them."
BERT WILLIAMS
Born: Bilston, January 30, 1920
1953-4 appearances 34

Without a doubt, Williams was one of the finest goalkeepers in football history, yet his career had humble beginnings. In a couple of seasons before the war he played 26 League and Cup games for Walsall before joining Wolves in September, 1945, having served in the RAF. It was not known at the time but he confirmed in later years that Chelsea were very interested in signing him. He had talks with the Londoners before opting to stay in his native West Midlands and go to Molineux.

A member of the 1949 FA Cup-winning side, Williams won his first full cap, as successor to the great Frank Swift, three weeks after the Cup Final in a 3-1 win over France at Colombes Stadium in Paris when Billy Wright scored a rare goal. Williams's international career could hardly have got off to a worse start. He was at fault as France took the lead in the opening minute but redeemed himself later in the game with several good saves. Later that year, he and clubmates Wright and Jesse Pye were in the team unexpectedly beaten 2-0 by the Republic of Ireland at Goodison Park – the first time England had lost to foreign opposition on home soil. However, Williams's display against Italy in the 2-0 win at White Hart Lane on November 30, 1949, was hailed as one of the greatest by an England keeper and earned him the nickname 'The Cat.' Stan Cullis recalled that match in his autobiography, All For The Wolves (Ruper Hart-Davis, 1960). "He made save after save which was right out of the range of any other goalkeeper and I regard this performance as the finest I have ever seen from any goalkeeper in the world."

There was another shock result ahead, though, as Williams was in goal when England were sensationally beaten 1-0 by the USA in the 1950 World Cup finals in Belo Horizonte, Brazil. He eventually lost his England place in 1951 to Birmingham's Gil Merrick but was recalled in December, 1954, to face new world champions West Germany at Wembley. He eventually took his total number of caps to 24 which at the time was just one short of Harry Hibbs's record for an England keeper. Williams is now president of Wolves Former Players' Association. Williams also played in two Wartime and two Victory internationals. The first of those Victory Internationals, against Wales at The Hawthorns, in October, 1945, saw Wolves provide both goalkeepers, with Cyril Sidlow between the sticks for the Welsh.

If one counts the 30 appearances he made in the First Division South in the first season after the War, Williams totalled 450 competitive games for Wolves, a club record for a goalkeeper.

Williams might never have become a goalkeeping legend. "When I was working at Thompson Brothers in Great Bridge, I broke my finger in one of the grinding machines," he recalls. "I went to hospital and they wanted to amputate the finger on my right hand but my dad would not let them. I don't know how it would have affected my keeping but there was goalkeeper who played for Leicester, Ian McGraw, he had to have a finger amputated and he was never as good a player after that."

112

Although he became one of the greatest names in Wolves' history, Williams was an Albion fan as a youngster. His father, Walter, used to take him to watch them in the 1930s. "We used to go on Benny Smith's coaches. I was always an Albion fan as a kid. I would have joined them but an Albion scout at Thompson Brothers said he would not recommend me for a trial. He said I was too small. Many years later I went back to Thompson's and saw this fella and he said: 'What a mistake I made with you. Whatever was I doing?'"

Having played for Bilston Boys, the young Williams was spotted by Walsall and signed by Fellows Park manager Andy Wilson, the former Middlesbrough, Chelsea and Scotland inside-forward. One of Williams's first games was for Walsall reserves against Albion reserves at The Hawthorns. "My dad, who had been a goalkeeper but never got anywhere because he wore glasses, was a big help to me and supported me all my life. I used to wear his cap and he said if Albion get a penalty throw your cap into the back of the net to show them you mean business.

"Well they got a penalty, and so I did as my dad said and tossed my cap into the back of the net and lined up for this penalty. Harry Kinsell, who went on to play in Albion's first team, took the kick and it went past me like a bullet. So much for dad's advice! It was the only goal of the game, as well." Williams could have been excused if he'd discarded the cap there and then for bringing him bad luck. He did just the opposite. "I wore it, when I needed to, all through my career with Wolves and England."

113

Williams served in the RAF during the War and it was while stationed at Ludford Magna in Lincolnshire that he played a number of games for Nottingham Forest. When he was transferred to RAF Wing, he began playing for Chelsea. "Their manager Billy Birrell was very keen to sign me but then Wolves wanted me and Jack Howley, the secretary, came over to Fellows Park and asked me to sign. I told them I had talked to Chelsea but I said I would talk it over with my wife. I caught the bus back to Bilston and I think my wife Evelyn had had an accident or was ill or something and I thought I would not like to be down in London away from her. I got the bus back to Walsall and said I'd sign for Wolves. Jack Howley must have been waiting for me about two and a half hours." Chelsea, at the time, were looking for a replacement for England goalkeeper Vic Woodley.

"I never regretted joining Wolves. Everybody there respected and cared for the club. Not just the manager, trainers and players but people like the secretary Jack Howley, Albert Tye the groundsman. Wolves were very lucky to have people like Jack and the others. We had good players but the spirit which ran all through the club was a big factor in our success."

What others said

Dennis Wilshaw: "Bert was a great keeper. He was very agile and I think he was better than Ted Ditchburn of Tottenham who was also bidding to be Frank Swift's successor in the England team. He was, and still is, my best friend. We used to sleep together – separate beds, of course! He was my room mate if we had to stay anywhere overnight."

Roy Swinbourne: "It was incredible really the way he would take off going one way, like a salmon and then turn in mid air and flick the ball over the other side of the goal. Bert pulled off some incredible saves. He was athletic really. He was also one of the quickest players on our books though big Angus McLean was the quickest of all of us when we got our spikes on and did sprinting. Bert was never far behind, though."

Norman Deeley: "He was a fantastic goalkeeper. He did a lot to help us youngsters. He was a good trainer and helped me a lot along the way."

Ron Flowers: "Bert made the best save I've ever seen. It was England against Spain and Kubala, who was born in Hungary but moved to Spain, fired in this free kick from about 30 yards. The continentals used to use a different ball from us, more like what is used today, and his shot wavered a bit but Bert leapt and caught the ball near the top right hand corner. I have this vision of seeing Bert virtually horizontal with the cross bar and clutching the ball. It was a great save – but that was Bert, a tremendous goalkeeper.

"He was part-time, I think, when I arrived and he used to put me through my paces. We'd go back to the ground about 2 o'clock and he'd have me banging balls at him and afterwards he would give me some exercises to do for about half an hour. He was a PE instructor during the war and knew what he was doing.

114

"Bert was also one of the nicest people you could wish to meet. I remember telling him I was going to buy a car – I wanted to take my mom and dad on holiday – but Bert just said 'Who do you think you are to have a car? Keep your money and look after it. You can use the bus or walk!' I think I still got the car but I never forgot what he said about looking after my money."

Bill Slater: "He was a lovely man. He was very special as a person and as a goalkeeper.

Nigel Sims: "I was his understudy for a long time and two or three times he was thinking about retiring but came back to play on. He was a lovely fella and he was a brilliant goalkeeper. I didn't model myself on him, though, because our styles were very different."

Bill Shorthouse: "He went to the same school as me – St Martin's in Bradley – though he was older and he always said he wished we'd both won caps. It would have been great for St Martin's It's difficult to know what to say about him apart from he was a very good goalkeeper. He has to be one of the best ever."

Eddie Stuart: "Bert was not only fit he was fast. Bert, Jimmy Mullen and I could all do the 100 yards in about 10.2 seconds. He used to say that anything in the six-yard box was his. If the opposition scored from inside the six-yard area it was his fault. Mind you he would rib me sometime saying the back passes I gave him frightened him. I can only repeat what others have said – he was a fantastic goalkeeper and one of the nicest people I've ever met in football."

Stan Cullis: "The finest save, I think, which I ever saw, was made by Bert when Wolves met Newcastle United in a first Division match at St James' Park. Jackie Milburn, the Newcastle forward, was one of the hardest shots in the Football League at that time. Here he drove the ball for the top corner of the net and Williams began to jump for it. On its way, the ball was deflected by an outstretched boot to the other side of the goal. Somehow, Bert changed direction and managed to push the shot away. Milburn – and 50,000 spectators – could not believe their eyes."

ROY PRITCHARD
Born: Dawley, Shropshire, May 9, 1925
1953-4 appearances 27

A Bevin Boy – one of the lads who worked in the coalmines during the Second World War – Pritchard joined the club in 1941, making 23 wartime appearances. As a schoolboy he played outside right and once scored 10 goals in a game but it was at full-back that he made his mark at Molineux.

He made his league debut on October 12, 1946, in a 6-1 win over Huddersfield. He made three more appearances that season and 20 in 1947-8. The following season he was a regular and gained an FA Cup winner's medal after the 3-1 defeat of Leicester City at Wembley. He was virtually first choice from then on and played 27 games in the title-winning season.

However, Pritchard's first team days were numbered – Eddie Stuart made the right-back spot his the following season while Bill Shorthouse was switched to left-back so Billy Wright could play in his England position of centre half. Pritchard eventually moved to Villa but broke his jaw in his first game for them and made only three first team appearances in three seasons before moving to Notts County and then Port Vale.

What others said

Dennis Wilshaw: "Roy was a really hard player. He was a good guy to have in your side. He did have a habit of going over the ball but he did not know he was doing it. At the end of our careers I played for Stoke and he played at Port Vale and in one match he did me. I was carried off and afterwards he came into our dressing room in tears. He said: 'I'm so sorry – I did not know it was you!'"

Roy Swinbourne: "When I came down from Yorkshire the secretary Jack Howley found me digs in Evans Street, Whitmore Reans in Wolverhampton and I was there with Angus McLean and Roy. They were Bevin Boys, they'd worked down the mine. Our landlady was Mrs Nuth who was also in charge of the waitresses at the Victoria Hotel."

"My first night in Wolverhampton Pritch says 'what are you doing tonight?' Bearing in mind I'm 16 and just arrived in Wolverhampton, I had nothing planned. So he said 'you'd better come with me' and he took me to Monmore Green dogs. That was my introduction to Wolverhampton. He was a lovely lad, made me welcome straight away."

Norman Deeley: "Roy liked to get a bit of blood on his boots! He was not a dirty player but he was really hard."

Ron Flowers: "Roy was quick and hard and he was one of the very few blokes that Stanley Matthews had trouble against. Pritch always bottled him up. I don't think Stan ever got the better of him."

Bill Slater: "He was not spectacular but very solid and secure. He could turn quickly and was not a clumsy player They always said he was the one player Stan Matthews did not like to play against."

Nigel Sims: "When I made my debut against Sheffield United (at Bramall Lane on Easter Monday, 1949), my dad was there to watch me and he said to Roy before the game 'Now you look after him' and Roy certainly did. He looked after me in a lot of other ways. I was just a young lad from a mining village and when we were staying at a hotel and having a meal, I wouldn't know which knife to use – that sort of thing – and Roy would say 'Just watch me.' As a player I thought he was marvellous, a grand full-back. A good tackler, read the game well – I thought he was still good enough to get in the Wolves team when they transferred him to Villa."

Bill Shorthouse: "Roy was always out in front when we went training. He could run for ever. He was really fit and used to enjoy a game of tennis, as well. He had a good left foot and was a good club man, like Jack Short."

116

Eddie Stuart: "I always rated Roy as one of the best left-backs Wolves have ever had. I think he felt Stan Cullis should have pushed him for an England place, which he was probably worth, and may have spoken out of turn with Stan once or twice which did not help him."

Bert Williams: "Roy was a born comedian. I recollect when we were going to play Blackpool and Ted Vizard, who was manager then, took him out on to the pitch and said: 'Now, I want to show you what to do when you face Stanley Matthews. Now I'm Matthews, you come in for the ball.' Well Pritch went in ever so gently so Ted said 'You wouldn't go in on Saturday, like that, against Matthews, would you? Show me how you'd really go in.' So Pritch tackles him again with such force that he sent him flying! In fact, he always played well against Matthews. Pritch was a very quick, very underrated player. He had a natural left foot and was a very useful player but he never seemed to take things too seriously."

JACK SHORT
Born: Barnsley, February 18, 1928
1953-4 appearances 26

Made his debut on December 2, 1950, when Wolves beat Albion 3-1, thanks to a Johnny Hancocks hat-trick. Short kept his place for virtually the rest of the season as Wolves reached the FA Cup semi-final only to lose to Newcastle in a replay. The FA Cup brought his only goals for the club on January 14, 1952, when he was played as an emergency centre forward.

He scored twice in a 4-1 replay win over Manchester City at Molineux and then played up front for the next three games but failed to score again.

Short played 26 of Wolves' first 30 games in the 1953-4 season before Eddie Stuart gained favour. He later had successful spells with Stoke and his native Barnsley.
What others said

Dennis Wilshaw: "Jack was a hard player, like Roy Pritchard."

Roy Swinbourne: "Jack was pal of mine. We were in digs together as he came form Yorkshire like me. He was a very fit player and looked after himself. He was very conscious of the fact that he had to keep himself fit to keep in the team."

Norman Deeley: "He was a delicate player, I thought, though he stood no nonsense. He had a lot of speed, as well."

Ron Flowers: "I liked Jack. He came down from Wath Wanderers like me. He'd worked in the mines and he was a typical Barnsley lad. He was a good strong player and a good tackler."

Bill Slater: "As I played right-half in those days I usually played in front of Jack and found him very reliable and a solid."

Nigel Sims: "Jack was a very good player, strong and read the game well, like Roy Pritchard. He was so fit and so dedicated. Jack and I were in digs together in Vincent Street – I think it's long since gone but it was just off Molineux Street and we only had to walk a few yards to the ground."

Bill Shorthouse: "There was nothing spectacular about him. He kept things simple which is what Stan Cullis made him do. Stan said to him once: 'Jack, why don't you play your normal game? You're not Alf Ramsey. You're good in the tackle, just get the ball off them and get it upfield.' Jack did as he was told and he was a good club man, too, easy to get on with."

Eddie Stuart: "I took Jack's place when he was having a poor run of form but there was never any nastiness from him, never any jealousy. He was a true professional. He had all the qualities needed for a good full-back."

Bert Williams: "Jack was not a regular first team player but he had a good run during that 1953-4 season. He was strong and a determined player. He was typical Wolverhampton Wanderers – gave everything to the club. He was another who came from Wath Wanderers and I think Wolves made a mistake when they severed connections with Wath."

RON FLOWERS
Born: Edlington, July 28, 1934
1953-4 appearances 15

He was, at 19, the baby among the nucleus of Wolves' title-winning side. He had made his debut on September 20, 1952, when Wolves lost 5-2 at home to Blackpool. Flowers was named at centre-half that day but switched with left-half Billy Wright soon after the kick-off and marked his debut with a goal, heading home a Johnny Hancocks corner. Two games later he was recalled at right-half in place of 1949 FA Cup final star Billy Crook and for the rest of the season disputed possession of the No 4 shirt with Bill Baxter. However, the right-half position was allocated to Bill Slater when the new season began. Flowers eventually played 15 games in the title-winning season but established himself during the following campaign and played for England under-23s against Italy under-23s at Stamford Bridge on January 19, 1955. He was selected for England's close-season tour and made his full debut against France in Paris. Flowers had a poor game that day in 1955 and had to wait three years for his next cap, replacing colleague Bill Slater, whom he had earlier replaced in the Wolves side. He became an England regular, taking his total of caps to 49. Although he was an attacking wing-half by nature he adopted a defensive role alongside Peter Swan of Sheffield Wednesday in the 4-2-4 formation which brought England so much success in the 1960-1 season.

Flowers played in the 1962 World Cup finals and was in the 1966 squad. He also captained his country on three occasions and his prowess from the penalty spot helped him score 10 goals at international level. He was a member of Wolves' 1957-8 and 1958-9 title-winning sides and the 1960 FA Cup-winning team. Later he played for Northampton and Telford and has run a successful sports outfitters business in Wolverhampton for many years.

118

As a schoolboy, Flowers, the son of a miner, was an inside right and won a place in the Doncaster Schools side where his wing partner was Alan Finney, later to play for Sheffield Wednesday. It was Wednesday who took an early interest in Flowers and he went with his father to look around Hillsborough but decided he would prefer to pursue his football locally and so signed for Doncaster Rovers, who were then managed by the former Manchester City and Ireland inside forward star Peter Doherty. The club also helped him get a job in the British Railways loco sheds at Doncaster. However, it did not work out at Rovers and Flowers was disillusioned by their apparent lack of interest in his career. Once his amateur registration had lapsed he accepted an approach from Wath Wanderers, Wolves' nursery club managed by ex-player Mark Crook.

Flowers was still an inside forward but when Wath were short of their regular left-half for a game, he was switched and he settled down well in his new role despite a painful beginning. He stooped to head a low ball and got a kick in the mouth which robbed him of his two front teeth. After being sent down to Molineux for three trial matches, he finally signed for Wolves as a professional. Among those who accompanied him from Wath was Dick Neal, who did not make the grade at Molineux but carved out a very successful career with Birmingham City.

What others said

Dennis Wilshaw: "Ron came into the side towards the end of the season. There were always a lot of good players around in the reserves. That's why you did not want to get injured you knew that someone would come in and you might not get your place back."

Roy Swinbourne: "When Ron came into the team he was still young but you could see he was going to be good. He was strong and well-built. Our half-back line was the engine room with players like Ron, Bill Slater, Billy Wright and Bill Shorthouse."

Norman Deeley: "He was big and strong but a good footballer as well. He was strong in the tackle a good header of the ball and had great distribution."

Bill Slater: "Ron was like many of the players at Wolves, hard but fair. Yet I can't remember anyone ever getting booked or sent off. I used to be more defensive but Ron liked to come surging through and have a shot at goal. He scored a few, as well. Ron never got flustered and if he could not see a player to pass to he had that ability to bring the ball out of defence."

Nigel Sims: "A great player – he was strong and just seemed to win everything He was a lovely passer of the ball, as well."

Bill Shorthouse: "I sometimes had to get on to him a bit when he first came into the team if he fell asleep and was out of position. But he'd always listen, was always willing to learn and he really came good as a player."

Eddie Stuart: "Ron was a wonderful wing-half. He was a tremendous passer of the ball, had a strong physique and was just an all-round perfectionist. We had four England international half-backs on our books in the late 1950s – and I don't think that had never happened at any club before."

119

Bert Williams: "Ron was one of the strongest tacklers you'd ever see in your life. He was a big man and ideal for Wolves' style of play. He could cross the ball out to the wing and always find his man. He was a nice person to know and I was ever so disappointed he did not get a World Cup medal in 1966. He was a tower of strength in any side."

EDDIE STUART
Born: South Africa, May 12, 1931
1953-4 appearances 12

Having made his debut on April 15, 1952, scoring Wolves' goal in a 4-1 home defeat by Albion, Stuart's career in English football was put on hold the following season when struck down by a mystery illness. He made a full recovery and repaid the club's care and consideration by giving them stalwart service for a decade.

Stuart had the distinction of being the first man to captain Wolves in a floodlit friendly. When the tourists from his native South Africa – Stuart had been signed from Johannesburg Rangers – visited Molineux on September 30, 1953, he was named centre-half and skipper, Bill Shorthouse agreeing to stand down.

Stuart also faced the tourists at Highbury on November 9 that year when a team of Anglo South Africans won 6-1. He was left-half and scored one of the goals. Stuart came into the championship-winning side at right-back for the final 12 matches and was a virtual ever-present for the next five seasons, picking up championship medals in 1957-8 and 1958-9.

When Billy Wright retired in 1959, it was Stuart to whom manager Stanley Cullis handed the captaincy of the club. However, loss of form saw him lose his full-back spot to George Showell and it was Bill Slater who skippered the side in the FA Cup final at Wembley that season.
Stuart eventually joined Stoke in 1962 where he was again given the captaincy as a Stanley-Matthews inspired Potters won the Second Division title. Nearing the veteran stage, Stuart still had plenty of football left in him and had a couple of seasons with both Tranmere and Stockport, winning the Fourth Division title with the latter in 1967.

"I was playing for Johannesburg Rangers when I was 16," Stuart recalls, "and became the youngest player to win a South African Cup winner's medal. Billy Butler, the old Bolton player from pre-War days, was with Rangers and also scouting for English clubs. He recommended me to some English clubs, including Wolves and Villa. It was Wolves I fancied as they had been on tour to South Africa and had made a big impression."

After, giving up his career as a bank clerk, joining Wolves and earning himself a first team debut, Stuart returned to South Africa in the summer of 1952 but became ill on his return. "I picked up an infection somewhere. I always believe it was in Egypt where we stopped off during the flight. It was diagnosed as some tropical virus and it baffled all the medical brains and top specialists." Stuart was in the Queen Victoria Nursing Institute in Wolverhampton – always known locally as the QVNI – and so serious was his condition that Wolves flew in his mother from South Africa. "She stayed six weeks, sometimes sleeping at the hospital. At one stage doctors said I might have only two hours to live but I recovered. Throughout it all, Wolves footed the bill."

120

Stuart never played for South Africa but he nearly played for Scotland. He impressed for Wolves in a friendly against Celtic in 1959 and was named in a Scottish squad of 15. "My grandfather on my father's side was from Inverness and it was thought that would qualify me. Then it was ruled that it was not a good enough qualification – your father or mother needed to be Scottish. It would have been different today – now they go back five generations!"

Stuart was very proud to have been handed the Wolves captaincy by Stan Cullis in succession to Billy Wright and still has among his treasured possessions a cutting of an article by Cullis on the qualities needed by a skipper. In it Cullis says: "Eddie Stuart has all the qualities I admire in a club captain. I like captains who are thinkers and men of decision." Says Stuart: "When I re-read that I still get emotional. It means such a lot to think Stan thought so much of me."

The honour of the captaincy turned sour for Stuart, however. "In 1960 there were the Sharpeville shootings in South Africa when police opened fire and killed about 70 Africans. It had repercussions throughout he world. I started getting vile letters and phone calls. I should have put it down to cranks but I let it upset me. I even got booed when I led out the team. In the end it affected my play and I had to ask Cullis to rest me."

The sequel was that George Showell came in at right-back and Bill Slater took over the

captaincy as Wolves completed the journey to an FA Cup final – a journey begun under Stuart's leadership. Stuart was was twelfth man for the final when Blackburn were beaten 3-0. "I received a winner's medal but it was not the same as playing," says Stuart, who was boosted by letters from fans when word of his hate mail got out.
What others said

Dennis Wilshaw: "While Jack Short was a hard player and Roy Pritchard even harder, I always thought Eddie was a more classy type of full-back. He was tough, too, but there was a lot of football ability about him."

Roy Swinbourne: "Eddie was big and strong and fast. He was a bit hard too – and you've got to have those kind of players in your team."

Norman Deeley: "He was a really hard player, like Roy Pritchard."

Ron Flowers: "He was another defensive strong man. He was a handsome fella, very strong and commanding."

Bill Slater: "Eddie was like the other full-backs – solid and secure."

Bert Williams: "I think Eddie was one of the best full-backs we ever had. I liked playing behind him. He was strong, he was fast, he was a good player. I told Stan Cullis once that when I played for England they used to let me throw the ball to the full-back, Stan wasn't having any of that at first but Eddie and I persuaded him to let us do it. So first time I tried it, the ball did not get to Eddie quickly enough, the opposition bloke picked it up and fired it into the back of the net. Oh, my God! It's the first time I've known Stan speechless – for a while, at least. Needless to say, he never let us try it again. He preferred the long ball, though it was never aimless long balls up the field. They were accurately placed."

121

NIGEL SIMS
Born: Coton-in-Elms, August 9, 1931
1953-4 appearances 8

In a long spell at Molineux – he joined the club in 1948 – Sims made 39 League and Cup appearances but had to be content to be Bert Williams's understudy. He made eight appearances during the title-winning campaign, having made his debut on April 18, 1949 in a 1-1 draw at Sheffield United. He played in 13 league games in 1952-3 but it was clear Williams was still first choice.

His games for Wolves in 1953-4 obviously caught the eye of FA officialdom because he was chosen to play in a new eve-of-Cup Final game – Old England against Young England (technically it was over-30s v under-30s) at Highbury on Friday, April 30. Sims was in the youngsters team and opposed by a side who included Stanley Matthews, Wilf Mannion, Tommy Lawton and Len Shackleton. The old 'uns won 2-1. Sims joined Villa in March 1956, winning an FA Cup medal at Wembley when his new side beat Manchester United 2-1. Sims was a fine keeper and rated by many experts as unlucky never to be capped by England, though he was twice selected for the Football League.

In many ways Sims believes he was lucky to get a chance to join Wolves. "I used to play for my local team at Coton-in-Elms and then Stapenhill, near Burton. The Wolves scout for that area was Charlie Wheeler and he got me a trial for Wolves. We lost nine-nil – the team I was in were mostly youngsters and we were up against some experienced players. They murdered us. Then I got another trial in the A team and we lost 4-0. So I thought: 'That's the end of that.'

"Then out of the blue I was asked to play for the colts team. I think they'd got a lot of goalkeepers injured and it was one of the trainers, Jack Nelson, who remembered me so they sent for me. I must have done all right because Cullis asked me if I wanted to sign. Did I want to sign? It was like winning the lottery! But it was just fate. I was in the right place at the right time. I just went on from there, eventually got into the reserves and then became Bert's deputy. Once or twice Bert talked about retiring but then he'd decide to play on so eventually I moved to Villa."

What others said

Roy Swinbourne: "Nigel was a good goalkeeper. He should have won a cap. We had three international class goalkeepers at that time. As well as Bert and Nigel we also had Noel Dwyer who went on to play for Ireland but could only get into our A team in those days."

Norman Deeley: "Nigel was a great friend of mine and a very good goalkeeper. He was unlucky to be playing at the same time as Bert Williams but they knew they could always call on him and he would not let the team down, like all the reserves in those days."

Ron Flowers: "He used to say to me: 'Don't come anywhere in the six-yard box or you'll get your head knocked in – and don't blame me.' What he meant was the six-yard area was his territory and he'd look after any ball that dropped in there. He was that confident. He was a big fella but very agile and he ought to have played for England."

Bill Shorthouse: "We had to encourage him and say 'Come on, you've got the ability.' Sometimes he did not seem to have the confidence but once he overcame that he became a good keeper. He worked hard and deserved his success."

Eddie Stuart: "I though he was almost as good as Bert Williams. If you gave Bert a rating of 100 then Nigel was 98, He was that good and used to dominate the six-yard box."

Bert Williams: "Nigel was very agile for a big man. You knew you could bring him into the side and he would not let you down. When he went to Villa he proved to people how good he was."

RON STOCKIN
Born Birmingham, June 27, 1931
1953-4 appearances 6

A former Walsall inside forward, at one time on Albion's books, Stockin seemed to have made the inside right spot his own when he played in an unchanged Wolves forward line for the final 13 games of the 1952-3 season. However, after three games of the 1953-4 campaign he lost his place to Peter Broadbent although he was three times called in to deputise – for Wilshaw (twice) and Broadbent. He later played for Cardiff and Grimsby. When Wolves beat the Welsh side 9-1 in September, 1955, to equal the highest away win in England's top flight, it was Stockin who hit the home side's lone reply.

Ron Flowers: "He was similar to Bill Baxter in some ways. His style was not best suited to Wolves but he did very well once he went to Cardiff."

Bill Shorthouse: "He was like so many of the reserve players. You knew you could rely on him. We had a lot like that. They never asked for a transfer It was great to have players like that."

Bert Williams: "Ron was not as clever as Peter Broadbent. He was not a forceful player but he was still a very useful one."

NORMAN DEELEY
Born: Wednesbury, November 30, 1933
1953-4 appearances 6

The diminutive Deeley hardly had the physique for a half-back but that was where he began his Wolves career. A former England schoolboy international he had made his debut at right-half against Arsenal on August 25, 1951, and still remembers how the Gunners legendary skipper Joe Mercer wished him good luck before the kick-off.

In the title-winning season, Deeley was called on five times at half-back and once at inside-forward but when he switched to the wing he really made his name. He got his chance in 1957 when Harry Hooper fell out of favour and in three seasons Deeley won two championship medals and an FA Cup winner's medal, scoring twice against Blackburn Rovers in the 1960 final at Wembley. The year before, he had won two full caps on England's South American tour, making his debut against world champions Brazil in Rio.

Deeley left Wolves for Leyton Orient and in 1962 helped the Londoners win promotion to the First Division for the first time in their history.

"I was not available that much during 1953-4, I was doing my national service in the Army," recalls Deeley. I was in the South East Staffs Regiment, did my basic training in Northern Ireland and was later stationed in Germany and at Lichfield.

"I got just the one England schoolboy cap, against Wales at Coventry, but there were quite a few clubs interested in signing me – Tottenham Newcastle, Wolves, Albion Walsall and the Villa. My dad, Harry Deeley, was an Albion fan. He would have liked me to sign for them or the Villa but I wanted Wolves. I was always a Wolves fan. Ted Vizard saw me first but it was Stan Cullis who eventually signed me. He'd just taken over as manager.

"I'll always remember that first game against Arsenal. Joe Mercer came and wished me all the best during the morning because I was at the ground blowing up the balls. That was one of my jobs on the ground staff then, blowing up the caseballs. When I'd done that I went home – on the bus – for something to eat. Then I had to get the bus back to Molineux. I remember, standing in a long queue at the Bull Stake in Darlaston. When I was on the bus I just listened to the fans talking about the match. They did not know the bloke sitting behind them was playing that day. All the players wished me all the best and Johnny Hancocks just said: ' Make sure your first pass, whether it's 12 yards or 20 yards, goes to feet.' That was the only advice he gave me."

What others said

Roy Swinbourne: "He was a lovely ball player. He had a lot of skill but he had to because of his size."

Ron Flowers: "I think he was struggling a bit in 1953-4, because of his height and playing at half-back. He was not really the sort of half-back Stan Cullis wanted. He liked them big and strong but he played him on the wing in the reserves and that really was the making of him."

Nigel Sims: "Norman was very mobile as a wing-half and a good passer of the ball who read the game well. I was not surprised he did well when he switched to the wing."

Bill Shorthouse: "I remember Jack Davies, one of our trainers, telling me we've got a little lad here who's going to be a good player – and he was right. Norman was another of the good back-up players in 1953-4. He was perhaps a bit too small for a half-back but he did very well on the wing. We used to pull his leg a bit but he had a great sense of humour and he was one of those who was good for morale."

Eddie Stuart: "Norman was a very clever player. He did not have fantastic pace but he was good on the ball. He may not have been big enough to be a half-back but his distribution was certainly good enough."

Bert Williams: "Norman was bit too small for a wing-half when it came to dealing with high balls. Stan Cullis used to tell me to take him away, give him some exercises and help him grow. He was quick and skilful – clubs would cry out for a player like him today."

BILL BAXTER
Born: Methil, September 21, 1924
1953-4 appearances 5

Baxter made five appearances at half-back in the title-winning season . That took his total league appearances to 43, having made his debut against Everton in December, 1948. He moved to Villa Park in November, 1953, in time to play for Villa in their 2-1 win over his old club at Molineux on Christmas Eve, when he was made captain for the occasion. Baxter had joined Wolves In August, 1939, after leaving school. He served in the Navy during the War and made guest appearances for Leicester, Mansfield and Notts County. His best Wolves season was 1951-2 when he played in 23 League and Cup matches, scoring his only goal for the club in the 3-3 draw with Villa at Villa Park on Christmas Day, 1951. He could have been forgiven for thinking he had established himself in the first team but along came young Ron Flowers and amateur international Bill Slater to halt his progress. While his first-team games at Molineux were limited, he was a stalwart of the reserve team who won the Central League for three successive seasons, starting in 1950-1. He played 108 league and cup games for Villa.

Ron Flowers: "Bill had to be a good player to get into the Wolves side of those days and he was in the team when I first came down to Molineux. He liked to play a passing game, that's what suited him best, but I don't think it was what Stan Cullis wanted."

Nigel Sims: "He was not a great tackler, he was not built that way. He was a footballer who could read the game well and used the ball well."

Bill Shorthouse: "He was one of our best reserves. A good Wolves man. He could come into the team and would not let you down."

Eddie Stuart: "Bill might not have been in the Ron Flowers or Bill Slater bracket but he was a dedicated player you could always rely on."

Bert Williams: "Bill was a joker. He would buy stink bombs and he had a big pair of glasses with a clown's nose and if any photos were being taken he'd put them on and stand right next to a director. He was a character. Once he was injured and told Stan Cullis he could not play so Stan told him to change his style of running. I think we were up at Newcastle and he's crossing the road and walks with an exaggerated limp. Arthur Oakley said; 'What's the matter with you?' and Bill says: 'Mr Cullis has told me to change my style of running and I'm practising.' With any other club, he would have been in the first team. He was a genuinely good footballer but can you imagine the competition there was at that time with the half-backs we had?"

125

LESLIE SMITH
Born: Halesowen, December 24, 1927
1953-4 appearances 4 Goals 1

Being a winger at Molineux in the days of Hancocks and Mullen did not make first team chances easy to come by yet the talented Smith still made 98 league and cup appearances during his time with the club. In 1952-3 he had kept Hancocks out of the side for 15 successive games but his role in 1953-4 was as a reserve. Yet Smith was not done with and kept Mullen out of the side the following season when he made 38 league and cup appearances and was also on the left wing in the epic floodlit wins over Spartak Moscow and Hungarian maestros Honved.

Eventually he moved to Villa in February 1956 and made 129 first team appearances for them, including the 2-1 1957 FA Cup final win over Manchester United at Wembley.

What others said

Roy Swinbourne: "He was a great standby for either wing. We had so many good players. They talk now about having a squad but we had a squad in those days. We won the Central League three years in a row."

Nigel Sims: "Les was a good player as he showed when he came to Villa with me. He could dribble, he was quick and he could cross the ball well."

Bill Shorthouse: "A good lad. He was very nippy. He had some real pace . He kept Jimmy Mullen out for a time and people forget he played against Spartak and Honved."

Eddie Stuart: "At one time Les was first choice left-winger and you had to be good to keep Jimmy Mullen out. He was a good two-footed player. He could cut inside from the left-wing and crack a shot with his right foot."

Bert Williams: "He could play on the right or left wing and never complained at being an understudy for Johnny Hancocks and Jimmy Mullen. He would have been a certain choice at another club but our reserves never seemed to ask for a transfer. They were such good clubmen. Les had a lot of skill and proved what he could do when he went to Villa."

BILL GUTTRIDGE
Born: Darlaston, March 4, 1931
1953-4 appearances 2

A tough-tackling full-back, Guttridge was twice called upon in the title-winning season taking his total first-team appearances for the club to six. He came to Molineux as an amateur in 1947, turning professional the following year. He was one of the faithful second strings at Molineux who made the Central League side such a formidable one during the 1950s.

He joined Walsall in November, 1954, and made some 200 appearances for the Saddlers.

What others said

Norman Deeley: "He was a hard man. I played a lot with him in the reserves and he was a good man to have in your defence."

Nigel Sims: "Yes, Bill was a hard man. He would always do a steady job and he was one of the reasons why the reserves won the Central League three years in a row"

Bill Shorthouse: "Bill was another of those players you could bring in and you'd know he would do the job for us."

Eddie Stuart: "When he tackled you, you knew you had been tackled."

Bert Williams: "He always says how lucky he was to play at Wolves and know all those star players. He's very humble about it. He was a strong footballer and you knew you could rely on him. He was very unlucky that there were so many good players at the club."

EDDIE CLAMP

Born: Coalville, September 14, 1934
1953-4 appearances 2

A former England schoolboy international, Clamp would became a stalwart member of the side who won the championship in 1957-8 and 1958-9 and then the FA Cup in 1960. However, he was called upon only twice in 1953-4, one of the games out of position at inside-left.

Often used as a left-back in his early Molineux days, Clamp had not had the best of summers in 1953. He had gone with the Wolves youth squad to Switzerland where they played in a one-day tournament and also had a couple of full-length matches. The day after the second of those matches he was taken ill. He was taken immediately to hospital in Schaffhausen where it was found he had appendicitis. He had to undergo surgery and stayed in Switzerland for a couple of weeks to recover. While the rest of the party, headed by manager Stan Cullis and chairman James Baker, flew home to London, trainer Joe Gardiner remained behind for a few days to keep Clamp company.

Clamp won four England caps, forming an all-Wolves half-back line with Bill Slater and Billy Wright and playing in the 1958 World Cup finals in Sweden. He is remembered as a hard player but he also possessed a lot of skill. He was sold to Arsenal in November, 1961, but soon returned to the Midlands, joining Stoke's array of ageing stars before ending his career at Peterborough. He made 32 appearances for the Potters when they won the Second Division title in 1962-3.

What others said

Norman Deeley: "He was another of the club's hard players but he had a lot more skill than people gave him credit for."

Bill Slater: "He was his own man. There was no one quite like Eddie. He'd give us heart failure sometimes, turning up in the dressing room with only a few minutes to go to kick-off."

Ron Flowers: "He was a better player than people used to think. He had a reputation for being a hard man but there was a lot more to his game. He was a character on the field as well as off, though. I remember one match when it was very foggy, you could see only about 20 yards. The ball went out for a throw-in and because the referee was nowhere near Eddie booted the ball back into the crowd and then, when the ref came up, picked it up for the throw as if it had only just been thrown back from the crowd. We were only one-nil up and he wanted to waste a bit of time."

Nigel Sims: "I thought Eddie was a skilful player. I was at Peterborough when Gordon Clark was the manager and he signed Eddie in the mid 1960s. He was still a good player then, though some times he'd turn up for a game with his boots still dirty from the last one – but that was Eddie!"

Bill Shorthouse: "A lot of people saw him as a hard man man but he had a lot of ability. We

127

often had to tell him to stop fooling about, though. He'd take the ball to the corner flag and put his foot on it, things like that. His mum was a nice lady. She used to do the laundry at Molineux."

Eddie Stuart: "Eddie always had this thing where he liked to push the ball between an opponent's legs. He would always get upset if had not done it at least once in a match. He did not feel he was having a good game unless he'd done that. He was a character. When we were playing in Lancashire, we'd always have a light lunch at the Queen's Hotel in Manchester about noon. Eddie would always finish first and then dash out of the hotel and disappear for about an hour. We decided to follow him one day and we found he was going to a joke and novelty shop. There he would buy stink bombs, funny hats, cushions that made a noise and all sorts of things so he could pull off a stunt at someone else's expense. He liked cars, too. He bought a Jag just before he joined Arsenal. One day he came back from training to the car park at Highbury and found that the bonnet had been pinched. It was never recovered but for weeks Eddie would be riding around London in a spanking new Jag with a blanket over the bonnet."

Bert Williams: "However Eddie tackled, it was never with hatred. He was a good man to have in your side."

LEN GIBBONS

Born: Ellesmere Port, November 22, 1930
1953-4 appearances 1

He made his league debut against Portsmouth in September, 1951 and played in 26 league and cup games that season. He lost his place to Roy Pritchard the following season. Sadly, injury brought an early end to his career.

What others said

Nigel Sims: "I had good reason to remember Len. We were playing for Wolves third team at Oswestry. I was in the Army but Stan Cullis had told me I was going on Wolves' tour of South Africa and had got me special leave but in this game I dived, Len had his foot out, I fell on it and he broke his leg. Afterwards Cullis said something to me, I said something back and he said 'Right, you're not going to South Africa.' Len was very upset about it all."

Eddie Stuart: "He was yet another of our reserves who would have earned a first-team place if he'd been with another First Division club"

RAY CHATHAM

Born: Wolverhampton, July 20, 1924
1953-4 appearances 1

Signed professional for Wolves in 1945 and looked a highly promising centre half, playing in 86 league and cup games for club. He made his debut in the first season after World War II as deputy at centre-forward for Dennis Westcott. It was as a striker that he had made his mark at

Backroom maestro - Wolves secretary Jack Howley addresses guests at the tribute dinner held in his honour

Historic occasion - Eddie Stuart leads out Wolves against South Africa, the first floodlit match staged at Molineux

Bilston boys - Bert Williams (left) and Bill Shorthouse, who both went to St Martin's School, Bradley get to grips with the Football League trophy

The men behind the scenes - Stan Cullis talks to his backroom staff

The England squad for the historic match against Hungary at Wembley, November 1953. They included Wolves' Billy Wright (seated, centre), who was skipper and Bert Williams (back row, second left), who was among the substitutes

Joe Gardiner, as the Wolves' trainer, was highly regarded by all the players at Molineux

Joe looks on as manager Stan Cullis talks to the players during a break in training

Celebration time - Wolves skipper Billy Wright shows the Football League Championship trophy to the Mayor of Wolverhampton during the civic banquet at the town's Civic Hall. Johnny Hancocks and Stan Cullis look on

Capable reserve - Bill Baxter

Capable reserve - Ron Stockin

Capable reserve - Bill Guttridge

Capable reserve - Les Smith

Capable reserve - Nigel Sims

Capable reserve - Norman Deeley

SEASON 1953-4

How the other clubs heralded Wolves' visit

Arsenal

Aston Villa

Blackpool

Bolton

Burnley

Cardiff

Charlton

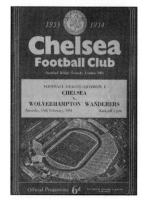

Chelsea

Huddersfield

Liverpool

Manchester City

Manchester United

Middlesbrough

Newcastle

Portsmouth

Preston

Sheffield United

Sheffield Wednesday

Sunderland

West Bromwich Albion

Wolves v South Africa

Wolves' Christmas Eve special

The team who figured in the final run-in to the season. Back (left to right) Joe Gardiner (trainer), Bill Slater, Bill Shorthouse, Bert Williams, Ron Flowers, Eddie Stuart; Front: Johnny Hancocks, Peter Broadbent, Roy Swinbourne, Billy Wright, Dennis Wilshaw, Jimmy Mullen

Fans invade the Molineux pitch after the final match of the season

Molineux and was the club's top scorer with 14 goals in the Football League South in the 1945-6 season, the last before normal league football resumed. His best seasons were 1950-1 and 1951-2 but he played in only one match during the title-winning season before joining Notts County for whom he had several good seasons.

What others said

Bill Shorthouse: "He was a good back-up player who could play anywhere in the half-back line. He would have walked into the first team at another club."

Eddie Stuart: "Ray was a very capable player."

Bert Williams: "Ray was a part-timer and Stan Cullis did not like part-time players. It was difficult for him with so many good half-backs at the club but you knew you could bring him in and he would not let the team down."

STANLEY CULLIS
Born: Ellesmere Port, October 25, 1916
Manager

Cullis is that football rarity – a man who could have the over-used word 'great' applied to both his playing career and his managerial career. His playing days were limited because of the Second World War, which brought League football to an end in 1939 at a time when centre-half Cullis was approaching his peak and the Wolves side he captained were the most talked-about club in the land. In the two seasons before the outbreak of hostilities Wolves had finished runners-up in the First Division and in 1939 were also beaten FA Cup finalists when unfancied Portsmouth caused a major Wembley upset by winning 4-1. Only Arsenal and Huddersfield had before had the twin disappointment of being runners-up in both competitions in the same season.

129

Cullis had been capped 12 times for England before the war and skippered his country against Romania in Bucharest on May 24, 1939, in what proved to be England's last full international for seven years. He went on to appear in 20 Wartime Internationals, ten of them as captain, forming a famous half-back line with Everton duo Cliff Britton and Joe Mercer.

Cullis scored only one goal for Wolves and it came long after his playing days were officially over, on the club's tour of South Africa in 1951, when he came out of retirement to play in the team who beat South Western Districts 11-0 at Mossel Bay.

After the war, Cullis had been tempted to move to Hull City as manager. The Yorkshire club had just moved from their Anlaby Road ground to the new Boothferry Park and were highly ambitious. Wolves directors, when they heard of the offer, made it clear they did not wish to lose him and persuaded him to play one more season on the understanding he would then be made assistant manager to Ted Vizard. It proved an epic last season, extended into June because of an horrendously severe winter which caused game after game to be postponed. The last day for Wolves arrived with them needing only a win over Liverpool at Molineux to be crowned champions. To add to the drama Cullis made it public before the match that it would be his last. Liverpool won 2-1 and, when Stoke failed to win their final game, eventually took the title. His temptation to join Hull was not the first time Cullis had been on the brink of leaving Molineux. He had joined the club in 1934 and at the end of his first season had the timerity to ask manager Major Frank Buckley for a rise of ten shillings (50p) on his weekly wage of £2 10s (£2.50). At first the manager and his board said no but when Cullis, showing the strength of will for which he became noted, made it clear he was willing to turn his back on Wolves and return home to Ellesmere Port, he got his way.

There is also a little known claim that Cullis might also have left Wolves in 1952. He had steered the club to an FA Cup final triumph over Leicester in 1949, after taking over from the sacked Vizard in 1948 – at 32, he remains the youngest ever Cup-winning manager – and then saw Wolves finish second in the First Division in 1949-50,. However, there followed two lean seasons with Wolves ending up 14th and then 16th. According to that doyen of Football writers Geoffrey Green in his book Soccer in the Fifties (Ian Allen) the Wolves board were on the point of dismissing Cullis. "Cullis was saved by the energetic advocacy of one of his directors, the bluff burly Jim Marshall, a powerful figure on the board, who owned a majority of shares in the club," wrote Green.

Green may well have had it right though in the the same book the one-time football correspondent of The Times wrote of Cullis: "That the Wolves style, based on his theories, did not please the press riled him to his very depths. 'All you bloody fellows from London can only see Spurs and Arsenal or Manchester United,' he would growl, giving us the thick edge of his Midland accent." Now Green, I venture to suggest, had it wrong on two counts there. Cullis may well have been angry that the London press did not give his team the credit he thought they deserved, but those who knew him well will confirm that he never swore and neither did he have a Midland accent – he retained that distinctive Ellesmere Port twang.

Assuming Green's story about Cullis being close to the sack in 1952 was correct, then the club's decision to stick by the boss was more than vindicated. As well as their title triumph in 1953-4, Wolves were also champions in 1957-8 and 1958-9 and won the FA Cup again in 1960, having just missed out on doing the Double. Cullis was an advocate of keeping the game simple and believed in getting the ball into the opposition penalty area as quickly as possible. His theory, perhaps not so firmly enforced in the early years as manager, was put rigidly into practice in the latter part of the 1950s. His ideas were reinforced by Commander Charles Reep from RAF Bridgnorth. Reep was doing fifty years ago what is commonplace now – keeping records during a game of passes and how many it took to create a goal. His findings showed that most goals came from moves of three or four passes and Cullis made sure his team realised that. Cullis was also a firm believer in having players supremely fit and that philosophy paid dividends in the number of times Wolves won or saved games late on because they had greater stamina than their opponents. His motto was on the dressing room wall for all to see: There is no substitute for hard work.

Tony Pawson, in his book The Football Managers (Eyre Methuen, 1973) endorses the famed Cullis work ethic for his Wolves players. "Cullis drove them on with relentless impassioned determination," wrote Pawson. "To be near him at a match was to experience total involvement, the torrent of words a meaningless chant to ease his tensions. Sitting in front of him once as Wolves overwhelmed Luton in an away Cup-tie was a painful experience as he kicked and tackled his way through the ninety minutes, living every second with his players."

Writing in his autobiography, One Hundred Caps and All That (Robert Hale Ltd, 1962), Billy Wright recalled what Cullis had said to his players in a meeting soon after his elevation to manager. "I want us to see eye to eye right from the start. I want, and I am going to get, one hundred per cent effort from you all, both on and off the field. If I get this support you can take it from me I will be one hundred per cent behind you. Nothing else is going to be enough." Wright added that the way Cullis made his point left all in no doubt that Cullis meant exactly what he said. From that moment on, continued Wright, Wolves' manager never forgave a player who didn't always try his hardest. "I do not think I am breaking any confidences when I say that this is the reason why more than a few players have since left Molineux. Cullis, on the other hand, always kept his part of the bargain. Playing, training and living conditions at Molineux have never been less than the best. Everyone's welfare, whether a player is a first-team star or a Worcestershire Combination hopeful, is zealously looked after."

It was almost inevitable that lean years would follow those of plenty and as the supply of quality home-grown players began to wear thin, Cullis resorted to buying established players to rebuild Wolves' fortunes. He had limited success and some home-grown youngsters like Fred Davies, Bobby Thomson, David Woodfield, Terry Wharton, Alan Hinton and Peter Knowles began to come through. However, a nightmare start to the 1964-5 season, when Wolves lost six and drew one of their first seven games, finally saw the unthinkable happen. Cullis was sacked.

131

He had a spell as manager of Birmingham City, though with no great success and perhaps his verdict on that spell at St Andrew's best sums up Cullis. My old Express & Star colleague David Harrison, a distinguished sports writer with the News of the World for some years now, once asked Cullis about his average success as Blues boss and Cullis replied: "In this world, you only have one life – and I gave mine to Wolves."

Fittingly, that Cullis quotation is on the plinth of a magnificent 9ft bronze statue of the manager, by sculptor James Butler, which was unveiled outside the Stan Culls Stand at Molinuex on Friday, August 8, 2003. It was donated by Wolves' president, chairman and owner Sir Jack Hayward, who, over the years, has ensured the name of Cullis will live on at the ground where he played. Before unveiling the statue, with the help of Cullis's son Andrew and daughter Susan, Sir Jack described Cullis as "the greatest manager Wolves have ever had in their illustrious history."

No one would argue with that verdict.

What others said

Dennis Wilshaw: "I had deep respect for Stan even though we did not always get on. As I look back I realise I must have been very hard to manage.
"Stan was a long ball advocate but not as a player. I played with Stan a couple of times and he

used to hit short balls to Tom Galley or Joe Gardiner or play square balls. If we did that when he was manager then we were in trouble. I remember, in one match, Tom Galley had received the umpteenth square ball from Stan and he told him 'Stan, kick the next effing ball up field, I'm effing tired.'"

Roy Swinbourne: "He was hard but he was fair – or tried to be fair, because it's very difficult when you've got 48 pros on the books and we did have something like 48 in those days.
"He could get so worked up during a match he would be wet through with sweat and he could lose his rag a bit at half-time. He could say what he liked to us but nobody else could say anything. If a director came in he'd soon make it clear he could not interfere. Nobody else could criticise us – but he could! He would always stand up for us if anybody else tried to say anything.
"When I'd scored those three hat-tricks on three successive Saturdays in 1955, and I was having a shower after training and he said 'How old are you now?' and I said 'Twenty-six' and he said 'I shall have to be looking for a replacement.' I was twenty-six in the August and this was only October – it was his way of keeping my feet on the ground. As it turned out, he did have to replace me because that was the season I got injured."

"We played the long ball game but I liked to play the ball a bit, I'd started as an outside right. But Stan said 'You're big, you're strong . . . if I wanted someone to play ball I'd have Ronnie Allen.' So that soon told me."

132

Norman Deeley: "I would not take anything away from Stan but I feel he had a team already made for him when he became manager. He inherited a good lot of players from Ted Vizard but he did make some good signings – like Peter Broadbent, Malcolm Finlayson and Bill Slater. But he made a few bad ones later.

"There's no doubt he was a great motivator and a bad loser, though we all are aren't we? I remember the 1960 FA Cup semi-fnal against Villa at the Albion. I'd had a groin injury and told him I was not fully fit but thought that I could play. So he brings in Gerry Mannion on the right wing, drops Des Horne and puts me on the left-wing to face Stan Lynn, who was a really hard man. I suppose that was his way of motivating me – and I did get the only goal of the game.

"He really lived every game from the touchline. In the 1960 Cup Final at Wembley he had to change his shirt in the dressing room at half-time because he'd got so worked up and had sweated so much."

Ron Flowers: "Stan knew what he wanted from his players and what he wanted them to do. He simplified things. He did not go in for jargon, it was all straight-forward. If you did what he wanted then you could not have a better friend but he would not tolerate people ignoring his instructions. I'm not saying he would not listen to your views, because he would and if he thought what you were saying made sense he would put it into practice.

"He could rant a bit but he would only have a real go at you if he thought you weren't giving 100 per cent effort. If you were just having one of those days, he could forgive you that. He would not allow defenders to play about with the ball and if you played it across the field he would go daft. He reckoned the more you passed the ball the greater the chance of a move breaking down. The more you passed the more time the opposition defenders had to get back and consolidate. I watch games now and the majority of goals still come from only three or four passes or fewer. We did not play so much a long ball game, we played direct football. We could change the direction of attack with long passes. If Jimmy Mullen had it on the left and was surrounded he would swing the ball over to the right and Johnny Hancocks would be in the clear. Or we could play a long ball up to Roy Swinbourne and know he could hold the ball up, which is only what centre-forwards do today."

Bill Slater: "Stan portrayed this image of being a hard and demanding manager and the players responded well to that. He would not have any dirty players and I cannot remember a single player being booked or sent off. He did not like us swearing around the club. He also did not like players to fall all over each other if we scored a goal. A handshake was enough. He had this idea that scoring goals was what we were supposed to be doing and, if you think about it, he was right. Underneath, however, I think he really felt for the players and had their interests at heart. I remember once when my wife was in hospital over Christmas, he invited me to his home for Christmas Day lunch. Not many managers would have done that."

Nigel Sims: "I did not get on with him that well. He sold me to Villa eventually. I also thought it was him who ended Billy Wright's career in 1959. He told Billy he would be playing in the reserves in the new season and that George Showell was going to be given his chance. Nothing against George, who was a good player, but Billy was still a star, still captain of England and I don't know how Cullis could do that to him. I know Billy gave other reasons at the time but I believe that was the real reason he decided to retire."

133

Bill Shorthouse: "I got on well with Stan. I thought he was very fair. He'd let you know what he wanted without any doubt but he never swore. The worst words he ever used were 'flippin' and 'floppin'. He was the one who recommended me for the first team. I was in the reserves and one day we'd won and the first team had lost and Stan – he was assistant manager then – thought they should have won. He told me he would talk to the manager (Ted Vizard) and on the Monday morning Stan told me 'You're training down with the first team from now on.' Stan also recommended me to the FA once I'd retired and become a coach. As well as helping the young players I also got called to help the full England squad before the World Cup in 1966. I was only on the fringes but I remember giving Gordon Banks some help. So I had a lot to thank Stan for. He would also listen if we'd got any problems. We had club houses in those days and if we told Stan something needed doing like painting or some repairs, he'd say 'Leave it to me' and there would be a man round the next day. He looked after his players."

Eddie Stuart: "He was a hard man but he certainly got results. I think the secret of his success, both as a player and manager, was that he was a perfectionist. He had drive and enthusiasm although when he took over the managerial reins he inherited a good team backed by a fine scouting staff. He was the master of Molineux and his word was virtually law. However, he had a very caring side. He ensured the club looked after me when I was ill and I shall never forget seeing him after the win over Spartak in 1954, I was in tears at the end of the game as we walked off and I saw Stan come on to give Billy Wright a hug and Stan was in tears as well."

Bert Williams: "Stan was in the same mould as the players, he gave 100 per cent for Wolves and would stand up for his players. If one of our players had been badly fouled I've known him wait after the game for the one who'd done it so he could tell him what he thought.

"Stan would not allow himself to get too close to the players but he always backed us. He believed in the same methods as Major Buckley and had the same strictness. He used to get so excited when he was first manager and so they stopped him sitting in the directors' box. Then he used to watch from a cover near the players' tunnel. It had a tin roof and I think he hit his head on the roof one day, jumping up and down. Then he tried watching from the boot-room which had a window looking out over the pitch but one day he kicked the window in. He was never still when he was watching a game.

"I got injured once in a game against Middlesbrough and was being treated by the first aid men with Stan there as well behind the goal. Then Wilf Mannion broke through and beat Sammy Smyth who'd gone in goal so Stan raced on to the pitch and tried to stop the ball going in. He didn't, but that was typical Stan to do something like that."

JOE GARDINER

134

Born: Bearpark, Durham, August 23, 1916
Trainer

The image of a 1950s trainer tends to conjure up a man with a cloth cap, dashing on to the field with a bucket of water and sponge to revive injured players. Gardiner was much more than that. As well as keeping the players fit and tending to injuries during a game, he was Cullis's right-hand man. His was often the calming influence on the Cullis fanaticism. Players knew he was a man to whom they could turn for help and advice.

Gardiner had been a fine player in his day. Signed by Major Buckley as a youngster in 1932, he made his first team debut a week after Stan Cullis had made his. Cullis was given his chance at right-half in the home game against Huddersfield on February 16, 1935 and a seven days later Gardiner made his bow at left-half against Albion at The Hawthorns, with Cullis again at right-half. While Cullis stayed in the team for one more game, Gardiner had to wait until the following season to make a real impact at Molineux. For the three seasons before the outbreak of World War II, Gardiner was first choice left-half.

With Tom Galley at right-half and Cullis at centre-half, they formed one of the best half-back lines in the First Division. While the other two gained full England caps, the only representative honour that came Gardiner's way was at Molineux in November, 1938, at left-half in the Football League XI who beat the Scottish League 3-1. That side included Stanley Matthews, then with Stoke, and young Everton centre-forward Tommy Lawton.

A member of the Wolves side who were runners-up in the First Division in 1937-8 and 1938-9 he also played in the side unexpectedly beaten 4-1 by Portsmouth in the 1939 FA Cup final at Wembley. In all he made 139 League and Cup appearances for Wolves as well as many in wartime before ending his playing days in 1944 to become a member of the Molineux training staff. Contrary to some sources, he did not follow Stan Cullis to Birmingham City, but stayed at Molineux until his retirement.

What others said

Dennis Wilshaw: "Joe and Stan Cullis made a wonderful pairing. Joe had an affinity with the players. If Stan upset someone, he was a shoulder to cry on. If you were having a problem with some aspect of your game he would always be willing to help you. I don't think Stan would have been as good without Joe. He really knew his football."

Roy Swinbourne: "Joe was a great foil for Stan. If Stan had had a go at someone, Joe would take them on one side and smooth things out. He knew his football, he was part of the set-up, part of the team. We would sneak off to the car park for a game and there would be one or two injuries through playing there. Joe would come and drag us off but he'd laugh about it. He was lovely chap."

Norman Deeley: "Joe WAS the Wolves in many ways. He was there from morning 'til night. He was there if you wanted to go back to do some extra training in the afternoon or work on your faults with you. He was a quiet man who just got on with the job. Everyone liked him and Cullis could go away for a few days if he had to and know Joe would look after things. Joe was so placid and the ideal man to put up with someone as intense as Stan."

135

Ron Flowers: "Joe was the best thing that happened to Cullis, Joe was the cooler down of things. If someone had had a rollicking from Stan he would not say 'Take no notice' but he would try to explain things in a more reasonable way and with a gentle voice. Joe did a lot to help me as a young player as did the coaches George Poyser and Harry Potts. They were very good so long as you showed an interest. If you wanted to learn they would help you and encourage you."

Bill Slater: "If I'd had a son who was showing promise at football and wanted to find a club and a coach he could feel safe with, then I would have sent him to Joe. I never heard him put a player down. He was always encouraging. He was a lovely man, who never swore, and one of those who made the club special. It was always a very happy club."

Nigel Sims: "Joe was his own man. I don't think he had many other interests outside football. Wolves was his life. He looked after all us players and I could not say a bad word about him."
Bill Shorthouse: "Joe was a good coach and got on well with all the players. We all liked him. He would always help you with your game and give you good hints about things you were doing. And if there was a problem he would sort it out."

Bert Williams: "Joe was a great bloke, very caring, very thoughtful. He never got married – I think he was married to football. He was more to do with the success of Wolves than a lot of people realise. He was a good player in his day and knew the game."

JACK HOWLEY
Born: Wolverhampton, June 12, 1907
Club secretary

He was part of the backroom team that helped make Molineux such a friendly place to be in the 1950s. He served the club for forty-five years. His father, also Jack, had been on Wolves books but it did not mean young Jack's future was mapped out when he left St Philip's Grammar School, Birmingham, in 1923. The post of office boy at Molineux was one of two offered him when he was taking a commercial course. The other was with a coal firm. Fortunately he chose football, a game at which he'd excelled during his school days. He'd captained his form, house and the first team at St Philip's. He later played for Newhampton Athletic in Wolverhampton's Heath Town League.

He began his service with Wolves when the club office was in Lichfield Street, Bert Hoskins was secretary and George Jobey manager. It was only on the appointment of Stan Cullis as manager in 1948 that Howley officially became secretary even though he had done the club's secretarial work for several years before. Not in good health, he retired in 1968, by which time his duties as secretary had been combined with that of general manager for five years. He died in 1971.

FIFA president Sir Stanley Rous was the principal guest when a dinner was held to honour Howley in 1964. A tribute to him in the programme for that event held at the Victoria Hotel said: "You can call him 'Loyal' Jack, 'Honest' Jack, or just 'Good old Jack' and they would all be fitting descriptions of a man whose backroom work has done as much as anything towards lifting the club to the position of pride they occupy in the football world. He has been recognised as the ideal secretary because he knows when to talk and – just as important – when not to, and he has come through many a testing experience without a sign of panic. Events of every kind at Molineux, large or small, all-ticket matches, those banes of club officials, have gone like clockwork, so have arrangements for internationals, FA Cup semi-finals and all those memorable Molineux floodlight Continental highlights of the 1950s. Jack has already been honoured with a Football League long service award but it is with an even greater sense of recognition that we honour him tonight."

His daughter, Christine Povey, says: "Dad was a pillar of the club. People like him, Joe Gardiner, Jack Dowen, the trainers, George Noakes, the chief scout, and George Palmer, the physiotherapist, helped make the club what it was – a family club.

"Dad never told me, but a lot of players have told me since how he'd help them when they were young lads – give them money out of his own pocket for bus fares or whatever. He was also very proud that he helped get Major Buckley to change his mind when he'd told Billy Wright he was too small and he would be sending him home. My dad was one of those who nagged the Major about it and got him to change his mind.

"Dad was very fond of Jimmy Mullen because he was a good player and was also a character – but he did not have a real favourite, he liked them all. "I think Dad ate drank and slept Wolves. He'd often work until 11 o'clock at night and on Sundays. I'd often go to Molineux with him

– from the age of about five. Many years later, I think it was at a do after they opened the Billy Wright Stand, Billy Wright shouted over to me 'I think we know our way round here, don't we?' "When Dad started at Molineux in 1923 they had one stand which seated 260 and 15,000 was a good gate. When they held that tribute dinner to him he was very proud of the fact Sir Stanley Rous flew in from Switzerland especially to be there. When he retired, the chairman John Ireland said it was the end of an era and that his devotion and service was unprecedented in the history of the club.

"Dad always got on well with the Press and TV blokes. He always treated them with courtesy and they had a great deal of affection for him. At one of the celebration dinners, held in London, a group of them at the end of the evening carried Dad up to his bedroom sitting on a chair – like a king on his throne. I think Kenneth Wolstenholme was one of those who did it. "Dad had to do a lot of organising of things in addition to the football – like when the Queen visited Molineux in the 1960s. He told me they had to equip a special bathroom for her – just in case she needed it.

"He knew a lot of showbusiness people, too. Once, Norman Wisdom came down to the club for treatment by George Palmer. Norman was appearing at the Grand Theatre and because he used to throw himself about so much in his act he had hurt himself." Wisdom was not the only famous comedian to visit Molineux.

137

"Another time I was in my seat in the stand just before kick-off and Eric Morecambe came up the stairs," recalls Mrs Povey. "The only empty seat was next to me so I knew he was going to sit there. It was wonderful – he joked with me all the way through the match. "When we won the Cup in 1960, Dad brought it to our house and slept with it under his bed. He was taking it to show the children at a school, I think, the following morning. "There are so many memories. I'm very proud of what he did for the club"

What others said

Bill Slater: "Jack was very supportive and appreciated all the implications having to do two jobs presented. When I was first at the club as an amateur I used to travel over from Birmingham as I was at the university and had to get my train fare from him – 2s 6d (12.5p) and he'd always say: 'Come for your half crown, have you?' I think the club would have done more to help me but I had to be careful as an amateur. Jack was a lovely man and very supportive which is why I warmed to him."

Ron Flowers: "He was one of the old type secretaries in a pin-stripe suit. He was a very nice fella but never got involved with the playing side apart from when we had to sign our contracts. He was a very approachable and an efficient bloke from what I gather. He'd always ensure we had our match tickets but if we wanted a few extra then it was a battle! He would always ask how the family was and would talk to you to make sure everything was OK."

Bert Williams: "You could always go in and have a chat with him. We were lucky in that people like Jack loved, respected and cared for Wolves."

CHAPTER EIGHT

THE RIVAL 21 CLUBS

Arsenal
Manager: Tom Whittaker
Ground: Highbury
Record attendance: 73,295 (Sunderland, League, March 9, 1935)

The Gunners won the 1952-3 First Division on goal average from Preston, both finishing on 54 points. That was the seventh time they had won the title which was then a record, ahead of Villa and Sunderland who had six to their name.

Welshman Jack Kelsey had established himself as first choice goalkeeper to the exclusion of veteran George Swindin while up front Cliff Holton made a major contribution to the title success with 19 goals in 21 league games. Former Walsall inside forward Doug Lishman had finished their top scorer with 22 league goals. Jimmy Logie, the other inside man, was the schemer of the side in a midfield which included Scottish powerhouse Alex Forbes.

Welsh international Ray Daniel was at the heart of the defence but was transferred to Sunderland in June, 1953, as the Roker Park club embarked on a spending spree. Daniel's departure would enable Bill Dodgin to take over at centre-half for the the 1953-4 season and he had the honour of captaining England's first ever under-23 side, who included Wolves' Peter Broadbent, when they lost to Italy under-23 in Bologna.

Skippered by Stan Cullis's old England pal Joe Mercer – they were both born in Ellesmere Port – Arsenal would sign veteran England centre-forward Tommy Lawton from Brentford before the season ended. They also signed Chelsea half-back Bill Dickson in October.

Alas, 1953-4, would not prove a happy one for Mercer, in his 40th year. He broke his leg in the game against Liverpool at Highbury in April and would never play again. That same day Welshman Derek Tapscott made his debut, scoring twice.

Aston Villa
Manager: Eric Houghton
Ground: Villa Park
Record attendance: 76,588 (Derby, FA Cup, February 2, 1946)

Danny Blanchflower, later to skipper Spurs to double glory in 1961, was still doing his best to revive former glories at Villa Park. Under manager George Martin, Villa had begun 1952-3 by losing five of their first seven games but rallied to finish eleventh. However, Martin quit the club at the end of the season and went to Luton as chief scout. Pre-war favourite Eric Houghton, a Villa outside-left who also played for England, returned to Villa Park as the new boss.

Johnny Dixon, a future FA Cup-winning skipper, had finished top scorer for the club in 1952-3 with 13 goals.

An emerging youngster in 1953 was Irishman Peter McParland, destined to score the two goals which saw Villa beat Manchester United 2-1 in the 1957 FA Cup final. He had made his debut in September, 1952, in the 1-0 home defeat by Wolves. By coincidence, his second first-team outing for Villa would also be against Wolves and he scored his side's winner in the Christmas Eve encounter at Molineux, retaining his place on the left-wing, where another Irishman, Norman Lockhart, had previously been the No 1 choice. After a successful Villa career, McParland moved to Molineux in January, 1962, signed by Stan Cullis to bolster a side struggling to avoid relegation.

Villa had a more experienced Ireland export in their ranks in 1953, Dave Walsh, who had made his name as a centre-forward with Albion. His strike partner at Villa was Tommy Thompson, already an England international. Harry Parkes remained a stalwart in defence where former Wolves man Dennis Parsons would begin the 1953-4 season in goal, before giving way to first choice Keith Jones. Another man was recruited from Wolves in November, 1953 – half-back Bill Baxter.

Blackpool
Manager: Joe Smith
Ground: Bloomfield Road
Record attendance: 36,259 (Preston, League, August 25, 1952)

Bloomfield Road was proudly displaying the FA Cup in the trophy cabinet after an epic FA Cup final victory over Bolton at Wembley. Trailing 3-1 they had scored three late goals as Stanley Matthews, the star of the win, had gained a winner's medal at last at the age of 38. The 'other' Stanley, England inside forward Stanley Mortensen, was credited with a hat-trick that day, though anyone who sees a TV replay of his first goal would probably agree it should go down as a Harold Hassall own goal as Morty's shot was going across the face of the goal before the Bolton man stuck out a foot and turned the ball into the net. Mortensen would make a brilliant goalscoring start to 1953-4 with 11 goals in eight games. He would also score in England's 6-3 humiliation by the Hungarian maestros at Wembley but that would prove to be his last international.

Unluckiest man at Blackpool was Allan Brown. The Scottish international had broken his leg scoring the 88th-minute winning goal in the 2-1 sixth round win over Arsenal at Highbury and had to miss the final. He had suffered a similar experience in 1951, playing in every round, including the semi-final, only to get injured three weeks before the final against Newcastle.

Blackpool could boast a host of internationals on their books, such as Scottish keeper George Farm, full-backs Tom Garrett and Eddie Shimwell, Hugh Kelly and veteran centre-half Harry Johnston while little Ernie Taylor would win his one and only cap in the Hungary debacle at Wembley in November, 1953. Inside forward Jackie Mudie and left-winger Bill Perry, scorer of the Cup Final winner against Bolton, would go on to become internationals later in the 1950s. In 1952-3, Blackpool had made a flying start to the season with seven wins and a draw in their first nine games, including an 8-4 home win over Charlton. They scored no fewer than 29 goals in that opening sequence including the rare feat of Matthews scoring in three successive matches. However, they faded as the Cup gradually become their No1 target, and finished seventh.

Bolton
Manager: Bill Ridding
Ground: Burnden Park
Record attendance: 69,912 (Manchester City, Cup, February 13, 1933)

Bolton had been in the First Division since 1935 without ever really threatening to take it by storm. However, they were beaten FA Cup finalists in 1953 and were set for better times. The 'other' Wanderers had the great Nat Lofthouse spearheading their attack and would come close to finishing third behind Wolves and Albion, only to miss out by losing their final game at Huddersfield, who duly took the 'bronze medal.'

Molineux had witnessed Lofthouse's scoring prowess the previous season when he hit six goals for the Football League in the 7-1 defeat of the Irish League on September 24, 1952. Scot Willie Moir and England international Harold Hassall were alongside the man nicknamed the "Lion of Vienna". Lofthouse hit 30 league and cup goals in 1952-3 and Moir 21.

Winger Doug Holden was a young man destined to win a full England cap as was young full-back Tommy Banks, operating in a defence marshalled by England cap Malcolm Barrass. Another youngster would clinch a first team place in 1953-4 – Ray Parry. He had made his debut against Wolves and written his name into Bolton history in October 20, 1951, when he became the club's youngest League player at the age of 15 years 267 days. Wolves made sure Bolton would have nothing else for which to remember that game when they won 5-1, Jesse Pye scoring three goals.

141

An injury to John Wheeler late in the 1953-4 season would let in Derek Hennin, another who would make his mark as a Burnden Park hard man.

Burnley
Manager: Frank Hill
Ground: Turf Moor
Record attendance: 54,775 (Huddersfield, Cup, February 24, 1924)

Burnley had gained promotion from the Second Division in the first League season after the War when they went close to emulating Albion's 1931 Double of winning promotion and the FA Cup in the same season. Burnley reached Wembley but lost 1-0 to Charlton in the final.

The Lancashire side were to enjoy a good season in 1953-4, building on their sixth place in 1952-3. They were helped by the silky skills of Northern Ireland inside forward Jimmy McIlroy. They also had a stalwart centre-half in Tommy Cummings and lively midfield men in Les Shannon and Jimmy Adamson. Shannon, was playing inside-forward in those days and hit 15 goals in 1952-3 when he and centre forward Bill Holden were both ever-presents.

Big man Holden was their top scorer in 1952-3 with 22 league goals while a future England winger Brian Pilkington was starting to make his name and would get his chance with the departure of Billy Elliott to Sunderland.

Cardiff City
Manager: Cyril Spiers
Ground: Ninian Park
Record attendance: 61,079 (Wales v England, October 25, 1949)

Cardiff had regained a place in the First Division in 1951-2 – but only narrowly. They were runners-up but only on goal average ahead of Birmingham City.

The Welsh club, whose only major honour was their 1927 FA Cup final win over Arsenal, enjoyed mid-table stability in 1952-3. They were managed by a former Wolves goalkeeper, Cyril Spiers, who had been a member of Major Buckley's training staff at Molineux.

Wales full-back Alf Sherwood was the key figure in defence where Derrick Sullivan had also gained a Welsh cap at half-back. City had Mike Tiddy, later in the '50s to sign for Arsenal, on the wing while their main striker was Ken Chisholm. Before Christmas, 1953, they would add Sunderland's swashbuckling Welsh centre-forward Trevor Ford to their ranks.

Charlton Athletic
Manager: Jimmy Seed
Ground: The Valley
Record attendance:75,031 (Villa, FA Cup, February 12, 1938)

142

By finishing fifth in the table in 1952-3, the Londoners had made themselves one of the division's most respected sides, under the management of Jimmy Seed, a member of the Tottenham side who beat Wolves in the 1921 FA Cup final at Stamford Bridge. The Addicks had won the FA Cup in1947, the only major trophy to come to The Valley.

Sam Bartram, so unlucky never to win an England cap, was still a fixture in goal, having begun his career before the war.

Eddie Firmani was beginning to show the goalscoring form which would later take him to fame and fortune in Italy.

At centre-half, Derek Ufton was pressing for international honours while Stuart Leary and Sid O'Linn, both fine cricketers, swelled the club's ranks of South African players.

Chelsea
Manager: Ted Drake
Ground: Stamford Bridge
Record attendance 82,905 (Arsenal, League, October 12, 1933)

The Pensioners had flirted with relegation in 1952-3 and showed little hint that two years later they would be First Division champions. However, the basis of the future title-winning side was taking shape, led by England striker Roy Bentley who had finished top scorer in 1952-3 with 17 league and cup goals. Youngsters on their books included future England winger Frank

Blunstone and striker Bobby Smith, later to make his name with the Spurs Double-winning side of 1961 as well as winning 15 England caps.

Ron Greenwood, later boss of West Ham then England, was vying for the centre-half spot with one-time Wolves man John Harris. Other key figures in defence were Ken Armstrong and Irishman Bill Dickson, the latter destined to move to Arsenal during the 1953-4 season.

Huddersfield Town
Manager: Andy Beattie
Ground: Leeds Road
Record attendance: 67,037 (Arsenal, FA Cup, February 27, 1932)

Relegated in 1951-2, Huddersfield bounced back as runners-up to Sheffield United but had six points to spare over third-placed Luton.

They set a remarkable record in regaining their top flight status. In the days when defences were clearly defined as goalkeeper, two full-backs and three half-backs, they had the same six players in those positions for all 42 league matches – Jack Wheeler, Ron Staniforth, ex-Wolves man Laurie Kelly, future Wolves boss Bill McGarry, Don McEvoy and Len Quested.

For good measure, England winger Vic Metcalfe was also an ever-present as Town used only 15 players to win promotion. Their top scorer in the league was Jimmy Glazzard with 30 goals and he duly maintained his eye for goal in the First Division.

143

Boss Andy Beattie, a former Scottish international, would make his mark at Molineux, taking over as caretaker manager following the sacking of Stan Cullis in 1964.

Liverpool
Manager: Don Welsh
Ground: Anfield
Record attendance: 61,905 (Wolves, FA Cup, February 2, 1952)

It is hard to imagine in 2003 but Liverpool fifty years ago were among the poor relations of the First Division, destined for relegation and a stay in the Second which only ended with the arrival of Bill Shankly.

The Reds were on a slippery slope after the immediate post-war years had seen them grab the championship from under Wolves' noses in 1946-7 and finish FA Cup runners-up in 1950.

Men who would later steer them to great heights, Bob Paisley and Ronnie Moran, were still on the playing staff as was Scotland wing wizard Billy Liddell. Future England winger Alan A'Court was also making his mark in a forward line that often featured Louis Bimpson, later to play for Blackburn against Wolves in the 1960 FA Cup final. Sammy Smyth, scorer of a memorable solo goal in Wolves' 1949 FA Cup final win over Leicester, was also at Anfield after a spell with Stoke.

Manchester City
Manager: Les McDowall
Ground: Maine Road
Record attendance: 84,569 (Stoke, FA Cup, March 3, 1934)

City finished just above the relegation places in 1952-3, a season which saw German goalkeeper Bert Trautmann an ever-present.

Don Revie, whose deep-lying centre-forward plan would in later years be a football talking point, was a key figure at Maine Road, turning out either at wing-half or inside-forward.

Rugged centre-half Dave Ewing was at the heart of their defence with Welsh international Roy Paul alongside him. Another Welsh international, Roy Clarke, was a star on the left wing, while future England full-back Jimmy Meadows would have several games at centre-forward during 1953-4. Ivor Broadis, an England international inside-forward, would move to Newcastle early in the 1953-4 season.

Manchester United
Manager: Matt Busby
Ground: Old Trafford
Record attendance: 76,962 (Wolves v Grimsby, FA Cup semi-final, March 25, 1939)

144

United had, with secretary Walter Crickmer taking on the duties of manager, won promotion to the First Division in 1937-8, edging Sheffield United into third place on goal average.

With Matt Busby as boss, they were runners-up in four of the first five seasons after the War, finally taking the title in 1951-2. They had also won the Cup in 1948, beating Blackpool 4-2 in one of Wembley's best-ever finals.

United had failed to hang on to their title, finishing eighth in 1952-3. The old guard, such as Johnny Carey, Henry Cockburn, Allenby Chilton, Stan Pearson and Jack Rowley were still around but the youngsters who would make Busby's side great were waiting in the wings.

Jackie Blanchflower had made his debut in 1951-2, his only game that season. He also made just one appearance in 1952-3 as did another newcomer Duncan Edwards. However, 17-year-old David Pegg had made nineteen appearances at outside-left and was in the side who beat Wolves 7-1 in the first leg of the FA Youth Cup final before drawing the return 2-2. Eddie Colman, Liam Whelan and Edwards were also in that final line-up. These young men represented the future of the club along with the others like Bill Foulkes and Dennis Viollet.

Roger Byrne, one of those fated to lose his life in the 1958 Munich Air Crash, was already an established member of the side as was centre-forward Tommy Taylor, who had been signed from Barnsley in 1952-3 and impressed sufficiently enough to be capped on England's close-season South American tour, along with club mate Johnny Berry.

Middlesbrough
Manager: Walter Rowley
Ground: Ayresome Park
Record attendance: 53,596 (Newcastle, League, December 27, 1949)

Boro had been in the top flight since winning the Second Division title in 1928-9 and had steadily improved during the 1930s to finish fourth in the last season before the War. However, since then they had made no real impact, apart from a sixth-placing in 1950-1. In 1952-3 they had looked good candidates for relegation for much of the season but saved themselves when they finished the campaign with a six-game unbeaten run. They would not be able to put off the inevitable in 1953-4, however.

Although former England inside-forward Wilf Mannion, one of Teesside's finest players, passed 35 in 1953, he was still a Boro first choice but playing in a struggling side.

It was to prove Boro's last season in the top flight for quite a while but Mannion, who had been the club's top league scorer in 1952-3 with 19 goals, would still be a thorn in Wolves' side in what proved to be his last season at Ayresome Park.

They also had a useful goalscoring winger or inside-forward in Jamaican-born Louis 'Lindy' Delapenha and a fine goalkeeper in Italian-born, but Scotland-raised, Rolando Ugolini who had previously played for Celtic. Former Wolves half-back Eddie Russell had played 20 matches for Boro in 1952-3 but left the club for Leicester in October.

145

In 1953-4, only Cardiff would score fewer than Boro's total of 60 goals and only Liverpool concede more than Boro's 91 against. Had they but known it, a young man was already on the books at Ayresome Park who would eventually deliver goals in abundance. He was busy doing his National Service with the RAF at that time. His name? Brian Clough.

Newcastle United
Manager: Stan Seymour
Ground: St James' Park
Record attendance: 68,386 (Chelsea, League, September 3, 1930)

Ace Cup fighters Newcastle, who had become the first team in the 20th century to win successive FA Cup finals – in 1951 and 1952 – had yet to make a sustained impact on the league since the War. They were promoted from the Second Division as runners-up in 1947-8.

They topped the First Division briefly the following season and looked like giving eventual champions Portsmouth a good run for their money. However, in the vital top-of-the-table clash with Pompey at St James' Park towards the end of the season the Geordies were humbled 5-0.

Three draws and two defeats in their last five games of the season saw Newcastle's challenge finally fade and they finished fourth. Title hopes were revived in 1950-1 and they led the table early on. The clash with the eventual champions again proved a chastening experience. They were beaten 7-0 by Spurs at White Hart Lane and they had to settle for a final placing of fourth once more.

Jackie Milburn was still the fans' idol but had played only 16 league games in 1952-3. Chilean striker George Robledo had departed for Cola Cola in his native Chile. Robledo had been Newcastle's top scorer in 1952-3 when the Geordies finished a disappointing 16th. To make up for Robledo's departure, England inside-forward Ivor Broadis was signed in October, 1953, from Manchester City for £20,000.

Bob Stokoe was making a breakthrough in a defence who had big Scottish centre-half Frank Brennan as their kingpin and experience at left-back in the form of Northern Ireland international Alf McMichael. Scottish winger Bobby Mitchell, was still weaving his magic while it was hoped the midfield would improve with the arrival of £22,500 club record signing Jimmy Scoular from Portsmouth.

Portsmouth
Manager: Eddie Lever
Ground: Fratton Park
Record attendance: 51,385 (Derby, FA Cup, February 26, 1949)

League champions in 1949 and 1950, Portsmouth still had some useful men in their line-up – like England left-half Jimmy Dickinson and versatile international Jack Froggatt who won England caps at centre-half and outside-left.

Peter Harris was a useful goalscoring winger – he hit 23 goals in 1952-3 – and 21-year-old Jackie Henderson was beginning to attract attention. A future Scottish international he was destined to sign for Wolves in 1958.

Pompey also had a reliable last line of defence in the shape of Irish goalkeeper Norman Uprichard who had joined them from Swindon Town. Another useful member of the squad was England international Len Phillips who could play inside-forward or half-back.

Preston
Manager: Scot Symon
Ground: Deepdale
Record attendance: 42,684 (Arsenal, League, April 23, 1930)

Preston had been relegated from the First Division in 1948-9, the season the legendary Bill Shankly ended his playing days. In 1950-1, North End gained promotion from the Second Division as champions, equalling a Football League record of fourteen successive wins on the way. Centre-forward Charlie Wayman, newly signed from Southampton, was their leading league scorer that season with 27. He hit another 24 league goals the following season.

In 1952-3, Preston went desperately close to winning the First Division. They finished on 54 points with Arsenal, but the Gunners took the title on goal average. Not surprisingly, North

146

End were one of the teams tipped for honours in 1953-4. They had two of the game's greatest post-War names still in their pomp – Scottish half-back Tommy Docherty and England wing maestro Tom Finney.

They were the men around whom a useful side had been built, spearheaded by Wayman, top scorer for the club with 23 league goals in 1952-3.

Their centre-half Joe Marston was an Australian and there were few of them playing in English football in those days. Full-back Willie Cunningham was destined to win caps for Scotland. Wayman, Marston and Angus Morrison had played in all 42 league games in 1952-3.

Sheffield Wednesday
Manager: Eric Taylor
Ground: Hillsborough
Record attendance: 72,841 (Manchester City, FA Cup, February 17, 1934)

Wednesday were still reeling from the blow of losing star centre-forward Derek Dooley. He broke his leg in a game against Preston in February, 1953, and when gangrene set in had to have the leg amputated.

The Owls finished mighty close to the relegation places in 1952-3 in what could have been a remarkable sequence for they had been promoted from the Second Division in 1949-50, relegated the following season and then promoted again in 1951-2. Despite their struggles, they had plenty of talent in their side – like England striker Jackie Sewell whose 1951 signing from Notts County for £34,000 in 1951 was still a record at the start of 1953-4.

The quaintly named Redfern Froggatt had won England caps and many experts were predicting big things for fair-haired ball-juggling inside-forward Albert Quixall, who celebrated his 20th birthday in August, 1953. Quixall would eventually be signed by Manchester United in September, 1958, for a record £45,000.

147

Sheffield United
Manager: Reg Freeman
Ground: Bramall Lane
Record attendance: 68,287 (Leeds, FA Cup, February 15, 1936)

The Blades won promotion from the Second Division in 1952-3 as champions with eight points to spare over third-placed Luton. They had been relegated from the First Division in 1948-9 and almost bounced straight back the following season, being edged into third place by neighbours Wednesday, only on goal average.

Republic of Ireland international Alf Ringstead had finished top scorer with 22 goals 1952-3. The brains of their attack was Jimmy Hagan. A star for England during wartime internationals, Hagan gained only one official cap. Destined to manage Albion, he was still a much-feared midfield presence.

The reliable Joe Shaw and Graham Shaw, at centre-half and full-back respectively, were key men in defence in front of a useful goalkeeper, Ted Burgin.

Sunderland
Manager: Bill Murray
Ground: Roker Park
Record attendance: 75,118 (Derby, FA Cup, March 8, 1933)

The big spenders of Roker Park had failed to buy success, finishing only ninth in 1952-3. Their response was to spend again, signing centre-half Ray Daniel from Arsenal, winger Billy Elliott from Burnley and goalkeeper Jimmy Cowan from Morton for a total of £61,000 – big money in those days.

Sunderland had one of the game's greatest attractions in Len Shackleton whose ball skills and trickery earned him the name of 'Clown Prince of Soccer'.

Rugged Welsh centre-forward Trevor Ford was the scourge of many a goalkeeper but was to leave for Cardiff in December, 1953, Willie Watson, a hero for his country on the cricket field in 1953, was about to start his final season with the club as young Stan Anderson began to make an impact in midfield.

Tottenham
Manager: Arthur Rowe
Ground: White Hart Lane
Record attendance: 75,038 (Sunderland, FA Cup, March 5, 1938)

Spurs' famous push-and-run style had brought them the Second Division title in 1949-50 and the following season they took the First Division by storm, bringing the championship to White Hart Lane for the first time. The 1951-2 season had seen them runners-up.

Highlight of the 1952-3 season had been their FA Cup run, which featured a sixth-round second replay win over Birmingham at Molineux before nearly 51,000 spectators. However, Spurs were beaten in the semi-final by Blackpool. By the time 1953-4 came along they were an ageing side. Alf Ramsey was still good enough to get into the England side at right-back and they had one of the country's best goalkeepers, Ted Ditchburn. At half-back were Welshman Ronnie Burgess and Englishman Bill Nicholson, both internationals, either side of big centre-half Harry Clarke.

A young amateur named Vic Groves, later to make his name with Leyton Orient and Arsenal, was on their books as was that diminutive box of tricks Tommy Harmer. Guernsey-born Len Duquemin had been their top scorer in 1952-3 with 24 league and cup goals, many of them set up by England inside forward Eddie Baily. Outside-left Les Medley, six times capped by England, had called it a day at the end of 1952-3 and emigrated to Canada. His wife was a Canadian. Medley's departure gave former England amateur international George Robb his chance

West Bromwich Albion
Manager: Vic Buckingham
Ground: The Hawthorns
Record attendance: 64,815 (Arsenal, FA Cup, March 6, 1937)

While Wolves were winning the FA Cup in 1949, Albion were clinching promotion from the Second Division under the managership of one-time Wolves full-back Jack Smith. Their promotion, clinched in an exciting finish which saw them edge Southampton into third place by a point, ended their longest absence from the top flight – ten years.

Their first three seasons back in the First Division saw Albion fourteenth, sixteenth and thirteenth. Smith resigned in 1952 and former Blackburn and Newcastle centre-half Jesse Carver was appointed coach. He had worked in Italy and would return there after just nine months but is given much credit, during his brief spell, for refining the club's style of play. The seeds he sowed would flourish when Albion put Vic Buckingham in charge. A former Spurs half-back, Buckingham placed the emphasis firmly on a passing game and in 1952-3 Albion figured prominently in the title race. They led the First Division at one stage before fading to fourth. However, it was clear they were a growing force.

Albion were to have a great 1953-4 season. Under Buckingham they were a stylish attacking side from Len Millard, their veteran full-back, to George Lee at outside-left.

Centre-forward Ronnie Allen, later to manage Wolves, had already been capped by England as an outside-right and had found a real partner in goals in the shape of Wolverhampton-born Johnny Nicholls.

Irishman Reg Ryan and right-winger Frank Griffin completed a splendid forward line, prompted by fine half-backs Jimmy Dudley and Ray Barlow. Jimmy Dugdale would force his way into the side at centre-half, where Joe Kennedy had seemed a fixture, while right-back Stan Rickaby would be capped by England during the season.

CHAPTER NINE

1953-4 LEAGUE RESULTS

In 1953-4 a win was worth only two points and teams level on points were separated not by goal difference but by goal average (the number of goals scored divided by those conceded). Gates are those officially registered with the Football League and may differ from the record books of individual clubs.

Football League Division One

	P	W	D	L	F	A	P
Sheff Wed	2	2	0	0	4	1	4
Charlton	2	2	0	0	8	4	4
West Brom	2	1	1	0	3	1	3
Cardiff	2	1	1	0	2	1	3
Huddersfield	2	1	1	0	2	1	3
Liverpool	2	1	1	0	7	5	3
Preston	2	1	0	1	5	2	2
Blackpool	1	1	0	0	2	1	2
Newcastle	1	1	0	0	2	1	2
Sheff Utd	1	1	0	0	4	3	2
WOLVES	**2**	**1**	**0**	**1**	**5**	**4**	**2**
Burnley	2	1	0	1	5	4	2
Tottenham	2	1	0	1	2	2	2
Man Utd	2	0	2	0	5	5	2
Bolton	1	0	1	0	1	1	1
Chelsea	2	0	1	1	2	3	1
Arsenal	2	0	1	1	0	2	1
Middlesbro	2	0	1	1	0	4	1
Portsmouth	2	0	0	2	4	7	0
Sunderland	2	0	0	2	4	7	0
Aston Villa	2	0	0	2	1	3	0
Man City	2	0	0	2	0	6	0

Wednesday, August 19, 1953

Burnley 4 Shannon 2, Holden, Pilkington — **Wolves 1** Swinbourne — Att: 32,822

Charlton 5 Firmani 2, Hammond, Leary, Lock (pen) — **Sunderland 3** T Wright, Ford 2 — Att: 49,742

Liverpool 3 Jones 2, Liddell — **Portsmouth 1** Henderson — Att: 39,662

Man Utd 1 Pearson — **Chelsea 1** McNichol — Att: 30,759

Middlesbrough 0 — **Cardiff 0** — Att: 33,726

Preston 1 Foster — **Huddersfield 2** Watson 2 — Att: 35,925

Sheff Wed 2 Jordan, Sewell — **Man City 0** — Att: 39,586

Tottenham 1 Parkes OG — **Aston Villa 0** — Att: 50,202

West Brom 2 Nicholls 2 — **Arsenal 0** — Att: 41,655

Saturday, August 22, 1953

Arsenal 0 — **Huddersfield 0** — Att: 54,847

Blackpool 2 Mortensen 2 — **Chelsea 1** Lewis — Att: 28,440

Cardiff 2 Rainford, P Thomas — **Aston Villa 1** Dixon — Att: 36,671

Charlton 3 Kiernan, Firmani, Leary — **Burnley 1** McIlroy — Att: 24,802

Liverpool 4 Bimpson 3, Jones — **Man Utd 4** Rowley, Byrne, Lewis, Taylor — Att: 46,725

Man City 0 — **Wolves 4** Wilshaw, Slater, Swinbourne 2 — Att: 22,729

Middlesbrough 0 — **Preston 4** Wayman, Foster 3 — Att: 32,891

Newcastle 2 Mitchell (pen), Keeble — **Sunderland 1** Shackleton — Att: 58,516

Portsmouth 3 Reid, Vaughan, Harris — **Sheff Utd 4** Hawksworth 2, Brook, Ringstead — Att: 32,259

Sheff Wed 2 Sewell 2 — **Tottenham 1** Walters — Att: 38,114

West Brom 1 Barlow — **Bolton 1** Moir — Att: 28,975

Football League Division One

	P	W	D	L	F	A	P
Huddersfield	3	2	1	0	4	1	5
West Brom	3	2	1	0	6	2	5
Preston	3	2	0	1	11	2	4
Sheff Utd	2	2	0	0	5	3	4
Tottenham	3	2	0	1	5	3	4
Burnley	3	2	0	1	7	5	4
Charlton	3	2	0	1	9	7	4
Liverpool	3	1	2	0	9	7	4
Sheff Wed	3	2	0	1	4	7	4
Newcastle	2	1	1	0	4	3	3
Bolton	2	1	1	0	4	3	3
Chelsea	3	1	1	1	6	6	3
Cardiff	3	1	1	1	2	3	3
Aston Villa	3	1	0	2	4	3	2
WOLVES	**3**	**1**	**0**	**2**	**7**	**7**	**2**
Blackpool	2	1	0	1	3	3	2
Sunderland	3	1	0	2	7	9	2
Man Utd	3	0	2	1	6	8	2
Arsenal	3	0	2	1	0	3	1
Middlesbro	3	0	1	2	2	7	1
Portsmouth	3	0	0	3	7	11	0
Man City	3	0	0	3	0	9	0

Monday, August 24, 1953

Aston Villa 3   **Man City 0**   Att: 21,194
Blanchflower, Thompson 2

Sheff Utd 1   **Arsenal 0**   Att: 50,723
Browning

Tuesday, August 25, 1953

Burnley 2   **Blackpool 1**   Att: 41,574
Pilkington, Shimwell, OG   Mortensen

Chelsea 4   **Portsmouth 3**   Att: 40,090
Lewis 3, McNichol   Harris, Henderson, McKight OG

Wednesday, August 26, 1953

Bolton 3   **Middlesbrough 2**   Att: 29,502
Hassall 2 (1 pen), Webster   Mannion, Delapenha

Huddersfield 2   **Cardiff 0**   Att: 30,089
Watson, Metcalfe

Liverpool 2   **Newcastle 2**   Att: 47,263
Baron 2   Hannah, Davies

Man Utd 1   **West Bromwich 3**   Att: 33,652
Taylor   Dudley, Nicholls, Lee

Preston 6   **Sheff Wed 0**   Att: 33,118
Baxter 3, Finney, Foster, Wayman

Sunderland 3   **Wolves 2**   Att: 57,135
T Wright, Shackleton, Ford   Hancocks (pen), Wilshaw

Tottenham 3   **Charlton 1**   Att: 48,035
Baily, Robb 2   Kiernan

1953-4 LEAGUE RESULTS

Football League Division One

	P	W	D	L	F	A	P
Huddersfield	4	3	1	0	9	2	7
West Brom	4	3	1	0	8	2	7
Tottenham	4	3	0	1	9	4	6
Burnley	4	3	0	1	11	6	6
Bolton	3	2	1	0	6	3	5
Chelsea	4	2	1	1	9	7	5
Preston	4	2	0	2	11	4	4
Aston Villa	4	2	0	2	6	4	4
WOLVES	**4**	**2**	**0**	**2**	**10**	**8**	**4**
Newcastle	3	1	2	0	5	4	4
Blackpool	3	2	0	1	7	6	4
Sheff Utd	3	2	0	1	8	7	4
Liverpool	4	1	2	1	9	9	4
Charlton	4	2	0	2	10	10	4
Sheff Wed	4	2	0	2	5	11	4
Man Utd	4	0	3	1	7	9	3
Cardiff	4	1	1	2	3	6	3
Sunderland	4	1	0	3	11	14	2
Man City	4	1	0	3	5	13	2
Middlesbro	4	0	1	3	3	11	1
Arsenal	4	0	1	3	1	5	1
Portsmouth	4	0	0	4	8	16	0

Saturday, August 29, 1953

Aston Villa 2
Walsh, Dixon
Att: 33,731

Bolton 2
Moir, Webster
Liverpool 0
Att: 27,258

Burnley 4
Pilkington 2, Gray 2
Sheff Wed 1
Froggatt
Att: 25,813

Chelsea 3
McNichol 2, Bentley
Charlton 1
Leary
Att: 49,245

Huddersfield 5
Glazzard 3, Davie, Watson
Portsmouth 1
Phillips
Att: 22,474

Man United 1
Chilton
Newcastle 1
Hannah
Att: 29,676

Preston 0
West Bromwich 2
Nicholls 2
Att: 30,462

Sheff Utd 3
Hagan, Wragg 2
Blackpool 4
Mortensen 3, Mudie
Att: 35,171

Sunderland 4
Shackleton, T Wright, A Wright, Branagan OG
Man City 5
Hart 2, Anders, Clarke, Whitfield
Att: 49,434

Tottenham 4
Walters, Bennett, Robb, Duquemin
Middlesbrough 1
Delapenha
Att: 44,911

Wolves 3
Wilshaw, Mullen, Hancocks (pen)
Cardiff 1
Grant
Att: 33,221

153

Football League Division One

	P	W	D	L	F	A	P
West Brom	5	4	1	0	10	2	9
Tottenham	5	4	0	1	10	4	8
Huddersfield	5	3	1	1	10	4	7
Newcastle	4	2	2	0	9	4	6
Aston Villa	5	3	0	2	7	4	6
Blackpool	4	3	0	1	9	6	6
Burnley	5	3	0	2	11	8	6
WOLVES	**5**	**3**	**0**	**2**	**13**	**9**	**6**
Sheff Wed	5	3	0	2	9	13	6
Bolton	4	2	1	1	8	6	5
Chelsea	5	2	1	2	11	10	5
Sheff Utd	4	2	1	1	9	8	5
Cardiff	5	2	1	2	5	7	5
Preston	5	2	0	3	13	8	4
Charlton	5	2	0	3	10	11	4
Liverpool	5	1	2	2	9	13	4
Man Utd	5	0	3	2	7	11	3
Middlesbro	5	1	1	3	6	13	3
Sunderland	5	1	0	4	12	17	2
Man City	5	1	0	4	5	14	2
Portsmouth	5	1	0	4	11	18	2
Arsenal	5	0	2	3	2	6	2

154

Monday, August 31, 1953

Blackpool 2 **Burnley 0**
Mortensen 2
Att: 18,113

Wolves 3 **Sunderland 1**
Wilshaw, Mullen, Swinbourne / T Wright
Att: 41,442

Tuesday, September 1, 1953

Arsenal 1 S **heff Utd 1**
Shaw, OG / Browning
Att: 42,077

Wednesday, September 2, 1953

Cardiff 2 **Huddersfield 1**
Grant, Chisholm / Glazzard
Att: 29,446

Man City 0 **Aston Villa 1**
Walsh
Att: 24,918

Middlesbrough 3 **Bolton 2**
Delapenha 2, Mannion / Wheeler, Hassall
Att: 25,458

Newcastle 4 **Liverpool 0**
Keeble, Mitchell, Milburn 2
Att: 48,439

Portsmouth 3 **Chelsea 2**
Harris 2, Gordon / Armstrong, Hall OG
Att: 29,571

Sheff Wed 4 **Preston 2**
Froggatt, Marriott, Shaw, Woodhead / Finney, Foster
Att: 36,976

West Bromwich 2 **Man Utd 0**
Allen, Hodgkisson
Att: 28,892

Thursday, September 3 1953

Charlton 0 **Tottenham 1**
Groves
Att: 37,609

Football League Division One

	P	W	D	L	F	A	P
West Brom	6	5	1	0	13	2	11
Blackpool	5	4	0	1	12	7	8
Burnley	6	4	0	2	14	9	8
WOLVES	**6**	**4**	**0**	**2**	**16**	**11**	**8**
Tottenham	6	4	0	2	10	7	8
Huddersfield	6	3	1	2	11	7	7
Bolton	5	3	1	1	11	8	7
Sheff Utd	5	3	1	1	11	9	7
Preston	6	3	0	3	18	9	6
Newcastle	5	2	2	1	11	7	6
Aston Villa	6	3	0	3	8	6	6
Charlton	6	3	0	3	12	6	6
Cardiff	6	2	2	2	6	8	6
Sheff Wed	6	3	0	3	10	15	6
Chelsea	6	2	1	3	12	12	5
Portsmouth	6	2	0	4	13	19	4
Man City	6	2	0	4	7	14	4
Liverpool	6	1	2	3	10	18	4
Man Utd	6	0	3	3	7	13	3
Sunderland	6	1	1	4	13	18	3
Middlesbro	6	1	1	4	7	16	3
Arsenal	6	0	2	4	4	9	2

155

Saturday, September 5, 1953

Wolves 3 Broadbent, Wilshaw, Hancocks — **Arsenal 2** Roper, Holton — Att: 60,460

Huddersfield 1 Davie — **Blackpool 3** Mortensen, Mudie, Fenton — Att: 34,507

Sunderland 1 T Wright — **Cardiff 1** Chisholm — Att: 42,002

Sheff Utd 2 Hagan 2 — **Chelsea 1** McNichol — Att: 49,824

Preston 5 Foster, Kaile, Finney 2, Wayman — **Liverpool 1** Jones — Att: 46,928

Man Utd 0 — **Man City 2** Hart, Revie — Att: 53,097

Burnley 3 Holden, Stephenson, Gray — **Middlesbrough 1** Edwards — Att: 32,597

Bolton 3 Webster 2, Hassall — **Newcastle 2** Mitchell, Hannah — Att: 61,321

Aston Villa 1 Walsh — **Portsmouth 2** Harris, Froggatt — Att: 31,871

Charlton 2 Leary, Hurst — **Sheff Wed 1** Woodhead — Att: 40,936

Tottenham 0 — **West Bromwich 3** Allen, Nicholls, Ramsey OG — Att: 42,959

Football League Division One

	P	W	D	L	F	A	P
West Brom	7	5	2	0	15	4	12
Burnley	7	5	0	2	18	11	10
WOLVES	**7**	**5**	**0**	**2**	**18**	**12**	**10**
Blackpool	6	4	1	1	13	8	9
Bolton	6	4	1	1	13	9	9
Preston	7	4	0	3	20	9	8
Huddersfield	7	3	2	2	12	8	8
Tottenham	7	4	0	3	12	11	8
Cardiff	7	3	2	2	7	8	8
Newcastle	6	2	3	1	13	9	7
Sheff Utd	6	3	1	2	11	10	7
Chelsea	7	3	1	3	14	13	7
Aston Villa	6	3	0	3	8	6	6
Charlton	7	3	0	4	12	14	6
Sheff Wed	7	3	0	4	11	17	6
Portsmouth	7	2	1	4	14	20	5
Man City	7	2	1	4	8	15	5
Man Utd	7	0	4	3	9	15	4
Liverpool	7	1	2	4	11	20	4
Middlesbro	7	1	2	4	9	18	4
Sunderland	6	1	1	4	13	18	3
Arsenal	7	0	2	5	5	11	2

156

Monday, September 7, 1953

Blackpool 1   **Portsmouth 1**
Mudie   Vaughan   Att: 30,914

Burnley 4   **Tottenham 2**
Gray 3, McIlroy   Robb, Walters   Att: 34,280

Sheff Utd 0   **Cardiff 1**
Edwards   Att: 34,043

Wolves 2   **Liverpool 1**
Swinbourne, Broadbent   Jackson   Att: 35,701

Tuesday September 8, 1953

Arsenal 1   **Chelsea 2**
Holton   Bentley, Lewis   Att: 54,946

Wednesday, September 9, 1953

Bolton 2   **Sheff Wed 1**
Moir, Hassall (pen)   Froggatt   Att: 31,143

Huddersfield 1   **Man City 1**
Metcalfe   Little   Att: 24,341

Man Utd 2   **Middlesbrough 2**
Rowley 2   Fitzsimons, Delapenha   Att: 19,893

Preston 2   **Charlton 0**
Foster, Baxter   Att: 28,055

West Bromwich 2   **Newcastle 2**
Ryan, Barlow   Keeble, Mitchell   Att: 32,780

Football League Division One

	P	W	D	L	F	A	P
West Brom	8	6	2	0	19	5	14
WOLVES	**8**	**6**	**0**	**2**	**22**	**15**	**12**
Huddersfield	8	4	2	2	15	9	10
Bolton	7	4	2	1	13	9	10
Burnley	8	5	0	3	19	15	10
Tottenham	8	5	0	3	14	12	10
Preston	8	4	1	3	22	11	9
Blackpool	7	4	1	2	14	10	9
Sheff Utd	7	4	1	2	13	10	9
Cardiff	8	3	3	2	8	9	9
Aston Villa	7	4	0	3	10	7	8
Charlton	8	4	0	4	20	15	8
Newcastle	7	2	4	1	15	11	8
Chelsea	8	3	1	4	15	16	7
Man City	8	2	2	4	9	16	6
Sheff Wed	8	3	0	5	11	19	6
Sunderland	7	2	1	4	20	19	5
Man Utd	8	0	5	3	9	15	5
Portsmouth	8	2	1	5	17	24	5
Liverpool	8	1	2	5	12	22	4
Middlesbro	8	1	2	5	10	26	4
Arsenal	8	0	2	6	6	18	2

Saturday, September 12, 1953

Aston Villa 2
Thompson, Walsh
Blackpool 1
Mortensen
Att: 37,284

Bolton 0
Man Utd 0
Att: 48,591

Burnley 1
Stephenson
West Bromwich 4
Allen, Nicholls 2, Ryan
Att: 38,948

Charlton 8
O'Linn 2, Firmani 3, Hurst 2, Leary
Middlesbrough 1
Spuhler
Att: 23,790

Huddersfield 3
Davie, Glazzard, Watson
Chelsea 1
Stubbs
Att: 29,631

Man City 1
Montgomery OG
Cardiff 1
Edwards
Att: 31,915

Preston 2
Baxter (pen), Finney
Newcastle 2
Milburn, Keeble
Att: 36,035

Sheff Utd 2
Hagan, Hawksworth
Sheff Wed 0
Att: 45,463

Sunderland 7
Ford 3, Elliott, Shackleton, T Wright 2
Arsenal 1
Lishman
Att: 59,784

Tottenham 2
Ramsey, Walters
Liverpool 1
Jones
Att: 47,535

Wolves 4
Wilshaw 3, Swinbourne
Portsmouth 3
Gordon 2, Harris
Att: 36,524

Football League Division One

	P	W	D	L	F	A	P
West Brom	9	7	2	0	26	8	16
WOLVES	**9**	**6**	**1**	**2**	**23**	**16**	**13**
Huddersfield	9	5	2	2	16	9	12
Burnley	9	6	0	3	22	17	12
Cardiff	9	4	3	2	10	9	11
Tottenham	9	5	0	4	16	15	10
Blackpool	8	4	2	2	18	14	10
Bolton	8	4	2	2	14	11	10
Aston Villa	8	5	0	3	13	8	10
Charlton	9	5	0	4	22	16	10
Preston	9	4	1	4	23	13	9
Sheff Utd	8	4	1	3	13	12	9
Newcastle	8	2	4	2	18	18	8
Sheff Wed	9	4	0	5	13	20	8
Chelsea	9	3	1	5	15	18	7
Man Utd	9	1	5	3	13	16	7
Portsmouth	9	2	2	5	21	28	6
Man City	9	2	2	5	9	17	6
Sunderland	8	2	1	5	21	22	5
Liverpool	9	1	3	5	13	23	5
Middlesbro	9	1	2	6	11	30	4
Arsenal	9	1	2	6	8	18	4

Monday, September 14, 1953

Aston Villa 3
Thompson, Dixon 2
Sunderland 1
T Wright
Att: 35,722

Tuesday, September 15, 1953

Chelsea 0
Arsenal 2
Lishman 2
Att: 60,652

Wednesday, September 16, 1953

Cardiff 2
Edwards, Grant
Sheff Utd 0
Att: 27,350

Liverpool 1
Jones
Wolves 1
Wilshaw
Att: 29,848

Man City 0
Huddersfield 1
McGarry
Att: 24,580

Middlesbrough 1
Delapenha (pen)
Man Utd 4
Taylor 2, Byrne, Rowley
Att: 23,791

Newcastle 3
Keeble, Mitchell 2
West Brom 7
Nicholls 3, Allen 2, Griffin, Ryan
Att: 57,838

Portsmouth 4
Harris, Vaughan 2, Gordon
Blackpool 4
Mudie 2, Mortensen, Perry
Att: 28,703

Sheff Wed 2
Sewell, Woodhead
Bolton 1
Hassall
Att: 26,025

Tottenham 2
Duquemin 2
Burnley 3
McIlroy 2, Gray
Att: 30,472

Thursday, September 17, 1953

Charlton 2
Kiernan, Leary
Preston 1
Finney
Att: 18,208

Saturday, September 19, 1953

Arsenal 2 — **Man City 2**
Lishman 2 / Hart, Spurdle
Att: 65,869

Blackpool 0 — **Wolves 0**
Att: 35,074

Cardiff 1 — **Bolton 1**
Chisholm / Hassall
Att: 35,788

Chelsea 1 — **Aston Villa 2**
A Moss OG / Walsh, Lockhart
Att: 47,487

Liverpool 4 — **Burnley 0**
Bimpson 4
Att: 36,643

Man Utd 1 — **Preston 0**
Byrne
Att: 43,003

Middlesbrough 4 — **Sheff Wed 1**
Mannion, Spuhler, Gannon OG, Delapenha / Jordan
Att: 22,638

Newcastle 1 — **Tottenham 3**
Milburn / Walters, Robb, Baily
Att: 53,056

Portsmouth 4 — **Sunderland 1**
Gordon 2, Vaughan, McNeil OG / T Wright
Att: 38,873

Sheff Utd 3 — **Huddersfield 6**
Hagan, Hawksworth, Ringstead / Glazzard 3, Metcalfe 2, Davie
Att: 40,263

West Brom 2 — **Charlton 3**
Barlow, Griffin / Evans 2, Leary
Att: 43,619

Football League Division One

	P	W	D	L	F	A	P
West Brom	10	7	2	1	28	11	16
Huddersfield	10	6	2	2	22	12	14
WOLVES	**10**	**6**	**2**	**2**	**23**	**16**	**14**
Aston Villa	9	6	0	3	15	9	12
Charlton	10	6	0	4	25	18	12
Tottenham	10	6	0	4	19	16	12
Cardiff	10	4	4	2	11	10	12
Burnley	10	6	0	4	22	21	12
Blackpool	9	4	3	2	18	14	11
Bolton	9	4	3	2	15	12	11
Preston	10	4	1	5	23	14	9
Man Utd	10	2	5	3	14	16	9
Sheff Utd	9	4	1	4	16	18	9
Newcastle	9	2	4	3	19	21	8
Portsmouth	10	3	2	5	25	29	8
Sheff Wed	10	4	0	6	14	24	8
Chelsea	10	3	1	6	16	20	7
Liverpool	10	2	3	5	17	23	7
Man City	10	2	3	5	11	19	7
Middlesbro	10	2	2	6	15	31	6
Sunderland	9	2	1	6	22	26	5
Arsenal	10	1	3	6	10	20	5

159

Football League Division One

	P	W	D	L	F	A	P
West Brom	11	8	2	1	31	13	18
Huddersfield	11	7	2	2	24	13	16
WOLVES	**11**	**7**	**2**	**2**	**31**	**17**	**16**
Aston Villa	10	7	0	3	19	9	14
Charlton	11	7	0	4	31	18	14
Tottenham	11	6	1	4	20	17	13
Burnley	11	6	0	5	23	23	12
Cardiff	11	4	4	3	11	13	12
Preston	11	5	1	5	26	15	11
Blackpool	10	4	3	3	20	17	11
Bolton	10	4	3	3	16	15	11
Man Utd	11	2	6	3	15	17	10
Newcastle	11	3	4	4	21	25	10
Sheff Wed	12	5	0	7	19	27	10
Sheff Utd	10	4	1	5	16	22	9
Man City	11	3	3	5	13	20	9
Portsmouth	11	3	2	6	26	31	8
Sunderland	10	3	1	6	25	28	7
Arsenal	11	2	3	6	13	20	7
Chelsea	11	3	1	7	17	28	7
Liverpool	11	2	3	6	17	29	7
Middlesbro	11	2	2	7	16	33	6

Wednesday, September 23, 1953

Sheff Wed 3   **Newcastle 0**   Att: 28,297
Jordan 2, Marriott

Saturday, September 26, 1953

Aston Villa 4   **Sheff Utd 0**   Att: 39,586
Walsh 2, Thompson, Lockhart

Burnley 1   **Newcastle 2**   Att: 33,688
Holden   Milburn, Keery

Cardiff 0   **Arsenal 3**   Att: 49,137
Lishman 2, Mansell OG

Charlton 6   **Liverpool 0**   Att: 31,258
Evans 2, Leary 4 (1 pen)

Huddersfield 2   **Middlesbrough 1**   Att: 37,054
Glazzard 2   Mannion

Man City 2   **Portsmouth 1**   Att: 35,688
Hart, Revie   Reid

Preston 3   **Bolton 1**   Att: 39,553
Wayman, Baxter (pen), Hatsell   Moir

Sheff Wed 2   **West Bromwich 3**   Att: 44,573
Sewell, Woodhead   Griffin, Nicholls, Lee

Sunderland 3   **Blackpool 2**   Att: 60,998
Ford 2, Daniel   Perry, Mudie

Tottenham 1   **Man Utd 1**   Att: 52,837
Duquemin   Rowley

Wolves 8   **Chelsea 1**   Att: 36,134
Hancocks 3 (1 pen), Wilshaw, Swinbourne 2   Bentley
Broadbent, Mullen

Saturday, October 3, 1953

Arsenal 3
Roper 2, Barnes (pen) | **Preston 2**
Hatsell 2 | Att: 61,807

Blackpool 2
Mudie 2 | **Man City 0** | Att: 35,666

Bolton 2
Lofthouse, Hassall | **Tottenham 0** | Att: 39,842

Chelsea 2
Bentley, Lewis | **Sunderland 2**
T Wright, Kemp | Att: 56,685

Huddersfield 4
Glazzard 3, Metcalfe | **Aston Villa 0** | Att: 36,534

Sheff Wed 2
Sewell, Woodhead | **Liverpool 2**
Paisley, Bimpson | Att: 38,647

Burnley 2
Stephenson, Gray | **Man Utd 1**
Pearson | Att: 39,550

Charlton 2
Leary, Fenton (pen) | **Newcastle 0** | Att: 47,516

Portsmouth 1
Vaughan | **Cardiff 1**
Sullivan | Att: 31,766

Sheff Utd 3
Ringstead 2, Bottom | **Wolves 3**
Hancocks, Wilshaw, Swinbourne | Att: 35,961

West Bromwich 2
Nicholls, Lee | **Middlesbrough 1**
Spuhler | Att: 36,865

Football League Division One

	P	W	D	L	F	A	P
West Brom	12	9	2	1	33	14	20
Huddersfield	12	8	2	2	28	13	18
WOLVES	**12**	**7**	**3**	**2**	**34**	**20**	**17**
Charlton	12	8	0	4	33	18	16
Burnley	12	7	0	5	25	24	14
Aston Villa	11	7	0	4	19	13	14
Blackpool	11	5	3	3	22	17	13
Tottenham	12	6	1	5	20	19	13
Bolton	11	5	3	3	18	15	13
Cardiff	12	4	5	3	12	14	13
Preston	12	5	1	6	28	18	11
Sheff Wed	13	5	1	7	21	29	11
Man Utd	12	2	6	4	16	19	10
Newcastle	12	3	4	5	21	27	10
Sheff Utd	11	4	2	5	19	25	10
Portsmouth	12	3	3	6	27	32	9
Arsenal	12	3	3	6	16	22	9
Man City	12	3	3	6	13	22	9
Sunderland	11	3	2	6	27	30	8
Chelsea	12	3	2	7	19	30	8
Liverpool	12	2	4	6	19	31	8
Middlesbro	12	2	2	8	17	35	6

Football League Division One

	P	W	D	L	F	A	P
West Brom	13	10	2	1	37	14	22
WOLVES	**13**	**8**	**3**	**2**	**36**	**21**	**19**
Charlton	13	9	0	4	37	20	18
Huddersfield	13	8	2	3	28	17	18
Burnley	13	8	0	5	26	24	16
Bolton	12	6	3	3	21	17	15
Cardiff	13	5	5	3	14	15	15
Aston Villa	12	7	0	5	20	19	14
Blackpool	12	5	3	4	24	21	13
Tottenham	13	6	1	6	21	23	13
Sheff Wed	14	6	1	7	23	29	13
Man Utd	13	3	6	4	17	19	12
Preston	13	5	1	7	29	20	11
Arsenal	13	4	3	6	20	23	11
Liverpool	13	3	4	6	25	32	10
Newcastle	13	3	4	6	22	29	10
Sheff Utd	12	4	2	6	19	27	10
Portsmouth	13	3	3	7	27	33	9
Man City	13	3	3	7	15	25	9
Sunderland	12	3	2	7	27	31	8
Chelsea	13	3	2	8	19	32	8
Middlesbro	13	3	2	8	19	35	8

162

Saturday, October 10, 1953

Bolton 3 **Man City 2**
Alcock 2, Moir — Revie 2
Att: 34,443

Burnley 1 **Portsmouth 0**
McIlroy
Att: 28,142

Charlton 4 **Blackpool 2**
O'Linn, Leary, Evans 2 — Mortensen, Fenton (pen)
Att: 56,664

Liverpool 6 **Aston Villa 1**
Smyth 2, Liddell, Paisley, Payne, Blanchflower OG — Walsh
Att: 37,759

Man Utd 1 **Sunderland 0**
Rowley
Att: 36,482

Middlesbrough 2 **Sheff Utd 0**
Mannion 2
Att: 26,136

Newcastle 1 **Wolves 2**
Mulgrew — Smith, Swinbourne
Att: 39,913

Preston 1 **Cardiff 2**
Hatsell — Chisholm 2
Att: 23,500

Sheff Wed 2 **Chelsea 0**
Finney, Shaw
Att: 32,214

Tottenham 1 **Arsenal 4**
Robb — Logie 2, Milton, Forbes
Att: 69,821

West Bromwich 4 **Huddersfield 0**
Allen 3, Nicholls
Att: 46,872

Saturday, October 17, 1953

Arsenal 2
Forbes, Roper

Burnley 5
Holden 3, Stephenson 2

Att: 47,353

Aston Villa 1
Thompson

Newcastle 2
Milburn, Davies

Att: 38,366

Blackpool 1
Mortensen

Sheff Wed 2
Fenton OG, Finney

Att: 35,910

Cardiff 1
Grant (pen)

Tottenham 0

Att: 41,083

Chelsea 1
Lewis

Middlesbrough 1
Rayment

Att: 23,513

Huddersfield 2
Glazzard, Metcalfe

Liverpool 0

Att: 30,115

Man City 1
Anders

Preston 4
Hatsell, Wayman 2, Finney

Att: 43,295

Portsmouth 3
Harris 2, Gordon

Charlton 1
Kiernan

Att: 30,933

Sheff Utd 1
Hagan

West Bromwich 2
Allen, Nicholls

Att: 38,367

Sunderland 1
Bingham

Bolton 2
Wheeler, Lofthouse

Att: 45,358

Wolves 3
Hancocks (pen), Broadbent, Swinbourne

Man Utd 1
Taylor

Att: 40,084

Football League Division One

	P	W	D	L	F	A	P
West Brom	14	11	2	1	39	15	24
WOLVES	14	9	3	2	39	22	21
Huddersfield	14	9	2	3	30	17	20
Charlton	14	9	0	5	38	23	18
Burnley	14	9	0	5	31	26	18
Bolton	13	7	3	3	23	18	17
Cardiff	14	6	5	3	15	15	17
Sheff Wed	15	7	1	7	25	30	15
Aston Villa	13	7	0	6	21	21	14
Preston	14	6	1	7	33	21	13
Blackpool	13	5	3	5	25	23	13
Tottenham	14	6	1	7	21	24	13
Man Utd	14	3	6	5	18	22	12
Newcastle	14	4	4	6	24	30	12
Portsmouth	14	4	3	7	30	34	11
Arsenal	14	4	3	7	22	28	11
Liverpool	14	3	4	7	25	34	10
Sheff Utd	13	4	2	7	20	29	10
Chelsea	14	3	3	8	20	33	9
Middlesbro	14	3	3	8	20	36	9
Man City	14	3	3	8	16	29	9
Sunderland	13	3	2	8	28	33	8

163

Saturday, October 24, 1953

Bolton 1   **Wolves 1**
Moir   Hancocks
Att: 40,027

Burnley 3   **Cardiff 0**
Gray, McIlroy, Pilkingorn
Att: 29,539

Charlton 1   **Arsenal 5**
Hurst   Marden 3, Roper, Holton
Att: 60,259

Liverpool 3   **Sheff Utd 0**
Smyth 2, Payne
Att: 37,978

Man Utd 1   **Aston Villa 0**
Berry
Att: 32,106

Middlesbrough 0   **Blackpool 1**
Taylor
Att: 39,416

Newcastle 0   **Huddersfield 2**
Glazzard, Brennan OG
Att: 46,644

Preston 6   **Sunderland 2**
Wayman 3, Baxter, Hatsell, Morrison   T Wright 2
Att: 34,466

Sheff Wed 4   **Portsmouth 4**
Jordan 2, Sewell 2   Vaughan, Gordon 3
Att: 36,500

Tottenham 3   **Man City 0**
Duquemin, Robb 2
Att: 37,577

West Bromwich 5   **Chelsea 2**
Allen 3, Nicholls, Lee   Bentley 2
Att: 35,254

Football League Division One

	P	W	D	L	F	A	P
West Brom	15	12	2	1	44	17	26
Huddersfield	15	10	2	3	32	17	22
WOLVES	**15**	**9**	**4**	**2**	**40**	**23**	**22**
Burnley	15	10	0	5	34	26	20
Charlton	15	9	0	6	39	28	18
Bolton	14	7	4	3	24	19	18
Cardiff	15	6	5	4	15	18	17
Sheff Wed	16	7	2	7	29	34	16
Preston	15	7	1	7	39	23	15
Blackpool	14	6	3	5	26	23	15
Tottenham	15	7	1	7	24	24	15
Aston Villa	14	7	0	7	21	22	14
Man Utd	15	4	6	5	19	22	14
Arsenal	15	5	3	7	27	29	13
Portsmouth	15	4	4	7	34	38	12
Liverpool	15	4	4	7	28	34	12
Newcastle	15	4	4	7	24	32	12
Sheff Utd	14	4	2	8	20	32	10
Chelsea	15	3	3	9	22	38	9
Middlesbro	15	3	3	9	20	37	9
Man City	15	3	3	9	16	32	9
Sunderland	14	3	2	9	30	39	8

1953-4 LEAGUE RESULTS

Football League Division One

	P	W	D	L	F	A	P
West Brom	16	12	2	2	45	21	26
WOLVES	**16**	**10**	**4**	**2**	**41**	**23**	**24**
Huddersfield	16	10	3	3	32	17	23
Burnley	16	10	0	6	36	29	20
Bolton	15	7	5	3	26	21	19
Cardiff	16	7	5	4	20	18	19
Charlton	16	9	0	7	39	33	18
Blackpool	15	7	3	5	30	24	17
Sheff Wed	17	7	2	8	30	38	16
Preston	16	7	1	8	39	24	15
Arsenal	16	6	3	7	31	30	15
Tottenham	16	7	1	8	27	28	15
Aston Villa	15	7	1	7	23	24	15
Man Utd	16	4	7	5	19	22	15
Newcastle	16	4	4	8	25	35	12
Portsmouth	16	4	4	8	34	40	12
Liverpool	16	4	4	8	30	39	12
Sheff Utd	15	5	2	8	23	33	12
Chelsea	16	4	3	9	27	40	11
Man City	16	4	3	9	19	34	11
Middlesbro	16	4	3	9	22	37	11
Sunderland	15	4	2	9	34	42	10

Saturday, October 31, 1953

Arsenal 4 — Holton 2, Logie 2
Sheff Wed 1 — Woodhead
Att: 52,543

Aston Villa 2 — Roberts, Walsh
Bolton 2 — Moir, Lofthouse
Att: 25,325

Blackpool 4 — Mortensen, Taylor 2, Perry
West Bromwich 1 — Allen
Att: 27,106

Cardiff 5 — Dudley, Chisholm 3, Tiddy
Charlton 0
Att: 25,340

Chelsea 5 — Bentley 2, Armstrong, Stubbs, Blunstone
Liverpool 2 — Smyth 2
Att: 32,867

Huddersfield 0
Man Utd 0
Att: 34,175

Man City 3 — Meadows 2, Cunliffe
Burnley 2 — Adamson, Gray
Att: 32,353

Portsmouth 0
Middlesbrough 2 — Fitzsimons, McPherson
Att: 24,342

Sheff Utd 3 — Brook 2, Hawksworth
Newcastle 1 — Hannah
Att: 30,070

Sunderland 4 — T Wright, Elliott, Bingham, Ford
Tottenham 3 — Robb, Duquemin, Walters
Att: 38,345

Wolves 1 — Wilshaw
Preston 0
Att: 34,211

Saturday, November 7, 1953

Bolton 6   **Portsmouth 1**   Att: 22,441
Lofthouse 2, Hassall 3 (1 pen), Holden   Harris

Burnley 2   **Sheff Utd 1**   Att: 15,846
McIlroy 2   Brook

Charlton 2   **Huddersfield 1**   Att: 23,733
Evans, Hurst   Glazzard

Liverpool 2   **Man City 2**   Att: 30,917
Bimpson, Baron   Hart, Meadows

Man Utd 2   **Arsenal 2**   Att: 29,914
Rowley, Blanchflower   Holton, Roper

Middlesbrough 3   **Wolves 3**   Att: 24,284
Fitzsimons, McPherson, Hartnett   Swinbourne, Hancocks, Wilshaw

Newcastle 4   **Cardiff 0**   Att: 42,355
Milburn, Broadis 2, Hannah

Preston 2   **Blackpool 3**   Att: 31,886
Morrison, Baxter   Fenton (pen), Brown, Mortensen

Sheff Wed 3   **Aston Villa 1**   Att: 30,687
Quixall, Shaw, Finney   Thompson

Tottenham 2   **Chelsea 1**   Att: 44,795
Baily, Walters   Stubbs

West Bromwich 2   **Sunderland 0**   Att: 37,553
Barlow, Lee

Football League Division One

	P	W	D	L	F	A	P
West Brom	17	13	2	2	47	21	28
WOLVES	17	10	5	2	44	26	25
Huddersfield	17	10	3	4	33	19	23
Burnley	17	11	0	6	38	30	22
Bolton	16	8	5	3	32	22	21
Charlton	17	10	0	7	41	34	20
Blackpool	16	8	3	5	33	26	19
Cardiff	17	7	5	5	20	22	19
Sheff Wed	18	8	2	8	33	39	18
Tottenham	17	8	1	8	29	29	17
Arsenal	17	6	4	7	33	32	16
Man Utd	17	4	8	5	21	24	16
Preston	17	7	1	9	41	27	15
Aston Villa	16	7	1	8	24	27	15
Newcastle	17	5	4	8	29	35	14
Liverpool	17	4	5	8	32	41	13
Portsmouth	17	4	4	9	35	46	12
Sheff Utd	16	5	2	9	24	35	12
Middlesbro	17	4	4	9	25	40	12
Man City	17	4	4	9	21	36	12
Chelsea	17	4	3	10	28	42	11
Sunderland	16	4	2	10	34	44	10

Football League Division One

	P	W	D	L	F	A	P
West Brom	18	13	2	3	47	22	28
WOLVES	**18**	**11**	**5**	**2**	**45**	**26**	**27**
Huddersfield	18	11	3	4	35	19	25
Burnley	18	11	0	7	39	32	22
Charlton	18	10	1	7	42	35	21
Blackpool	17	9	3	5	34	26	21
Bolton	17	8	5	4	35	26	21
Cardiff	18	7	5	6	21	28	19
Man Utd	18	5	8	5	27	25	18
Arsenal	18	7	4	7	37	35	18
Sheff Wed	19	8	2	9	33	41	18
Preston	18	8	1	9	44	28	17
Tottenham	18	8	1	9	29	30	17
Aston Villa	17	8	1	8	29	30	17
Newcastle	18	5	5	8	29	35	15
Liverpool	18	4	5	9	34	44	13
Chelsea	18	5	3	10	30	43	13
Sheff Utd	17	5	3	9	25	36	13
Man City	18	4	5	9	21	36	13
Sunderland	17	5	2	10	37	46	12
Portsmouth	18	4	4	10	36	49	12
Middlesbro	18	4	4	10	28	45	12

Saturday, November 14, 1953

Arsenal 4
Holton 3, Lishman
Bolton 3
Moir, Wheeler, Hassall (pen)
Att: 52,319

Aston Villa 5
Thompson 3, Walsh, Chapman
Middlesbrough 3
McPherson, Delapenha, Rayment
Att: 20,735

Blackpool 1
Taylor
Tottenham 0
Att: 19,667

Cardiff 1
Chisholm
Man Utd 6
Viollet 2, Pearson, Taylor, Blanchflower, Berry
Att: 26,844

Chelsea 2
McNichol, Bentley
Burnley 1
Stephenson
Att: 39,731

Huddersfield 2
Glazzard 2
Sheff Wed 0
Att: 30,671

Man City 0
Newcastle 0
Att: 34,150

Portsmouth 1
Dale
Preston 3
Morrison, Baxter (pen), Finney
Att: 30,734

Sheff Utd 1
Wragg
Charlton 1
Hurst
Att: 27,661

Sunderland 3
Aitken, Elliott 2
Liverpool 2
Smyth 2
Att: 36,537

Wolves 1
Mullen
West Bromwich 0
Att: 56,590

Football League Division One

	P	W	D	L	F	A	P
West Brom	19	14	2	3	53	23	30
WOLVES	19	12	5	2	47	26	29
Huddersfield	19	11	3	5	35	20	25
Burnley	19	12	0	7	42	34	24
Bolton	18	8	6	4	37	28	22
Blackpool	18	9	3	6	35	30	21
Charlton	19	10	1	8	42	37	21
Man Utd	19	6	8	5	31	26	20
Arsenal	19	8	4	7	39	36	20
Preston	19	9	1	9	46	29	19
Tottenham	19	9	1	9	30	30	19
Cardiff	19	7	5	7	22	34	19
Sheff Wed	20	8	3	9	35	43	19
Aston Villa	18	8	1	9	31	33	17
Newcastle	19	5	6	8	30	36	16
Man City	19	5	5	9	22	36	15
Chelsea	19	5	4	10	32	45	14
Sunderland	18	5	3	10	39	48	13
Portsmouth	19	4	5	10	37	50	13
Liverpool	19	4	5	10	35	46	13
Sheff Utd	18	5	3	10	26	38	13
Middlesbro	19	4	4	11	28	46	12

168

Saturday, November 21, 1953

Bolton 2
Lofthouse, Wheeler
Chelsea 2
McNichol 2
Att: 30,635

Burnley 3
Stephenson, Gray, McIlroy
Aston Villa 2
Chapman 2
Att: 26,868

Charlton 0
Wolves 2
Broadbent, Hancocks
Att: 35,595

Liverpool 1
Bimpson
Arsenal 2
Logie, Lishman
Att: 47,814

Man Utd 4
Taylor 3, Viollet
Blackpool 1
Perry
Att: 51,688

Middlesbrough 0
Man City 1
Robinson OG
Att: 22,099

Newcastle 1
Milburn
Portsmouth 1
Harris
Att: 48,853

Preston 2
Wayman, Evans
Sheff Utd 1
Brook
Att: 23,703

Sheff Wed 2
Woodhead, Sewell
Sunderland 2
T Wright, Davis
Att: 37,446

Tottenham 1
Duquemin
Huddersfield 0
Att: 42,503

West Bromwich 6
Allen 4, Nicholls 2
Cardiff 1
Chisholm
Att: 39,444

Football League Division One

	P	W	D	L	F	A	P
West Brom	20	15	2	3	56	25	32
WOLVES	**20**	**13**	**5**	**2**	**51**	**27**	**31**
Huddersfield	20	12	3	5	38	21	27
Burnley	20	12	0	8	43	37	24
Bolton	19	8	7	4	37	28	23
Arsenal	20	9	4	7	41	37	22
Blackpool	19	9	4	6	35	30	22
Charlton	20	10	1	9	43	39	21
Man Utd	20	6	9	5	32	27	21
Cardiff	20	8	5	7	25	35	21
Preston	20	9	1	10	46	30	19
Sheff Wed	21	8	3	10	36	47	19
Aston Villa	19	9	1	9	33	34	19
Tottenham	20	9	1	10	32	35	19
Chelsea	20	6	4	10	33	45	16
Newcastle	20	5	6	9	31	38	16
Sheff Utd	19	6	3	10	31	40	15
Man City	20	5	5	10	24	39	15
Portsmouth	20	4	6	10	38	51	14
Middlesbro	20	5	4	11	30	46	14
Sunderland	19	5	3	11	39	50	13
Liverpool	20	4	5	11	36	49	13

Saturday, November 28, 1953

Arsenal 2   **Newcastle 1**
Holton, Forbes   Milburn   Att: 62,456

Aston Villa 2   **Charlton 1**
Dixon, Thompson   Ayre   Att: 30,205

Blackpool 0   **Bolton 0**
Att: 29,464

Cardiff 3   **Liverpool 1**
Grant, Chisholm, Edwards   Bimpson   Att: 21,284

Chelsea 1   **Preston 0**
Bentley   Att: 40,922

Huddersfield 3   **Burnley 1**
Glazzard, Davie 2   Shannon   Att: 34,666

Man City 2   **West Bromwich 3**
Hart, Revie   Lee, Allen, Nicholls   Att: 40,753

Portsmouth 1   **Man Utd 1**
Froggatt   Taylor   Att: 29,236

Sheff Utd 5   **Tottenham 2**
Ringstead 3, Brook, Hawksworth   Walters, Bennett   Att: 31,337

Sunderland 0   **Middlesbrough 2**
Walker 2   Att: 41,538

Wolves 4   **Sheff Wed 1**
Wilshaw, Hancocks (pen), Swinbourne 2   Woodhead   Att: 35,154

Football League Division One

	P	W	D	L	F	A	P
WOLVES	**21**	**14**	**5**	**2**	**54**	**29**	**33**
West Brom	21	15	2	4	58	28	32
Huddersfield	21	12	4	5	38	21	28
Burnley	21	13	0	8	48	38	26
Bolton	20	8	8	4	37	28	24
Charlton	21	11	1	9	45	40	23
Man Utd	21	6	10	5	34	29	22
Blackpool	20	9	4	7	37	35	22
Arsenal	21	9	4	8	41	39	22
Sheff Wed	22	9	3	10	38	48	21
Cardiff	21	8	5	8	26	37	21
Preston	21	9	2	10	47	31	20
Aston Villa	20	9	2	9	34	35	20
Tottenham	21	9	1	11	34	38	19
Newcastle	21	5	7	9	32	39	17
Chelsea	21	6	5	10	34	46	17
Sheff Utd	20	6	4	10	33	42	16
Portsmouth	21	5	6	10	41	53	16
Middlesbro	21	6	4	11	32	46	16
Liverpool	21	5	5	11	41	51	15
Man City	21	5	5	11	25	41	15
Sunderland	20	5	3	12	40	55	13

Saturday, December 5, 1953

Bolton 0   **Huddersfield 0**   Att: 36,077

Burnley 5   **Sunderland 1**   Att: 27,839
Shannon, Gray, Holden, Adamson, McIlroy   Shackleton

Charlton 2   **Man City 1**   Att: 17,813
Fenton, Leary   Meadows

Liverpool 5   **Blackpool 2**   Att: 47,320
A'Court 2, Payne, Arnell, Smyth   Taylor 2

Man Utd 2   **Sheff Utd 2**   Att: 33,524
Blanchflower 2   Toner, Hawksworth

Middlesbrough 2   **Arsenal 0**   Att: 30,085
Spuhler 2

Newcastle 1   **Chelsea 1**   Att: 41,728
Mitchell   Stubbs

Preston 1   **Aston Villa 1**   Att: 20,590
Hatsell   Thompson

Sheff Wed 2   **Cardiff 1**   Att: 26,597
Froggatt, Sewell   Chisholm

Tottenham 2   **Wolves 3**   Att: 48,164
Bennett, Duquemin   Wilshaw, Broadbent, Hancocks

West Bromwich 2   **Portsmouth 3**   Att: 29,492
Nicholls, Allen   Gordon 2, Harris

1953-4 LEAGUE RESULTS

Football League Division One

	P	W	D	L	F	A	P
West Brom	22	15	3	4	60	30	33
WOLVES	**22**	**14**	**5**	**3**	**55**	**31**	**33**
Huddersfield	22	12	5	5	40	23	29
Burnley	22	14	0	8	50	39	28
Bolton	21	8	8	5	37	31	24
Charlton	22	11	1	10	46	42	23
Arsenal	22	9	5	8	43	41	23
Cardiff	22	9	5	8	27	37	23
Blackpool	21	9	4	8	38	37	22
Man Utd	22	6	10	8	35	38	22
Preston	22	9	3	10	49	33	21
Tottenham	22	10	1	11	36	39	21
Sheff Wed	23	9	3	11	40	51	21
Aston Villa	21	9	2	10	35	37	20
Newcastle	22	6	7	9	35	40	19
Chelsea	22	7	5	10	37	47	19
Portsmouth	22	6	6	10	46	54	18
Sheff Utd	21	7	4	10	36	42	18
Man City	22	6	5	11	28	43	17
Middlesbro	22	6	4	12	32	47	16
Liverpool	22	5	5	12	42	56	15
Sunderland	21	6	3	12	42	56	15

Saturday, December 12, 1953

Arsenal 2
Lishman 2

West Bromwich 2
Nicholls 2   Att: 55,264

Aston Villa 1
Blanchflower

Tottenham 2
Baily, Walters   Att: 27,480

Blackpool 1
Perry

Newcastle 3
Broadis, Hannah, Mitchell   Att: 19,896

Cardiff 1
Ford

Middlesbrough 0   Att: 31,776

Chelsea 3
McNichol 2, Parsons

Man Utd 1
Berry   Att: 37,153

Huddersfield 2
Cavanagh, Metcalfe (pen)

Preston 2
Wayman, Morrison   Att: 26,972

Man City 3
Davies, Little, Revie

Sheff Wed 2
Froggatt, Curtis (pen)   Att: 27,710

Portsmouth 5
Gordon, Harris 3, Vaughan

Liverpool 1
Smyth   Att: 23,709

Sheff Utd 3
Hawksworth, Ringstead, Toner

Bolton 0   Att: 27,769

Sunderland 2
Shackleton 2

Charlton 1
Hurst   Att: 29,652

Wolves 1
Hancocks

Burnley 2
Holden 2   Att: 35,043

Football League Division One

	P	W	D	L	F	A	P
WOLVES	**23**	**15**	**5**	**3**	**58**	**32**	**35**
West Brom	23	15	3	5	61	32	33
Huddersfield	23	12	6	5	42	25	30
Burnley	23	15	0	8	52	39	30
Bolton	22	9	8	5	39	32	26
Cardiff	23	10	5	8	29	38	25
Man Utd	23	7	10	6	40	33	24
Arsenal	23	9	6	8	45	43	24
Preston	23	10	3	10	50	33	23
Charlton	23	11	1	11	46	44	23
Tottenham	23	11	1	11	39	40	23
Blackpool	22	9	4	9	39	43	22
Chelsea	23	8	5	10	42	48	21
Sheff Wed	24	9	3	12	41	54	21
Sheff Utd	22	8	4	10	39	43	20
Aston Villa	22	9	2	11	36	39	20
Newcastle	23	6	8	9	36	41	20
Portsmouth	23	6	6	11	47	57	18
Man City	23	6	5	12	29	46	17
Sunderland	22	6	4	12	43	57	16
Middlesbro	23	6	4	13	32	48	16
Liverpool	23	5	5	13	43	61	15

172

Saturday, December 19, 1953

Aston Villa 1
Dixon
Cardiff 2
Northcott 2
Att: 27,012

Bolton 2
Lofthouse, Wheeler
West Bromwich 1
Ryan
Att: 32,246

Burnley 2
Shannon, McIlroy
Charlton 0
Att: 25,369

Chelsea 5
McNichol 3, Bentley, Stubbs
Blackpool 1
Mudie
Att: 34,865

Huddersfield 2
Glazzard 2
Arsenal 2
Milton, Lishman
Att: 34,018

Man Utd 5
Taylor 2, Blanchflower 2, Viollet
Liverpool 1
Bimpson
Att: 27,916

Preston 1
Wayman
Middlesbrough 0
Att:18,909

Sheff Utd 3
Furniss 2 (2 pen), Wragg
Portsmouth 1
Gordon
Att: 25,346

Sunderland 1
Anderson
Newcastle 1
Broadis
Att: 49,822

Tottenham 3
Curtis OG, Duquemin, Baker
Sheff Wed 1
Froggatt
Att: 25,957

Man City 1
Davies
Wolves 3
Hancocks 2 (1 pen), Wilshaw
Att: 27,606

Football League Division One

	P	W	D	L	F	A	P
West Brom	24	16	3	5	66	34	35
WOLVES	**24**	**15**	**5**	**4**	**59**	**34**	**35**
Burnley	24	16	0	8	54	40	32
Huddersfield	24	12	7	5	43	26	31
Man Utd	24	8	10	6	45	35	26
Bolton	23	9	8	6	39	33	26
Charlton	24	12	1	11	47	44	25
Cardiff	23	10	5	8	29	38	25
Arsenal	23	9	6	8	45	43	24
Tottenham	24	11	2	11	40	41	24
Preston	24	10	3	11	51	35	23
Aston Villa	23	10	2	11	38	40	22
Blackpool	22	9	4	9	39	43	22
Newcastle	24	7	8	9	39	43	22
Sheff Utd	23	8	5	10	41	45	21
Chelsea	23	8	5	10	42	48	21
Sheff Wed	25	9	3	13	43	59	21
Portsmouth	24	6	7	11	48	58	19
Man City	24	6	6	12	31	48	18
Sunderland	23	6	5	12	44	58	17
Middlesbro	24	6	4	14	34	51	16
Liverpool	24	5	5	14	45	66	15

Thursday, December 24, 1953

Wolves 1 Aston Villa 2
Wilshaw Dixon, McParland
Att: 40,536

Friday, December 25, 1953

Burnley 2 Preston 1
Pilkington, Shannon Morrison
Att: 33,398

Charlton 1 Bolton 0
Hewie
Att: 19,226

Man Utd 5 Sheff Wed 2
Taylor 3, Viollet, Blanchflower Gannon, Woodhead
Att: 28,953

Middlesbrough 2 Newcastle 3
Walker, Spuler Mitchell, Scoular, Monkhouse
Att: 28,138

Sheff Utd 2 Man City 2
Hawksworth, Brook Hart, Revie
Att: 32,787

Sunderland 1 Huddersfield 1
Hall Watson
Att: 36,751

Tottenham 1 Portsmouth 1
Brooks Harris
Att: 36,502

Sheff Utd 2 Man City 2
Hawksworth, Brook (pen) Hart, Revie
Att: 32,787

West Bromwich 5 Liverpool 2
Nicholls, Barlow, Griffin 2, Allen A'Court, Lambert (pen)
Att: 30,287

Football League Division One

	P	W	D	L	F	A	P
WOLVES	**25**	**16**	**5**	**4**	**61**	**35**	**37**
West Brom	25	16	4	5	66	34	36
Huddersfield	25	13	7	5	45	27	33
Burnley	25	16	0	9	55	42	32
Man Utd	25	9	10	6	46	35	28
Bolton	24	10	8	6	42	34	28
Preston	25	11	3	11	53	36	25
Arsenal	24	9	7	8	47	45	25
Charlton	25	12	1	12	48	47	25
Tottenham	25	11	3	11	41	42	25
Cardiff	24	10	5	9	29	40	25
Chelsea	24	9	5	10	44	48	23
Blackpool	23	9	5	9	41	45	23
Aston Villa	24	10	2	12	39	42	22
Newcastle	25	7	8	10	41	46	22
Sheff Utd	24	8	5	11	42	47	21
Sheff Wed	26	9	3	14	43	60	21
Portsmouth	25	6	8	11	49	59	20
Man City	25	7	6	12	33	49	20
Middlesbro	25	7	4	14	37	53	18
Sunderland	24	6	5	13	45	60	17
Liverpool	25	5	6	14	45	66	16

Saturday, December 26, 1953

Aston Villa 1
Thompson
Wolves 2
Hancocks, Wilshaw
Att: 49,123

Blackpool 2
Brown 2
Arsenal 2
Lishman, Roper
Att: 29,347

Bolton 3
Lofthouse, Moir, Wheeler
Charlton 1
Hewie
Att: 36,065

Chelsea 0
Cardiff 0
Att: 61,336

Huddersfield 2
Cavanagh, Metcalfe
Sunderland 1
Shackleton
Att: 40,898

Liverpool 0
West Bromwich 0
Att: 51,167

Man City 2
Hart, Rawson OG
Sheff Utd 1
Ringstead
Att: 35,786

Newcastle 2
Broadis, Mitchell
Middlesbrough 3
Delapenha, O'Conell, Lawrie
Att: 43,750

Portsmouth 1
Vaughan
Tottenham 1
Walters
Att: 36,677

Preston 2
Wayman 2
Burnley 1
McIlroy
Att: 32,416

Sheff Wed 0
Man Utd 1
Viollet
Att: 43,526

Monday, December 28 1953

Arsenal 1   Att: 63,661
Roper
Cardiff 0

Blackpool 1   Att: 36,958
Perry
Chelsea 0

Football League Division One

	P	W	D	L	F	A	P
WOLVES	**25**	**16**	**5**	**4**	**61**	**35**	**37**
West Brom	25	16	4	5	66	34	36
Huddersfield	25	13	7	5	45	27	33
Burnley	25	16	0	9	55	42	32
Man Utd	25	9	10	6	46	35	28
Bolton	24	10	8	6	42	34	28
Arsenal	25	9	8	8	48	46	26
Cardiff	25	10	6	9	29	40	26
Preston	25	11	3	11	53	36	25
Charlton	25	12	1	12	48	47	25
Tottenham	25	11	3	11	41	42	25
Chelsea	25	9	6	10	44	48	24
Blackpool	24	9	6	9	42	46	24
Aston Villa	24	10	2	12	39	42	22
Newcastle	25	7	8	10	41	46	22
Sheff Utd	24	8	5	11	42	47	21
Sheff Wed	26	9	3	14	43	60	21
Portsmouth	25	6	8	11	49	59	20
Man City	25	7	6	12	33	49	20
Middlesbro	25	7	4	14	37	53	18
Sunderland	24	6	5	13	45	60	17
Liverpool	25	5	6	14	45	66	16

Friday, January 1, 1954

Bolton 2	Sheff Utd 1	Att: 37,484
Lofthouse, Coldwell OG	Brook	
Newcastle 2	Blackpool 1	Att: 44,343
Milburn 2	Brown	
Sunderland 2	Aston Villa 0	Att: 44,337
Shackleton, Chisholm		

Football League Division One

	P	W	D	L	F	A	P
WOLVES	**25**	**16**	**5**	**4**	**61**	**35**	**37**
West Brom	25	16	4	5	66	34	36
Huddersfield	25	13	7	5	45	27	33
Burnley	25	16	0	9	55	42	32
Bolton	25	11	8	6	44	35	30
Man Utd	25	9	10	6	46	35	28
Arsenal	25	9	8	8	48	46	26
Cardiff	25	10	6	9	29	40	26
Preston	25	11	3	11	53	36	25
Charlton	25	12	1	12	48	47	25
Tottenham	25	11	3	11	41	42	25
Chelsea	25	9	6	10	44	48	24
Newcastle	26	8	8	10	43	47	24
Blackpool	25	9	6	10	43	48	24
Aston Villa	25	10	2	13	39	44	22
Sheff Utd	25	8	5	11	43	49	21
Sheff Wed	26	9	3	14	43	60	21
Portsmouth	25	6	8	11	49	59	20
Man City	25	7	6	12	33	49	20
Middlesbro	25	7	4	14	37	53	18
Sunderland	25	7	5	13	47	60	19
Liverpool	25	5	6	14	45	66	16

Football League Division One

	P	W	D	L	F	A	P
WOLVES	26	17	5	4	64	36	39
West Brom	26	17	4	5	69	36	38
Huddersfield	26	13	7	6	47	32	33
Burnley	26	16	0	10	55	44	32
Bolton	26	12	8	6	46	36	32
Man Utd	26	10	10	6	48	36	30
Arsenal	25	9	8	8	48	46	26
Charlton	26	12	2	12	49	48	26
Cardiff	26	10	6	10	30	43	26
Preston	26	11	3	12	55	39	25
Chelsea	26	9	7	10	45	49	25
Tottenham	26	11	3	12	41	45	25
Blackpool	26	9	7	10	45	50	25
Newcastle	27	8	8	11	44	49	24
Sheff Wed	27	10	3	14	45	60	23
Aston Villa	25	10	2	13	39	44	22
Sheff Utd	26	8	6	12	45	51	22
Man City	26	8	6	12	35	50	22
Portsmouth	26	7	8	11	54	61	22
Middlesbro	26	8	4	14	40	53	20
Sunderland	26	7	5	14	48	62	19
Liverpool	26	5	6	15	46	68	16

177

Saturday, January 2, 1954

Arsenal 3
(abandoned, 23 minutes – fog)
Holton 2, Lawton
Aston Villa 0
Att: 30,000

Blackpool 2
Taylor 2
Sheff Utd 2
Ringstead, Hawksworth
Att: 20,470

Cardiff 1
Nugent,
Wolves 3
Swinbourne, Wilshaw, Hancocks
Att: 42,521

Charlton 1
Hewie
Chelsea 1
McNichol
Att: 29,017

Liverpool 1
Evans
Bolton 2
Moir, Stevens
Att: 44,383

Man City 2
McAdams, Revie
Sunderland 1
T Wright
Att: 23,742

Middlesbrough 3
Spuhler, Lawrie, O'Connell
Tottenham 0
Att: 35,141

Newcastle 1
Broadis
Man Utd 2
Foulkes, Blanchflower
Att: 56,034

Portsmouth 5
Vaughan 3, Harris, Henderson
Huddersfield 2
Mansell OG, Quested
Att: 27,215

Sheff Wed 2
Quixall, Woodhead
Burnley 0
Att: 33,061

West Bromwich 3
Allen 2, Nicholls
Preston 2
Wayman, Morrison
Att: 20,174

Football League Division One

	P	W	D	L	F	A	P
West Brom	27	18	4	5	70	36	40
WOLVES	27	17	5	5	64	38	**39**
Huddersfield	27	13	8	6	47	32	34
Burnley	27	17	0	10	60	44	34
Bolton	27	12	9	6	48	38	33
Man Utd	27	10	11	6	49	37	31
Arsenal	26	10	8	8	50	46	28
Charlton	27	13	2	12	53	50	28
Preston	27	12	3	12	57	40	27
Chelsea	27	10	7	10	48	50	27
Blackpool	27	9	8	10	45	50	26
Cardiff	27	10	6	11	30	48	26
Newcastle	28	8	9	11	46	51	25
Tottenham	27	11	3	13	41	46	25
Aston Villa	26	10	3	13	40	45	23
Portsmouth	27	7	9	11	55	62	23
Sheff Wed	28	10	3	15	47	64	23
Man City	27	8	7	12	36	51	23
Sheff Utd	27	8	6	13	46	54	22
Sunderland	27	8	5	14	53	62	21
Middlesbro	27	8	4	15	40	58	20
Liverpool	27	5	6	16	47	70	16

178

Saturday, January 16, 1954

Aston Villa 1
Thompson
Portsmouth 1
Harris
Att: 24,802

Bolton 2
Moir, Lofthouse
Newcastle 2
Keeble, Broadis
Att: 29,476

Burnley 5
Holden, Gray 3, McIlroy
Middlesbrough 0
Att: 23,481

Charlton 4
Leary 2, Ayre, Kiernan
Sheff Wed 2
Sewell, Shaw
Att: 19,655

Huddersfield 0
Blackpool 0
Att: 25,733

Man Utd 1
Berry
Man City 1
McAdams
Att: 48,216

Preston 2
Foster, Wayman
Liverpool 1
Baron
Att: 26,128

Sheff Utd 1
Wragg
Chelsea 3
Parsons, Stubbs, Blunstone
Att: 22,569

Sunderland 5
T Wright 2, Shackleton, Purdon 2
Cardiff 0
Att: 40,629

Tottenham 0
West Bromwich 1
Allen
Att: 48,812

Wolves 0
Arsenal 2
Logie, Lishman
Att: 45,974

Saturday, January 23, 1954

Arsenal 1
Holton
Sunderland 4
Purdon 3, T Wright
Att: 60,218

Blackpool 3
Stephenson, Perry 2
Aston Villa 2
Thompson 2
Att: 16,629

Cardiff 0
Man City 3
Anders, Clarke, Revie
Att: 22,516

Chelsea 2
Bentley, McNichol
Huddersfield 2
Glazzard 2
Att: 45,041

Liverpool 2
Liddell, Evans
Tottenham 2
Walters, Lock, OG
Att: 43,592

Man Utd 1
Taylor
Bolton 5
Lofthouse 2, Parry 2, Moir
Att: 48,505

Middlesbrough 0
Charlton 2
Leary 2
Att: 19,327

Newcastle 0
Preston 4
Wayman 2, Foster, Baxter
Att: 40,340

Portsmouth 2
Dickinson, Reid
Wolves 0
Att: 35,312

Sheff Wed 3
Sewell, Shaw 2
Sheff Utd 2
Brook 2
Att: 42,889

West Bromwich 0
Burnley 0
Att: 42,644

Football League Division One

	P	W	D	L	F	A	P
West Brom	28	18	5	5	70	36	41
WOLVES	**28**	**17**	**5**	**6**	**64**	**40**	**39**
Huddersfield	28	13	9	6	49	34	35
Burnley	28	17	1	10	60	44	35
Bolton	28	13	9	6	53	39	35
Man Utd	28	10	11	7	50	42	31
Charlton	28	14	2	12	55	50	30
Preston	28	13	3	12	61	40	29
Arsenal	27	10	8	9	51	50	28
Chelsea	28	10	8	10	50	52	28
Blackpool	28	10	8	10	48	52	28
Tottenham	28	11	4	13	43	48	26
Cardiff	28	10	6	12	30	51	26
Portsmouth	28	10	5	11	57	62	25
Newcastle	29	8	9	12	46	55	25
Man City	28	9	7	12	39	51	25
Sheff Wed	29	11	3	15	50	66	25
Sunderland	28	9	5	14	57	63	23
Aston Villa	27	10	3	14	42	48	23
Sheff Utd	28	8	6	14	48	48	22
Middlesbro	28	8	4	16	40	57	20
Liverpool	28	5	7	16	49	72	17

Saturday, February 6, 1954

Aston Villa 2   **Chelsea 2**
Roberts, Blanchflower (pen)   McNichol, Bentley   Att: 20,625

Bolton 3   **Cardiff 0**
Lofthouse, Moir, Stevens   Att: 30,777

Burnley 1   **Liverpool 1**
Pilkington   Anderson   Att: 24,025

Charlton 1   **West Bromwich 1**
Ayre   Allen   Att: 27,553

Huddersfield 2   **Sheff Utd 2**
Frear 2   Cross, Staniforth OG   Att: 27,335

Man City 0   **Arsenal 0**
Att: 39,503

Preston 1   **Man Utd 3**
Baxter (pen)   Blanchflower, Rowley, Taylor   Att: 30,064

Sheff Wed 4   **Middlesbrough 2**
Sewell, Woodhead 2, Shaw   Delapenha 2   Att: 30,856

Sunderland 3   **Portsmouth 1**
Elliott, Shackleton, Purdon   Henderson   Att: 45,935

Tottenham 3   **Newcastle 0**
Robb 2, Walters   Att: 35,798

Wolves 4   **Blackpool 1**
Swinbourne 3, Hancocks   Stephenson   Att: 27,795

Football League Division One

	P	W	D	L	F	A	P
West Brom	29	18	6	5	71	37	42
WOLVES	29	18	5	6	68	41	41
Bolton	29	14	9	6	56	39	37
Huddersfield	29	13	10	6	51	36	36
Burnley	29	17	2	10	61	45	36
Man Utd	29	11	11	7	53	43	33
Charlton	29	14	3	12	56	51	31
Preston	29	13	3	13	62	43	29
Arsenal	28	10	9	9	51	50	29
Chelsea	29	10	9	10	52	54	29
Tottenham	29	12	4	13	46	48	28
Blackpool	29	10	8	11	49	56	28
Sheff Wed	30	12	3	15	54	68	27
Man City	29	9	8	12	39	51	26
Cardiff	29	10	6	13	30	54	26
Sunderland	29	10	5	14	60	64	25
Portsmouth	29	8	9	12	58	65	25
Newcastle	30	8	9	13	46	58	25
Aston Villa	28	10	4	14	44	50	24
Sheff Utd	29	8	7	14	50	59	23
Middlesbro	29	8	4	17	42	64	20
Liverpool	29	5	8	16	50	73	18

Saturday, February 13, 1954

Arsenal 1 Lishman	**Cardiff 1** Ford	Att: 45,497
Blackpool 3 Perry, Brown 2	**Sunderland 0**	Att: 23,058
Bolton 0	**Preston 2** Baxter, Finney	Att: 44,639
Chelsea 4 Bentley 2, Parsons, Stubbs	**Wolves 2** Swinbourne, Wilshaw	Att: 60,289
Liverpool 2 Evans, Anderson	**Charlton 3** Firmani 2, O'Linn	Att: 47,657
Man Utd 2 Rowley, Taylor	**Tottenham 0**	Att: 37,289
Middlesbrough 0	**Huddersfield 3** Metcalfe, Burrell, Glazzard	Att:18,717
Newcastle 3 Broadis 2, Milburn	**Burnley 1** McIlroy	Att: 29,114
Portsmouth 4 Froggatt 2, Henderson 2	**Man City 1** McAdams	Att: 30,013
West Bromwich 4 Nicholls, Butler OG, Rickaby, Ryan	**Sheff Wed 2** Woodhead, Shaw	Att: 38,304

Football League Division One

	P	W	D	L	F	A	P
West Brom	30	19	6	5	75	39	44
WOLVES	**30**	**18**	**5**	**7**	**70**	**45**	**41**
Huddersfield	30	14	10	6	54	36	38
Bolton	30	14	9	7	56	41	37
Burnley	30	17	2	11	62	48	36
Man Utd	30	12	11	7	55	43	35
Charlton	30	15	3	12	59	53	33
Preston	30	14	3	13	64	43	31
Chelsea	30	11	9	10	56	56	31
Arsenal	29	10	10	9	52	51	30
Blackpool	30	11	8	11	52	56	30
Tottenham	30	12	4	14	46	50	28
Portsmouth	30	9	9	12	62	66	27
Newcastle	31	9	9	13	49	59	27
Sheff Wed	31	12	3	16	56	72	27
Cardiff	30	10	7	13	31	55	27
Man City	30	9	8	13	40	55	26
Sunderland	30	10	5	15	60	67	25
Aston Villa	28	10	4	14	44	50	24
Sheff Utd	29	8	7	14	50	59	23
Middlesbro	30	8	4	18	42	67	20
Liverpool	30	5	8	17	52	76	18

Football League Division One

	P	W	D	L	F	A	P
West Brom	30	19	6	5	75	39	44
WOLVES	**31**	**19**	**5**	**7**	**76**	**46**	**43**
Huddersfield	31	14	11	6	56	38	39
Burnley	31	18	2	11	64	48	38
Bolton	30	14	9	7	56	41	37
Man Utd	31	12	11	8	55	45	35
Charlton	30	15	3	12	59	53	33
Chelsea	31	12	9	10	58	57	33
Preston	30	14	3	13	64	43	31
Arsenal	29	10	10	9	52	51	30
Blackpool	30	11	8	11	52	56	30
Tottenham	30	12	4	14	46	50	28
Portsmouth	30	9	9	12	62	66	27
Newcastle	31	9	9	13	49	59	27
Sheff Wed	31	12	3	16	56	72	27
Cardiff	30	10	7	13	31	55	27
Man City	30	9	8	13	40	55	26
Sunderland	31	10	5	16	61	69	25
Aston Villa	29	10	5	14	46	52	25
Sheff Utd	30	8	7	15	51	65	23
Middlesbro	30	8	4	18	42	67	20
Liverpool	30	5	8	17	52	76	18

Saturday, February 20, 1954

Aston Villa 2
Thompson 2
Huddersfield 2
Metcalfe, Glazzard
Att: 24,451

Burnley 2
Gray 2
Man Utd 0
Att: 31,402

Sunderland 1
Chisholm
Chelsea 2
Parsons, Bentley
Att: 45,755

Wolves 6
Swinbourne 2, Hancocks 2, Broadbent, Wilshaw
Sheff Utd 1
Cross
Att: 27,823

Football League Division One

	P	W	D	L	F	A	P
West Brom	31	19	7	5	76	40	45
WOLVES	**31**	**19**	**5**	**7**	**76**	**46**	**43**
Huddersfield	31	14	11	6	56	38	39
Burnley	31	18	2	11	64	48	38
Bolton	30	14	9	7	56	41	37
Man Utd	31	12	11	8	55	45	35
Charlton	30	15	3	12	59	53	33
Chelsea	31	12	9	10	58	57	33
Arsenal	30	11	10	9	53	51	33
Blackpool	31	12	8	11	56	57	32
Preston	31	14	3	14	64	44	31
Tottenham	30	12	4	14	46	50	28
Sheff Wed	32	12	4	16	57	73	28
Portsmouth	30	9	9	12	62	66	27
Newcastle	31	9	9	13	49	59	27
Cardiff	30	10	7	13	31	55	27
Man City	31	9	8	14	41	59	26
Sunderland	31	10	5	16	61	69	25
Aston Villa	29	10	5	14	46	52	25
Sheff Utd	30	8	7	15	51	65	23
Middlesbro	31	8	5	18	43	68	21
Liverpool	31	5	9	17	53	77	19

Wednesday, February 24, 1954

Man City 1
Clarke
Blackpool 4
Matthews 2, Brown, Perry
Att: 22,515

Middlesbrough 1
Delapenha (pen)
West Bromwich 1
Allen
Att: 17,144

Preston 0
Arsenal 1
Lishman
Att: 25,633

Sheff Wed 1
Woodhead
Liverpool 1
Anderson
Att: 16,986

Football League Division One

	P	W	D	L	F	A	P
West Brom	32	20	7	5	78	40	47
WOLVES	**32**	**20**	**5**	**7**	**79**	**48**	**45**
Huddersfield	32	14	11	7	56	40	39
Burnley	32	18	2	12	66	51	38
Bolton	31	14	9	8	56	44	37
Man Utd	32	13	11	8	57	45	37
Charlton	32	15	4	13	60	56	34
Blackpool	32	13	8	11	59	58	34
Chelsea	32	12	9	11	58	58	33
Arsenal	31	11	10	10	53	54	32
Preston	32	14	3	15	65	46	31
Tottenham	31	13	4	14	49	50	30
Sheff Wed	33	13	4	16	58	73	30
Portsmouth	31	10	9	12	65	68	29
Cardiff	31	11	7	13	33	56	29
Man City	32	10	8	14	44	59	28
Newcastle	33	9	10	14	51	62	28
Aston Villa	30	11	5	14	48	53	27
Sunderland	32	10	5	17	61	71	25
Sheff Utd	31	8	8	15	53	67	24
Middlesbro	32	8	6	18	45	70	22
Liverpool	32	5	9	18	54	79	19

Thursday, February 25, 1954

Charlton 0   Newcastle 0   Att: 13,441

Saturday, February 27, 1954

Arsenal 0   **Tottenham 3**   Att: 64,311
Robb 2, Walters

Aston Villa 2   **Liverpool 1**   Att: 25,973
Thompson, Roberts   Bimpson

Blackpool 3   **Charlton 1**   Att: 21,619
Stephenson 2, Taylor   Firmani

Cardiff 2   **Preston 1**   Att: 30,502
Grant 2   Finney

Chelsea 0   **Sheff Wed 1**   Att: 54,498
Woodhead

Huddersfield 0   **West Bromwich 2**   Att: 48,237
Ryan, Nicholls

Man City 3   **Bolton 0**   Att: 39,340
McAdams, Meadows, Revie

Portsmouth 3   **Burnley 2**   Att: 24,155
Barnard, Gordon 2   McIlroy, Adamson

Sheff Utd 2   **Middlesbrough 2**   Att: 29,029
McNab, Cross   Delapenha, Mannion

Sunderland 0   **Man Utd 2**   Att: 38,400
Taylor, Blanchflower

Wolves 3   **Newcastle 2**   Att: 38,592
Broadbent, Wilshaw, Slater   Milburn, Broadis

Football League Division One

	P	W	D	L	F	A	P
West Brom	33	20	8	5	80	42	48
WOLVES	**33**	**20**	**5**	**8**	**79**	**49**	**45**
Huddersfield	33	15	11	7	59	41	41
Burnley	33	19	2	12	68	52	40
Man Utd	33	14	11	8	58	45	39
Bolton	33	15	9	9	61	48	39
Charlton	33	16	4	13	63	57	36
Blackpool	33	14	8	11	61	59	36
Chelsea	33	12	10	11	61	61	34
Preston	33	15	3	15	69	46	33
Cardiff	33	13	7	13	37	58	33
Arsenal	32	11	10	11	54	56	32
Tottenham	33	14	4	15	52	53	32
Sheff Wed	34	13	4	17	59	75	30
Portsmouth	33	10	9	14	68	74	29
Aston Villa	31	12	5	14	49	53	29
Newcastle	34	9	10	15	51	63	28
Man City	33	10	8	15	44	63	28
Sheff Utd	32	8	9	15	55	69	25
Sunderland	33	10	5	18	62	74	25
Middlesbro	33	8	7	18	48	73	23
Liverpool	33	5	9	19	55	82	19

Wednesday, March 3, 1954

Cardiff 3 — **Portsmouth 2**   Att: 17,842
Nugent, Tiddy, Grant — Reid, Pearson

Tottenham 3 — **Bolton 2**   Att: 16,720
Walters, Stokes, Dunmore — Moir, Lofthouse

Saturday, March 6, 1954

Bolton 3 — **Sunderland 1**   Att: 36,379
Stevens, Parry, Moir — Shackleton

Burnley 2 — **Arsenal 1**   Att: 22,726
Holden, Shannon — Holton

Charlton 3 — **Portsmouth 1**   Att: 37,598
Leary 2, Firmani — Barnard

Liverpool 1 — **Huddersfield 3**   Att: 46,074
Evans — Burrell 2, Cavanagh

Man Utd 1 — **Wolves 0**   Att: 40,774
Berry

Middlesbrough 3 — **Chelsea 3**   Att: 27,920
Spuhler, Delapenha 2 — Parsons 2, Bentley

Newcastle 0 — **Aston Villa 1**   Att: 36,847
Walsh

Preston 4 — **Man City 0**   Att: 23,669
Baxter (pen), Finney, Wayman 2

Sheff Wed 1 — **Blackpool 2**   Att: 41,619
Woodhead — Mudie, Brown

Tottenham 0 — **Cardiff 1**   Att: 45,248
Tiddy

West Bromwich 2 — **Sheff Utd 2**   Att: 37,472
Nicholls, Lee — Wragg 2

Football League Division One

	P	W	D	L	F	A	P
West Brom	33	20	8	5	80	42	48
WOLVES	**33**	**20**	**5**	**8**	**79**	**49**	**45**
Huddersfield	34	16	11	7	62	43	43
Burnley	34	19	2	13	68	53	40
Man Utd	34	14	12	8	60	47	40
Bolton	33	15	9	9	61	48	39
Charlton	34	16	5	13	66	60	37
Blackpool	34	14	9	11	61	59	37
Cardiff	34	14	7	13	38	58	35
Chelsea	33	12	10	11	61	61	34
Preston	33	15	3	15	69	46	33
Arsenal	33	11	11	11	57	59	33
Tottenham	33	14	4	15	52	53	32
Aston Villa	32	12	6	14	51	55	30
Sheff Wed	34	13	4	17	59	75	30
Portsmouth	33	10	9	14	68	74	29
Newcastle	35	9	10	16	53	66	28
Man City	33	10	8	14	44	63	28
Sheff Utd	33	9	9	15	58	70	27
Sunderland	33	10	5	18	62	74	25
Middlesbro	34	8	8	18	48	73	24
Liverpool	34	5	9	20	56	85	19

186

Saturday, March 13, 1954

Arsenal 3
Dickson, Holton, Lishman
Charlton 3
Leary 2, Hurst
Att: 41,256

Aston Villa 2
Thompson, Baxter
Man Utd 2
Taylor 2
Att: 26,023

Cardiff 1
Sullivan
Burnley 0
Att: 33,413

Blackpool 0
Middlesbrough 0
Att: 20,334

Huddersfield 3
Cavanagh 2, Glazzard
Newcastle 2
Monkhouse, Milburn
Att: 25,710

Sheff Utd 3
McNab, J Shaw, Twentyman, OG
Liverpool 1
Liddell (pen)
Att: 24,147

Football League Division One

	P	W	D	L	F	A	P
West Brom	34	20	8	6	80	47	48
WOLVES	**33**	**20**	**5**	**8**	**79**	**49**	**45**
Huddersfield	34	16	11	7	62	43	43
Burnley	34	19	2	13	68	53	40
Man Utd	34	14	12	8	60	47	40
Bolton	33	15	9	9	61	48	39
Charlton	34	16	5	13	66	60	37
Blackpool	34	14	9	11	61	59	37
Chelsea	34	13	10	11	66	61	36
Cardiff	34	14	7	13	38	58	35
Preston	33	15	3	15	69	46	33
Arsenal	33	11	11	11	57	59	33
Tottenham	34	14	4	16	53	57	32
Aston Villa	32	12	6	14	51	55	30
Sheff Wed	34	13	4	17	59	75	30
Man City	34	11	8	15	48	64	30
Portsmouth	33	10	9	14	68	74	29
Newcastle	35	9	10	16	53	66	28
Sheff Utd	33	9	9	15	58	70	27
Sunderland	33	10	5	18	62	74	25
Middlesbro	34	8	8	18	48	73	24
Liverpool	34	5	9	20	56	85	19

Wednesday, March 17, 1954

Chelsea 5   **Albion 0**   Att: 46,089
Saundrers, McNichol, Bentley, Stubbs, Lewis

Man City 4   **Tottenham 1**   Att: 9,984
Clarke, Hart, McAdams, Revie   Marchi

Football League Division One

	P	W	D	L	F	A	P
West Brom	35	21	8	6	82	48	50
WOLVES	**34**	**21**	**5**	**8**	**80**	**49**	**47**
Huddersfield	35	16	11	8	63	46	43
Burnley	35	20	2	13	71	54	42
Man Utd	35	15	12	8	63	48	42
Bolton	34	16	9	9	64	48	41
Charlton	35	17	5	13	69	62	39
Chelsea	35	13	11	11	67	62	37
Blackpool	35	14	9	12	62	61	37
Cardiff	35	14	7	14	40	61	35
Arsenal	34	11	11	12	58	61	33
Preston	34	15	3	16	69	47	33
Tottenham	35	14	4	17	53	60	32
Sheff Wed	35	14	4	17	61	76	32
Aston Villa	33	12	6	15	51	58	30
Portsmouth	34	10	10	14	70	76	30
Newcastle	36	10	10	16	57	67	30
Man City	35	11	8	16	49	67	30
Sunderland	34	11	5	18	65	74	27
Sheff Utd	34	9	9	16	59	74	27
Middlesbro	35	8	9	18	50	75	25
Liverpool	35	5	10	20	57	86	20

188

Saturday, March 20, 1954

Bolton 3   **Aston Villa 0**   Att: 26,292
Hassall 2, Stevens

Burnley 3   **Man City 1**   Att: 23,061
Holden, Gray, McIlroy   Hart

Charlton 3   **Cardiff 2**   Att: 20,717
Firmani, Hurst, Leary   Grant, Ford

Liverpool 1   **Chelsea 1**   Att: 35,947
Anderson   Parsons

Man Utd 3   **Huddersfield 1**   Att: 43,015
Blanchflower, Rowley, Viollet   Metcalfe (pen)

Middlesbrough 2   **Portsmouth 2**   Att: 20,743
Mannion, Harris   Barnard, Henderson

Newcastle 4   **Sheff Utd 1**   Att: 36,668
Monkhouse 3, Milburn   McNab

Preston 0   **Wolves 1**   Att: 24,376
  Wilshaw

Sheff Wed 2   **Arsenal 1**   Att: 41,194
Gannon, Sewell   Holton

Sunderland 3   **Tottenham 0**   Att: 39,393
Shackleton, Purdon, Chisholm

West Bromwich 2   **Blackpool 1**   Att: 53,019
Allen, Ryan   Mudie

Football League Division One

	P	W	D	L	F	A	P
West Brom	35	21	8	6	82	48	50
WOLVES	**36**	**21**	**6**	**9**	**83**	**54**	**48**
Huddersfield	36	17	11	8	67	47	45
Bolton	36	16	10	10	67	52	42
Burnley	36	20	2	14	72	56	42
Man Utd	36	15	12	9	64	51	42
Chelsea	36	14	11	11	68	62	39
Charlton	36	17	5	14	70	66	39
Blackpool	35	14	9	12	62	61	37
Cardiff	36	15	7	14	42	62	37
Arsenal	35	12	11	12	61	62	35
Preston	34	15	3	16	69	47	33
Portsmouth	35	11	10	14	73	78	32
Tottenham	36	14	4	18	53	61	32
Sheff Wed	35	14	4	17	61	76	32
Aston Villa	33	12	6	15	51	58	30
Man City	35	11	8	15	49	67	30
Newcastle	37	10	10	17	58	69	30
Sheff Utd	35	10	9	16	61	75	29
Sunderland	34	11	5	18	65	74	27
Middlesbro	36	9	9	18	54	77	27
Liverpool	35	5	10	20	57	86	20

Wednesday, March 24 1954

Wolves 1
Broadbent

Bolton 1
Lofthouse

Att: 19,617

Saturday, March 27, 1954

Arsenal 3
Logie 2, Holton

Man Utd 1
Taylor

Att: 42,735

Cardiff 2
Nugent, Tiddy

Newcastle 1
Monkhouse

Att: 26,242

Chelsea 1
McNichol

Tottenham 0

Att: 49,315

Huddersfield 4
McGarry, Frear 2, Cavanagh

Charlton 1
Ayre

Att: 20,896

Portsmouth 3
Gordon, Harris, Henderson

Bolton 2
Moir, Parry

Att: 22,784

Sheff Utd 2
Bottom, Ringstead

Burnley 1
McIlroy

Att: 20,000

Wolves 2
Broadbent 2

Middlesbrough 4
Watkin, McPherson 2 (1 pen), Delapenha

Att: 29,145

1953-4 LEAGUE RESULTS

190

Football League Division One

	P	W	D	L	F	A	P
West Brom	36	21	8	7	83	50	50
WOLVES	36	21	6	9	83	54	**48**
Huddersfield	36	17	11	8	67	47	45
Bolton	36	16	10	10	67	52	42
Burnley	36	20	2	14	72	56	42
Man Utd	36	15	12	9	64	51	42
Chelsea	36	14	11	11	68	62	39
Charlton	36	17	5	14	70	66	39
Blackpool	36	15	9	12	66	63	39
Cardiff	36	15	7	14	42	62	37
Arsenal	35	12	11	12	61	62	35
Preston	35	15	3	17	71	51	33
Portsmouth	35	11	10	14	73	78	32
Aston Villa	34	13	6	15	53	59	32
Tottenham	36	14	4	18	53	61	32
Sheff Wed	36	14	4	18	62	78	32
Man City	35	11	8	16	49	67	30
Newcastle	37	10	10	17	58	69	30
Sunderland	35	12	5	18	67	75	29
Sheff Utd	35	10	9	16	61	75	29
Middlesbro	36	9	9	18	54	77	27
Liverpool	35	5	10	20	57	86	20

Wednesday, March 31, 1954

Blackpool 4
Taylor 2, Durie, Mortensen

Preston 2
Foster, Wayman

Att: 16,674

Aston Villa 2
Thompson, Dixon

Sheff Wed 1
Woodhead

Att: 9,609

Sunderland 2
Purdon, Elliott

West Bromwich 1
Cox

Att: 26,632

Football League Division One

	P	W	D	L	F	A	P
West Brom	37	21	8	8	83	51	50
WOLVES	37	22	6	9	84	54	**50**
Huddersfield	37	18	11	8	71	48	47
Bolton	37	17	10	10	70	53	44
Burnley	37	20	2	15	73	58	42
Man Utd	37	15	12	10	66	54	42
Chelsea	37	15	11	11	70	63	41
Charlton	37	18	5	14	73	66	41
Blackpool	37	15	10	12	68	65	40
Cardiff	37	16	7	14	45	64	39
Preston	36	16	3	17	75	51	35
Arsenal	36	12	11	13	62	65	35
Tottenham	37	14	5	18	55	63	33
Aston Villa	35	13	6	16	54	61	32
Portsmouth	36	11	10	15	73	82	32
Newcastle	38	11	10	17	62	72	32
Sheff Wed	37	14	4	19	63	82	32
Man City	36	11	8	17	52	71	30
Sunderland	36	12	5	19	70	79	29
Sheff Utd	36	10	9	17	61	78	29
Middlesbro	37	10	9	18	56	78	29
Liverpool	36	6	10	20	61	89	22

Saturday, April 3, 1954

Bolton 3 Hassall (pen), Lofthouse, Moir — **Arsenal 1** Holton — Att: 30,525

Burnley 1 Gray — **Chelsea 2** Bentley, Lewis — Att: 20,312

Charlton 3 Ayre, Kiernan, Terry — **Sheff Utd 0** — Att: 16,845

Liverpool 4 Jackson, Evans, Liddell (pen), Anderson — **Sunderland 3** Shackleton, Chisholm, Purdon — Att: 30,417

Man Utd 2 Viollet, Rowley — **Cardiff 3** Grant 2, Sullivan — Att: 24,616

Middlesbrough 2 Mannion, McPherson — **Aston Villa 1** McParland — Att: 21,142

Newcastle 4 Monkhouse, Davies, Milburn 2 (2 pen) — **Man City 3** Clarke, Hart, McAdams — Att: 27,764

Preston 4 Foster 2, Wayman, Baxter (pen) — **Portsmouth 0** — Att: 15,464

Sheff Wed 1 Shaw — **Huddersfield 4** Glazzard, Frear 2 (1 pen), Cavanagh — Att: 30,837

Tottenham 2 Baily, Robb — **Blackpool 2** Perry, Mortensen — Att: 43,870

West Bromwich 0 — **Wolves 1** Swinbourne — Att: 49,669

191

Football League Division One

	P	W	D	L	F	A	P
WOLVES	38	23	6	9	89	54	52
West Brom	38	21	8	9	83	53	50
Huddersfield	38	17	11	9	73	53	47
Bolton	38	17	10	11	70	55	44
Chelsea	38	16	11	11	72	63	43
Burnley	38	20	2	16	74	63	42
Man Utd	38	15	12	11	66	56	42
Blackpool	38	16	10	12	70	65	42
Charlton	38	18	5	15	73	71	41
Cardiff	38	17	7	14	47	64	41
Arsenal	38	13	12	13	66	66	38
Preston	38	16	5	17	78	54	37
Portsmouth	38	13	10	15	77	83	36
Aston Villa	37	14	7	16	60	63	35
Tottenham	38	15	5	18	60	65	35
Sheff Wed	39	15	4	20	68	86	34
Newcastle	39	11	10	18	62	74	32
Man City	38	12	8	18	57	75	32
Sunderland	38	12	6	20	74	85	30
Sheff Utd	37	10	10	17	62	79	30
Middlesbro	38	10	9	19	58	83	29
Liverpool	38	7	10	21	63	92	24

Tuesday, April 6, 1954

Arsenal 1 **Aston Villa 1**
Lawton McParland Att: 14,619

Wednesday, April 7, 1954

Man City 0 **Liverpool 2**
Jackson, Dale Att: 12,593

Portsmouth 2 **Sheff Wed 1**
Gordon, Dale Shaw Att: 15,197

Sunderland 2 **Preston 2**
Chisholm, Elliott Wayman 2 Att: 31,143

Saturday, April 10, 1954

Arsenal 3 **Liverpool 0**
Tapscott 2, Roper Att: 33,578

Aston Villa 5 **Burnley 1**
Baxter, McParland, Gibson, Pace 2 Holden Att: 23,043

Blackpool 2 **Man Utd 0**
Mortensen, Perry Att: 25,996

Cardiff 2 **West Bromwich 0**
Grant, Ford Att: 43,614

Chelsea 2 **Bolton 0**
Parsons, Bentley Att: 49,433

Huddersfield 2 **Tottenham 5**
Glazzard, Shiner Brooks, Hutchinson, Robb 2, Harmer Att: 26,232

Man City 5 **Middlesbrough 2**
Clarke 2, Meadows 2, Revie Delapenha, Little OG Att: 28,445

Portsmouth 2 **Newcastle 0**
Barnard, Dale Att: 26,604

Sheff Utd 1 **Preston 1**
Hoyland Hatsell Att: 30,712

Sunderland 2 **Sheff Wed 4**
Elliott, Anderson Shaw 2, Froggatt 2 Att: 36,982

Wolves 5 **Charlton 0**
Hancocks 2, Wilshaw, Mullen 2 Att: 35,028

Football League Division One

	P	W	D	L	F	A	P
WOLVES	38	23	6	9	89	54	52
West Brom	38	21	8	9	83	53	50
Huddersfield	38	18	11	9	73	53	47
Bolton	39	17	11	11	70	55	45
Man Utd	39	16	12	11	68	56	44
Blackpool	39	17	10	12	74	66	44
Chelsea	39	16	11	12	72	64	43
Burnley	39	20	3	16	74	63	43
Charlton	39	18	5	16	73	73	41
Cardiff	39	17	7	15	48	68	41
Arsenal	39	14	12	13	69	66	40
Preston	39	17	5	17	80	55	39
Portsmouth	39	13	10	16	77	86	36
Aston Villa	37	14	7	16	60	63	35
Tottenham	39	15	5	19	61	67	35
Sheff Wed	40	15	4	21	68	89	34
Newcastle	40	12	10	18	65	74	34
Man City	39	13	8	18	58	75	34
Sunderland	39	12	7	20	76	87	31
Sheff Utd	38	10	11	17	64	81	31
Middlesbro	39	10	9	20	58	84	29
Liverpool	39	8	10	21	64	92	26

Friday, April 16, 1954

Arsenal 3　　　　**Portsmouth 0**　　Att: 44,948
Tapscott 2, Roper

Blackpool 4　　　**Cardiff 1**　　　Att: 26,194
Brown, Mortensen, Taylor, Perry　Ford

Bolton 0　　　　　**Burnley 0**　　　Att: 34,394

Chelsea 0　　　　**Man City 1**　　Att: 59,794
　　　　　　　　　　Meadows

Man Utd 2　　　　**Charlton 0**　　Att: 33,663
Aston, Viollet

Middlesbrough 0　**Liverpool 1**　　Att: 26,882
　　　　　　　　　　Smyth

Newcastle 3　　　**Sheff Wed 0**　Att: 43,945
Mitchell 2, Monkhouse

Preston 2　　　　**Tottenham 1**　Att: 24,521
Wayman, Forbes　　Harmer

Sunderland 2　　　**Sheff Utd 2**　Att: 49,419
Anderson, Bingham　Cross, Hawksworth

Saturday, April 17, 1954

Football League Division One

	P	W	D	L	F	A	P
WOLVES	**39**	**23**	**7**	**9**	**89**	**54**	**53**
West Brom	39	22	8	9	84	53	52
Huddersfield	39	18	11	10	74	55	47
Bolton	40	18	11	11	73	57	47
Man Utd	40	17	12	11	70	56	46
Burnley	40	21	3	16	76	64	45
Blackpool	40	17	10	13	76	69	44
Chelsea	40	16	11	13	72	65	43
Cardiff	40	18	7	15	49	68	43
Charlton	40	18	6	16	74	74	42
Preston	40	18	5	17	81	55	41
Arsenal	40	14	12	14	71	71	40
Tottenham	40	16	5	19	63	68	37
Aston Villa	38	14	8	16	61	64	36
Newcastle	41	13	10	18	70	76	36
Portsmouth	40	13	10	17	77	88	36
Sheff Wed	41	15	5	21	68	89	35
Man City	40	13	8	19	58	76	34
Sunderland	40	12	8	20	76	76	32
Sheff Utd	39	10	11	18	65	83	31
Middlesbro	40	10	10	20	58	84	30
Liverpool	40	8	10	22	64	93	26

Bolton 3   **Blackpool 2**
Moir, Lofthouse, Hassall   Brown, Perry
Att: 40,291

Burnley 2   **Huddersfield 1**
Adamson, Pilkington   Cavanagh
Att: 26,180

Charlton 1   **Aston Villa 1**
Leary   Pace
Att: 22,226

Liverpool 0   **Cardiff 1**
Northcott
Att: 41,340

Man Utd 2   **Portsmouth 0**
Blanchflower, Viollet
Att: 31,426

Middlesbrough 0   **Sunderland 0**
Att: 38,762

Newcastle 5   **Arsenal 2**
Davies 3, Hannah, White   Milton, Holton,
Att: 48,243

Preston 1   **Chelsea 0**
Foster
Att: 27,172

Sheff Wed 0   **Wolves 0**
Att: 40,707

Tottenham 2   **Sheff Utd 1**
Ramsey (pen), Brittan   Brook
Att: 35,105

West Bromwich 1   **Man City 0**
Allen (pen)
Att: 38,567

Football League Division One

	P	W	D	L	F	A	P
WOLVES	**40**	**24**	**7**	**9**	**93**	**54**	**55**
West Brom	40	22	9	9	85	54	53
Huddersfield	40	18	11	11	74	59	47
Bolton	41	18	12	11	74	58	48
Man Utd	41	17	12	12	70	57	46
Burnley	41	21	4	16	77	65	46
Blackpool	41	18	10	13	77	69	46
Chelsea	41	16	12	13	73	66	44
Charlton	41	19	6	16	75	74	44
Preston	41	19	5	17	87	57	43
Cardiff	41	18	7	16	49	69	43
Arsenal	41	14	13	14	72	72	41
Aston Villa	39	14	9	16	62	65	37
Tottenham	41	16	5	20	65	74	37
Portsmouth	41	13	11	17	78	89	37
Newcastle	41	13	10	18	70	76	36
Man City	41	13	9	19	59	77	35
Sheff Wed	41	15	5	21	68	89	35
Sunderland	41	13	8	20	79	88	34
Sheff Utd	40	10	11	19	66	86	31
Middlesbro	41	10	10	21	59	88	30
Liverpool	41	9	10	22	68	94	28

Monday, April 19, 1954

Burnley 1 Holden — **Bolton 1** Parry — Att: 25,857

Cardiff 0 — **Blackpool 1** Perry — Att: 44,508

Charlton 1 Firmani — **Man Utd 0** — Att: 19,111

Liverpool 4 Smyth 2, Rowley, Liddell — **Middlesbrough 1** Watkin — Att: 22,174

Man City 1 Branagan — **Chelsea 1** Bentley — vAtt: 30,620

Portsmouth 1 Barnard — **Arsenal 1** Roper — Att: 30,898

Sheff Utd 1 Hoyland — **Sunderland 3** Purdon 2, Elliott — Att: 31,387

Tottenham 2 Bennett, Dunmore — **Preston 6** Foster, Hatsell 3, Baxter (pen), Morrison — Att: 30,206

West Bromwich 1 Nicholls — **Aston Villa 1** McParland — Att: 45,816

Wolves 4 Mullen, Hancocks, Broadbent, Wilshaw — **Huddersfield 0** — Att: 42,862

Football League Division One
(top of table)

	P	W	D	L	F	A	P
WOLVES	**41**	**24**	**7**	**10**	**94**	**56**	**55**
West Brom	41	22	9	10	86	60	53
Huddersfield	41	19	11	11	76	60	49
Bolton	41	18	12	11	74	56	48
Man Utd	41	17	12	12	70	57	46
Burnley	41	21	4	16	77	65	46
Blackpool	41	18	10	13	77	69	46

Football League Division One

	P	W	D	L	F	A	P
WOLVES	**42**	**25**	**7**	**10**	**96**	**56**	**57**
West Brom	42	22	9	11	86	63	53
Huddersfield	42	20	11	11	78	61	51
Man Utd	42	18	12	12	73	58	48
Bolton	42	18	12	12	75	60	48
Blackpool	42	19	10	13	80	69	48
Burnley	42	21	4	17	78	67	46
Chelsea	42	16	12	14	74	68	44
Charlton	42	19	6	17	75	77	44
Cardiff	42	18	8	16	51	71	44
Preston	42	19	5	18	87	58	43
Arsenal	42	15	13	14	75	73	43
Aston Villa	41	16	9	16	69	66	41
Portsmouth	42	14	11	17	81	89	39
Newcastle	42	14	10	18	72	77	38
Tottenham	42	16	5	21	65	76	37
Man City	42	14	9	19	62	77	37
Sunderland	42	14	8	20	81	89	36
Sheff Wed	42	15	6	21	70	91	36
Sheff Utd	41	10	11	20	67	89	31
Middlesbro	42	10	10	22	60	91	30
Liverpool	42	9	10	23	68	97	28

196

Tuesday, April 20, 1954

Aston Villa 6 **West Bromwich 1** Att: 57,899
Pace 2, Tyrrell 2, Dixon, Blanchflower Griffin

Huddersfield 2 **Wolves 1** Att: 35,814
Glazzard, McGarry Wilshaw

Saturday, April 24, 1954

Arsenal 3 **Middlesbrough 1** Att: 35,069
Tapscott, Lishman, Roper Delapenha

Aston Villa 1 **Preston 0** Att: 31,495
Tyrrell

Blackpool 3 **Liverpool 0** Att:18,651
Mortensen 2, Brown

Cardiff 2 **Sheff Wed 2** Att: 15,777
Sherwood, Ford Sewell, Woodhead

Chelsea 1 **Newcastle 2** Att: 46,991
Parsons Mitchell, White

Huddersfield 2 **Bolton 1** Att: 25,635
McGarry (pen), Cavanagh Parry

Man City 3 **Charlton 0** Att: 19,549
McAdams 2, Spurdle

Portsmouth 3 **Albion 0** Att: 28,004
Harris 2, Reid

Sheff Utd 1 **Man Utd 3** Att: 29,189
Brook Aston, Blanchflower, Viollet

Sunderland 2 **Burnley 1** Att: 28,014
Chisholm 2 Adamson

Wolves 2 **Tottenham 0** Att: 44,055
Swinbourne 2

Football League Division One

	P	W	D	L	F	A	P
WOLVES	42	25	7	10	96	56	57
West Brom	42	22	9	11	86	63	53
Huddersfield	42	20	11	11	78	61	51
Man Utd	42	18	12	12	73	58	48
Bolton	42	18	12	12	75	60	48
Blackpool	42	19	10	13	80	69	48
Burnley	42	21	4	17	78	67	46
Chelsea	42	16	12	14	74	68	44
Charlton	42	19	6	17	75	77	44
Cardiff	42	18	8	16	51	71	44
Preston	42	19	5	18	87	58	43
Arsenal	42	15	13	14	75	73	43
Aston Villa	42	16	9	17	70	68	41
Portsmouth	42	14	11	17	81	89	39
Newcastle	42	14	10	18	72	77	38
Tottenham	42	16	5	21	65	76	37
Man City	42	14	9	19	62	77	37
Sunderland	42	14	8	20	81	89	36
Sheff Wed	42	15	6	21	70	91	36
Sheff Utd	42	11	11	20	69	90	33
Middlesbro	42	10	10	22	60	91	30
Liverpool	42	9	10	23	68	97	28

Monday, April 26, 1954

Aston Villa 1
Pace

Att: 12,796

Sheff Utd 2
Cross, Ringstead

CHAPTER TEN

SEASON FACTS

Playing record	P	W	D	L	F	A	Pt
Home	21	16	1	4	61	25	33
Away	21	9	6	6	35	31	24
Total	42	25	7	10	96	56	57

Appearances	League	Cup
Johnny Hancocks	42	1
Bill Shorthouse	40	1
Roy Swinbourne	40	1
Bill Slater	39	1
Dennis Wilshaw	39	1
Billy Wright	39	1
Jimmy Mullen	38	1
Peter Broadbent	36	1
Bert Williams	34	0
Roy Pritchard	27	1
Jack Short	26	1
Ron Flowers	15	0
Eddie Stuart	12	0
Nigel Sims	8	1
Norman Deeley	6	0
Ron Stockin	6	0
Bill Baxter	5	0
Les Smith	4	0
Eddie Clamp	2	0
Bill Guttridge	2	0
Ray Chatham	1	0
Len Gibbons	1	0

Goals	League	Cup
Dennis Wilshaw	26	1
Johnny Hancocks	24	0
Roy Swinbourne	24	0
Peter Broadbent	12	0
Jimmy Mullen	7	0
Bill Slater	2	0
Les Smith	1	0

Admission Prices	Adults	Juniors
South Bank	1s 9d (8.75p)	9d (3.75p)
North Bank	2s 0d (10p)	1s (5p)
Waterloo Road enclosure	3s 6d (17.5p)	1s 9d (8.75p)
Molineux Street enclosure	3s 6d (17.5p)	1s 9d (8.75p)
Waterloo Road Stand centre	7s 3d (31.25p)	
Waterloo Road Stand wing	5s 6d (27.5p)	
Molineux Street Stand centre	6s 0d (30p)	
Molineux Street Stand wing	5s 6d (27.5p)	

	Date	Opponents	Result	1	2	3	4	5	6	7	8	9	10	11
L	Aug 19	Burnley	A 1-4	Sims	Short	Pritchard	Slater	Shorthouse	Wright	Hancocks	Stockin	Swinbourne 1	Wilshaw	Mullen
W	Aug 22	Man City	A 4-0	Sims	Short	Pritchard	Slater 1	Shorthouse	Wright	Hancocks	Stockin	Swinbourne 2	Wilshaw 1	Mullen
L	Aug 26	Sunderland	A 2-3	Sims	Short	Pritchard	Slater	Shorthouse	Wright	Hancocks 1 (p)	Stockin	Swinbourne	Wilshaw 1	Mullen
W	Aug 29	Cardiff	H 3-1	Sims	Short	Pritchard	Slater	Shorthouse	Wright	Hancocks 1 (p)	Broadbent	Swinbourne	Wilshaw 1	Mullen 1
W	Aug 31	Sunderland	H 3-1	Sims	Short	Pritchard	Slater	Shorthouse	Wright	Hancocks 1	Broadbent	Swinbourne 1	Wilshaw 1	Mullen 1
W	Sept 5	Arsenal	A 3-2	Williams	Short	Pritchard	Slater	Shorthouse	Wright	Hancocks 1	Broadbent 1	Swinbourne 1	Wilshaw 1	Mullen
W	Sept 7	Liverpool	H 2-1	Williams	Short	Pritchard	Slater	Shorthouse	Wright	Hancocks	Broadbent 1	Swinbourne 1	Wilshaw	Mullen
W	Sept 12	Portsmouth	H 4-3	Williams	Gibbons	Pritchard	Deeley	Shorthouse	Wright	Hancocks	Broadbent	Swinbourne 1	Wilshaw 3	Mullen
D	Sept 16	Liverpool	A 1-1	Williams	Wright	Pritchard	Deeley	Shorthouse	Slater	Hancocks	Broadbent	Swinbourne	Wilshaw 1	Mullen
D	Sept 19	Blackpool	A 0-0	Williams	Wright	Pritchard	Chatham	Shorthouse	Baxter	Hancocks	Broadbent	Swinbourne	Wilshaw	Mullen
W	Sept 26	Chelsea	H 8-1	Williams	Short	Pritchard	Slater	Shorthouse	Wright	Hancocks 3(1p)	Broadbent 1	Swinbourne 2	Wilshaw 1	Mullen 1
D	Oct 3	Sheff Utd	A 3-3	Williams	Short	Pritchard	Slater	Shorthouse	Wright	Hancocks 1	Broadbent	Swinbourne 1	Wilshaw 1	Mullen
W	Oct 10	Newcastle	A 2-1	Williams	Short	Pritchard	Slater	Shorthouse	Flowers	Hancocks	Broadbent	Swinbourne 1	Stockin	Smith 1
W	Oct 17	Man Utd	H 3-1	Williams	Short	Guttridge	Slater	Shorthouse	Wright	Hancocks 1 (p)	Broadbent 1	Swinbourne 1	Wilshaw	Mullen
D	Oct 24	Bolton	A 1-1	Williams	Short	Guttridge	Baxter	Shorthouse	Slater	Hancocks 1	Broadbent	Swinbourne	Wilshaw	Mullen
W	Oct 31	Preston	H 1-0	Williams	Short	Wright	Baxter	Shorthouse	Slater	Hancocks	Broadbent	Wilshaw 1	Stockin	Mullen
D	Nov 7	Middlesbro	A 3-3	Williams	Short	Wright	Baxter	Shorthouse	Slater	Hancocks 1	Broadbent	Swinbourne 1	Wilshaw 1	Mullen 1
W	Nov 14	West Brom	H 1-0	Williams	Short	Pritchard	Baxter	Shorthouse	Wright	Hancocks 1	Broadbent	Swinbourne	Wilshaw	Mullen
W	Nov 21	Charlton	A 2-0	Williams	Short	Pritchard	Slater	Shorthouse	Wright	Hancocks 1	Stockin	Swinbourne	Wilshaw	Mullen 1
W	Nov 28	Sheff Wed	H 4-1	Williams	Short	Pritchard	Slater	Shorthouse	Wright	Hancocks 1 (p)	Broadbent 1	Swinbourne 2	Wilshaw 1	Mullen
W	Dec 5	Tottenham	A 3-2	Williams	Short	Pritchard	Slater	Shorthouse	Wright	Hancocks 1	Broadbent 1	Swinbourne	Wilshaw 1	Mullen
L	Dec 12	Burnley	H 1-2	Williams	Short	Pritchard	Slater	Shorthouse	Wright	Hancocks 1	Broadbent	Swinbourne	Wilshaw 1	Mullen
W	Dec 19	Man City	H 3-1	Williams	Short	Pritchard	Slater	Shorthouse	Wright	Hancocks 2(1p)	Broadbent	Swinbourne	Wilshaw	Mullen
L	Dec 24	Aston Villa	H 1-2	Sims	Short	Pritchard	Slater	Shorthouse	Wright	Hancocks	Broadbent	Swinbourne	Wilshaw 1	Mullen
W	Dec 26	Aston Villa	A 2-1	Sims	Short	Pritchard	Slater	Shorthouse	Wright	Hancocks 1	Broadbent	Swinbourne	Wilshaw 1	Mullen

SEASON FACTS

W	Jan 2	Cardiff	A 3-1	Sims	Wright	Pritchard	Slater	Shorthouse	Flowers	Hancocks 1	Broadbent	Swinbourne 1	Wilshaw 1	Mullen
L	Jan 16	Arsenal	H 0-2	Williams	Short	Pritchard	Slater	Wright	Flowers	Hancocks	Broadbent	Swinbourne	Wilshaw	Mullen
L	Jan 23	Portsmouth	A 0-2	Williams	Short	Wright	Slater	Shorthouse	Flowers	Hancocks	Deeley	Swinbourne	Broadbent	Mullen
W	Feb 6	Blackpool	H 4-1	Williams	Short	Pritchard	Slater	Shorthouse	Wright	Hancocks 1	Flowers	Swinbourne 3	Wilshaw	Mullen
L	Feb 13	Chelsea	A 2-4	Williams	Short	Pritchard	Slater	Shorthouse	Wright	Hancocks	Flowers	Swinbourne 1	Wilshaw 1	Mullen
W	Feb 20	Sheff Utd	H 6-1	Williams	Stuart	Pritchard	Slater	Wright	Flowers	Hancocks 2	Broadbent 1	Swinbourne 2	Wilshaw 1	Mullen
W	Feb 27	Newcastle	H 3-2	Williams	Stuart	Shorthouse	Slater 1	Wright	Flowers	Hancocks	Broadbent 1	Swinbourne	Wilshaw 1	Mullen
L	Mar 6	Man Utd	A 0-1	Williams	Stuart	Shorthouse	Slater	Wright	Clamp	Hancocks	Broadbent	Flowers	Wilshaw	Mullen
W	Mar 20	Preston	A 1-0	Williams	Stuart	Shorthouse	Slater	Wright	Deeley	Hancocks	Broadbent	Swinbourne	Wilshaw 1	Smith
D	Mar 24	Bolton	H 1-1	Williams	Stuart	Shorthouse	Slater	Wright	Deeley	Hancocks	Broadbent 1	Swinbourne	Clamp	Smith
L	Mar 27	Middlesbro	H 2-4	Williams	Stuart	Shorthouse	Slater	Wright	Deeley	Hancocks	Broadbent 2	Swinbourne	Wilshaw	Mullen
W	Apr 3	West Brom	A 1-0	Williams	Stuart	Pritchard	Slater	Shorthouse	Flowers	Smith	Broadbent	Swinbourne 1	Wilshaw	Hancocks
W	Apr 10	Charlton	H 5-0	Williams	Stuart	Wright	Slater	Shorthouse	Flowers	Hancocks 2	Broadbent	Swinbourne	Wilshaw 1	Mullen 2
D	Apr 17	Sheff Wed	A 0-0	Williams	Stuart	Wright	Slater	Shorthouse	Flowers	Hancocks	Broadbent	Swinbourne	Wilshaw	Mullen
W	Apr 19	Huddersfield	H 4-0	Williams	Stuart	Wright	Slater	Shorthouse	Flowers	Hancocks 1	Broadbent 1	Swinbourne	Wilshaw 1	Mullen 1
L	Apr 20	Huddersfield	A 1-2	Williams	Stuart	Wright	Slater	Shorthouse	Flowers	Hancocks	Broadbent	Swinbourne	Wilshaw 1	Mullen
W	Apr 24	Tottenham	H 2-0	Williams	Stuart	Wright	Slater	Shorthouse	Flowers	Hancocks	Broadbent	Swinbourne 2	Wilshaw	Mullen

FA Cup third round

L	Jan 9	Birmingham	H 1-2	Sims	Short	Pritchard	Slater	Shorthouse	Wright	Hancocks	Broadbent	Swinbourne	Wilshaw 1	Mullen

Friendlies

W	Sept 30	South Africa	H 3-1	Williams	Short	Pritchard	Slater	Stuart	Wright	Hancocks	Broadbent 1	Swinbourne 1	Stockin	Mullen
L	Oct 6	Bury	A 1-3	Sims	Clamp	Pritchard	Chatham	Shorthouse	Baxter	Hancocks	Broadbent	Swinbourne	Wilshaw	Stockin 1
W	Oct 15	Celtic	H 2-0	Sims	Short	Guttridge	Baxter	Shorthouse	Wright	Hancocks	Mason	Swinbourne	Wilshaw 2	Mullen
W	Mar 10	Racing Club	H 3-1 Buenos Aires	Williams	Stuart	Shorthouse	Slater	Wright	Deeley 1	Hancocks	Broadbent	Taylor 1	Wilshaw	Mullen 1